The Intext *Series in*

FINANCE

Consulting Editor

E. BRUCE FREDRIKSON
Syracuse University

Techniques of
Investment Analysis

Techniques of Investment Analysis

STANLEY S. C. HUANG

Associate Professor of Finance
Rider College

INTEXT EDUCATIONAL PUBLISHERS
College Division of Intext
Scranton   San Francisco   Toronto   London

ISBN 0-7002-2383-5

Library of Congress Catalog Card Number: 71-177312

Preface

This book is concerned with the techniques of investment analysis. It introduces a number of innovations in the use of investment techniques and in the arrangement of materials. The plan behind the organization of the materials in this book is influenced by the following:

First, securities markets are famous for fluctuating prices. They are strongly influenced by the short-term outlook of general business and corporate profits. Security analysts and portfolio managers must be knowledgeable in the analysis and forecast of trends in general business, corporate profits, and interest rates. Therefore some analytical techniques in these areas should be a part of the arsenal of working tools available to prospective security analysts and portfolio managers.

Second, before making a commitment one has to ascertain in his mind whether the security in question is over- or underpriced in the market. Additionally, he has to ask whether the general market is relatively high, low, or neutral. Therefore valuation of both individual securities and the general market forms the basis for intelligent investment decisions, and much effort should be devoted to the learning of valuation techniques.

Third, many lay securities buyers make their buy-and-sell decisions on the basis of the so called "technical approach" or market analysis. In recent years this approach has gained popularity even among many Wall Street professionals. Irrespective of one's inclinations, the technical or market approach should be thoroughly analyzed and evaluated in relation to its premises and claims.

The above are some of the thoughts behind the arrangement of materials in this book. Many of the techniques of analysis discussed in this book have been tested and accepted by both professionals and academicians. Some however are new, either untested empirically or not yet in general use. Nevertheless, they are considered to have sufficient merit to warrant careful consideration.

The author would like to take this opportunity to express his gratitude and appreciation to the many writers on investments whose books and articles he has read over the years. Particular thanks are due to Dr. C. H. Li for his help in running the multiple correlation on valuation, to Dr. Bruce Fredrikson for his valuable suggestions to improve the manuscript, and especially to my wife Aileen for her assistance in typing and other important details of manuscript preparation.

STANLEY HUANG

Trenton, N. J.
December, 1971

Contents

1. Introduction 1

The Nature of Investment Management. Areas for Critical Investment Analysis and Evaluation. Risks of Investment in
Securities. Questions and Problems.

2. Analysis and Forecast of Trend of General Business 6

Security Values and Economic Environment. Long-Term
Economic Forecasts. Evaluation of Kendrick's Long-Term
Forecasts. Short-Term Economic Forecast. Short-Term
Forecast on Basis of Economic Indicators. Short-Term Fore-
cast on Basis of Diffusion Index. Short-Term Forecast on
Basis of Business and Consumer Surveys. Short-Term Fore-
cast on Basis of National Income and Product Accounts. In-
put-Output Analysis. Suggested Readings. Questions and
Problems.

3. Analysis and Forecast of Trend of Corporate Profits 34

Determinants of Security Values—Long Run vs. Short Run.
Aggregate Measures of Corporate Profits. Corporate Profits
Level in Last Two Decades. Rates of Return on Equity, Net
Profit Margins, and Turnover Capital. Factors Affecting
Profit Margins. Rates of Return and Profit Margins in
Individual Industries. Long-Term Perspective of Corporate
Profits. Short-Term Profits Forecast. Suggested Readings.
Questions and Problems.

4. Analysis and Forecast of Trend of Interest Rates 49

Importance of Interest Rate Forecast. Structure of Interest
Rates. Trends and Cyclical Variations of Interest Rates. In-

fluence of Federal Reserve Policy on Short- and Long-Term Interest Rates. Forecast of Trend of Interest Rates by Supply and Demand Analysis. Financial Forecast for 1971. Estimates of Demand for and Sources of Funds. Implications for Interest Rates. Federal Reserve Policy and Levels of Interest Rates in 1969–70. Suggested Readings. Questions and Problems.

5.   **Industry Analysis** **74**

Changing Importance of Industries. Advantages of Faster-Growing Industries. Classification of the Economy into Industries. Stages of Industry Development. Structure and Operational Characteristics of the Industry. Yardstick of Management Performance of Individual Firms and Industries. Composite Industry Data. Industry Analysis and Investment Decisions. Industry Performance in the Stock Market 1965–68. Suggested Readings. Questions and Problems.

6.   **Company Analysis** **99**

Analysis of Record of Performance in the Most Relevant Past. Comparison of Record of Performance with Industry Average and Competitors. Management and Current Programs. Outlook of Sales and Profits. Appendix A. Suggested Readings. Questions and Problems.

7.   **Valuation of the "General Market"** **132**

The "General Market." Importance of the Valuation of the "General Market." Theories of Valuation of Common Stock. Earnings, Quarterly Price Indexes, Price-Earnings Ratios of DJIA, 1936–70. Valuation of DJIA on Basis of Earnings Record. Valuation of DJIA on Basis of Price-Actual Earnings Ratios. Valuation of Standard & Poor's 425 on Basis of Earnings Record. Valuation of DJIA in Terms of Present-Worth Approach. Valuation of DJIA on Basis of Anticipated Average Earning Power. Suggested Readings. Questions and Problems.

8.   **Valuation of Common Stocks** **150**

Present-Worth Approach and Discount Tables. The Capitalization Approach. Summary. Suggested Readings. Questions and Problems.

9.   **Market Analysis** **176**

Market Analysis vs. Security Analysis. The Dow Theory.
Technical Indicators of Stock Price Level. Technical Market
Analysis—Individual Stocks. Random-Walk Theory and Technical Market Analysis. Price vs. Volume Changes. Evaluation
of Technical Market Analysis. Suggested Readings. Questions
and Problems.

10.   **Portfolio Management** **202**

Financial Status and Requirements of the Investor, Individual
or Institutional. Portfolio Objectives and Risk Assumption.
Portfolio Policy and Management. Suggested Readings. Questions and Problems.

Index **211**

1. Introduction

Investment in securities, especially in common stocks, is a very challenging business. Although some have accumulated a great deal of wealth through this avenue, many others have lost most if not all of their hard-earned savings through either unwise investment or unwarranted speculation. This book is concerned with investment analysis and management. It is designed to improve the sophistication of the investor, thereby increasing his chance of success.

THE NATURE OF INVESTMENT MANAGEMENT

The nature of investment management can probably be best explained in the form of a chart, as in Figure 1-1.

Before making any commitment each investor should first establish his objectives in the light of his financial and personal circumstances (and legal restrictions in the case of institutional investors), and his ability to shoulder risks as shown in the chart. The objectives can include any mixture of (a) capital appreciation, (b) safety of principal, (c) a good and dependable current income, or (d) protection of purchasing power.

Once the investment objectives are established, the investment decision process can begin. The investment decision process consists of two aspects, security analysis and portfolio management. Security analysis deals with analysis of past performance and evaluation of future prospects of individual securities. In addition, the security analyst will also estimate a normal worth for the security on the basis of projected earnings and dividends for purpose of comparison with its market price. Portfolio management, on the other hand, decides in the light of portfolio objectives such questions as What types of securities and what grades are to be included? How many issues? In what proportions? What investment policy (aggressive, neutral, or defensive) to follow, in general and at different points of time? And last but not least, portfolio management determines the timing of purchase and sale of individual securities.

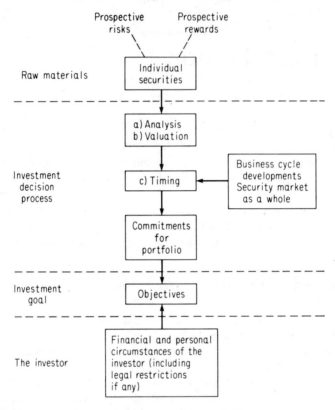

Figure 1-1
Schematic Presentation of the Nature of
Investment Management and Analysis

AREAS FOR CRITICAL INVESTMENT ANALYSIS AND EVALUATION

Admittedly the investment problem is a very complex one. Successful investment is both a science and an art. However, a complex problem can be made simpler if it is broken into several component parts for study. The author is firmly convinced that investment decision making can be greatly improved if the investment problem is broken down into several functional areas and each area critically studied. The functional areas which the author will deal with in the following chapters are

Analysis and forecast of trend of general business
Analysis and forecast of trend of corporate profits
Analysis and forecast of trend of interest rates
Industry analysis
Company analysis

Valuation of the "general market"
Valuation of common stocks
Market analysis
Portfolio management

Because common stocks constitute the most important media today for both institutional and individual investors, the analysis is heavily geared to the evaluation and management of common stocks.

RISKS OF INVESTMENT IN SECURITIES

Investments in securities are subject to a variety of risks. The kind of risks and the extent to which securities are exposed to them depends on the types and grades of securities. The risks involved are basically of five types.

Business or Financial Risk

By business or financial risk we mean that the price of the securities of a business may decline in the marketplace because of financial insolvency or declining profitability of the issuer. Of the two, the latter is found much more frequently than the former one. There can be a variety of reasons why a business is declining in its profitability. Some of the reasons are internal such as poor management, inefficiency in cost control, or lack of new products. Other factors, such as overcapacity in the industry, general business downturn, increasing competition from other industries, are external and subject less to the control of the corporation. Whether due to internal or external factors or a combination of them, the problem is the same—the issuing company is deteriorating in its ability to make profits. This is certainly one of the most common reasons why many common stocks have suffered sharp declines in market price in the past.

Price-Level Risk

This refers to the risk of losing purchasing power from returns of fixed income securities because of inflation. A person who bought, for example, a ten-year bond in 1959 at par for $1,000 found that when he cashed the bond in 1969, he had lost about 30 percent of the purchasing power of his original investment. In other words, the cost of living as measured by Consumer Price Index appreciated about 30 percent during the period from 101.5 in December 1959 to 131.3 in December 1969.

Interest-Rate Risk

The holders of fixed-income securities are exposed not only to risks from changes in price levels but also to changes in money rates. As money rates move up, the prices of existing fixed-income securities move down, and vice versa. This relationship is due to the fact that no buyer likes to buy a bond at par when its

fixed interest rate is lower than the prevailing interest rate on bonds of comparable grade. For instance, imagine that you bought a 5 percent 20-year GM bond
at par for $1,000 in 1966. Today the interest rate is much higher—say 7 percent
on comparable bonds. Suppose you want to sell your bond now; unless you are
willing to sell it for around $750, giving it a current yield of about 7 percent,
there will be little chance that you can find a buyer in the market place. The
changes in money rates can affect also the prices of common stocks but to a
lesser degree. The influence on prices of common stocks comes through changes
in relative attractiveness of yields between stocks and bonds.

Market Risk

Although the earning power of the issuing corporations remains unchanged,
the prices of their securities, especially common shares, can fluctuate widely
within a short span of time. The causes are varied, but mainly it is due to change
in investors' psychology toward equities in general, or toward certain types or
groups of securities at the time. Adverse political, social, or economic news or
rumors can affect investors' psychology and cause substantial declines in prices
in the securities markets.

Psychological Risk

This risk is akin to market risk, but remains distinct from it. The psychological risk refers to emotional instability of the investor. When the market is bullish, he is overly enthused; when the market is declining, his fear of loss grips
him; in time of panic, he will sell most or all of his securities irrespective of their
normal value in terms of actual and potential earnings. By the same token, he is
willing to pay excessive prices for securities without questioning their normal
worth during the later stage of a bull market.

These are the five major types of risks that investors encounter in their
commitment of funds to securities. In terms of the degree and extent of risks to
which various types and grades of securities are exposed, a few general statements can be made as follows:

High-grade bonds, both government and corporate, mortgages, and preferred
stocks are subject primarily to price-level and interest-rate risks and less to
market risk.

Common equities of all grades are subject primarily to business, market, and
psychological risks.

Medium- and lower-grade bonds, mortgages, and preferred stocks are subject
to business and market risks as well as price-level and interest rate risks.

QUESTIONS AND PROBLEMS

1. What type of risks is the investor exposed to when he purchases a popular
   growth stock?

2. What type of risks is the investor incurring when he purchases a portfolio of high-grade corporate bonds?

3. What are the principal types of risks involved in investment in securities? Which types in your opinion are the most important?

4. What are the advantages and disadvantages of common stock ownership?

5. Why should an investor first establish his investment objectives or goals before he commits his funds in securities?

6. Comment on the statement: "Since I don't have much money, I cannot get rich by buying "blue chip" stocks; I have to speculate on low-price stocks of little-known corporations."

7. As shown in Figure 1-1, timing of purchase and sale of securities is related to the evaluation of the position of the individual security, business-cycle developments at the time, and the security market as a whole. Why is it so?

8. Are common stocks a good hedge against inflation? Discuss.

9. Prepare a portfolio each composed of six securities having a total value of $20,000 for each of the following objectives: (a) Safety of principal and good current income; (b) Maximum appreciation possibility, (c) Moderate risk and moderate appreciation possibility; (d) Reasonable yield (current income) and protection against purchasing power risk.

10. Consult *Economic Reports of the President, Federal Reserve Bulletin, Barron's*, etc., and prepare a tabulation showing the cost of living, stock prices, bond prices, dividend yield (dividend/stock price), and bond yield (interest income/bond price) annually since 1950. What implications can you draw from this tabulation?

2. Analysis and Forecast of Trend of General Business

SECURITY VALUES AND ECONOMIC ENVIRONMENT

One of the most important determinants of security values is, of course, the income from the security, be it dividend or interest payment. The size and timing of the stream of dividends or of interest payments, in turn, depend much on the rate of secular growth of the economy and the frequency and amplitude of cyclical fluctuation.

> Sound evaluation of the expansion or contraction in the national economy is essential to sound investment. The prosperity of an industry and a company, the market price of a security, and the trend of interest rates are affected and frequently determined by the strength of the economy. An investor, before he plans the purchase (or sale) of a security of a particular company in a particular industry at a given price level, must first reach a decision on the nation's economy. Is it headed for expansion or contraction? Is productivity increasing or decreasing, i.e., is the output of goods and services rising or falling?... Is the economy headed toward inflation or deflation? Is the population rising or falling?[1]

In Figure 2-1, stock prices, as measured by Standard & Poor's Common Stock Index, are compared to the Federal Reserve's Industrial Production Index and also to gross national product in current and constant dollars for two decades. It is interesting to note that the secular growth and cyclical fluctuation of industrial production had a very similar counterpart in stock prices over this period.

LONG-TERM ECONOMIC FORECASTS

The practice of making and periodically updating a long-term forecast of economic trends and security values is a useful one. Security prices in the mar-

[1] Julius Grodinsky, *Investments* (New York: The Ronald Press Company, 1953), p. 24.

Figure 2-1
GNP, Industrial Production Index, and Stock Prices

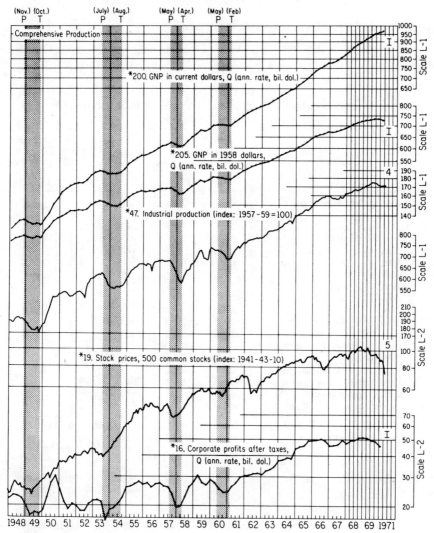

SOURCE: *Business Conditions Digest*, U.S. Department of Commerce, May 1970, adopted from tables in p. 21 and 37.

ketplace are highly volatile, and investors need bench marks for reference. The long-term economic and financial projections provide not only long-term perspective but also a frame of reference for near-term market fluctuations. A good example of long-term economic and financial forecast both in terms of quality of forecast and methodology was provided by Professor John W. Kendrick in 1961 in his forecast of the coming decade to 1970.[2]

Method of Long-Term Economic Projection

As shown in Table 2-1, to develop an economic projection of GNP in constant dollar in some years ahead requires the assumption and quantification

TABLE 2-1
Labor Supply, Productivity, and Real National Product Estimates for
1950 and 1960; Projection to 1970

Line No.	Actual		Projected 1970	Average Annual Percent Rates of Change	
	1950	1960		1950-60	1960-70
1 Total labor force (millions)	65.1	72.8	86.2	1.1	1.7
2 Armed forces	1.7	2.5	2.2	3.3	-1.3
3 Civilian labor force	63.4	70.3	84.0	1.0	1.8
4 Unemployment (millions)	3.3	3.9	3.4	1.6	-1.4
5 Percent of civilian labor force .	5.2	5.6	4.0	0.7	-3.4
6 Civilian employment	60.1	66.4	80.6	1.0	2.0
7 Government	5.5	7.9	9.6	3.8	1.9
8 Private	54.6	58.5	71.0	0.7	2.0
Average hours worked:					
9 Per week	41.0	38.9	37.0	-0.5	-0.5
10 Per year.	2134.0	2022.0	1924.0	-0.5	-0.5
11 Total man-hours (billions)	116.5	118.2	136.6	0.1	1.5
12 Real private product per man-hour (1960 dollars).	2.82	3.86	5.19	3.2	3.0
13 Real private product (billions 1960 dollars)	328.8	456.4	709.0	3.3	4.5
14 Real government product	33.6	46.8	53.0	3.4	1.3
15 Total real product (GNP).	362.3	503.2	762.0	3.3	4.2

SOURCE: John W. Kendrick, "Investment Implications of Long-Run Economic Trends," *Financial Analysts Journal*, September–October 1961, p. 30.

of two basic factors as follows:
1. Labor time—man-hours applied to production which in turn is determined by
   (a) Total labor force.
   (b) Employment between armed forces, government, and private sector.
   (c) Rate of unemployment in the private sector.
   (d) Average hours worked per week.
2. Productivity of labor force:
   (a) Government employment—held by convention at cost or proportional to labor time worked.
   (b) Private employment—depends on improvements in organization and technology of production, and capital investment for worker.

[2]John W. Kendrick, "Investment Implications of Long-Run Economic Trends," *Financial Analysts Journal*, September–October 1961, pp. 29–34.

TABLE 2-2
National Product, Corporate Profits, and Stock Market Averages Estimates for 1950 and 1960-61; Projection for 1970

Line No.	Actual 1950	Actual 1960	First Half* 1961	Projected 1970	Average Annual Percent Rates of Change 1950-60	Average Annual Percent Rates of Change 1960-70
1 Total real product (GNP)	362.3	503.2	503.2	762.0	3.3	4.2
2 Implicit price index, 1960 = 100	78.6	100.0	100.9	124.7	2.5	2.3
3 Private economy	80.2	100.0	N.A.†	122.0	2.2	2.0
4 Government	61.9	100.0	N.A.‡	162.0	5.0	5.0
5 GNP, current dollars (billions)	284.6	503.2	507.9	950.0	5.9	6.6
6 Private economy	263.8	456.4	460.9	865.0	5.6	6.6
7 Government	20.8	46.8	47.9	85.0	8.4	6.1
8 Total corporate profits, adjusted ($ billions)	35.7	45.0	41.5	80.0	2.3	5.9
9 Percent of private GNP	13.5	9.9	9.0	9.2	-2.9	-0.7
10 Reported, book profits	46.0	45.0	41.0	81.0	1.0	6.0
11 After tax	22.8	23.0	20.5	41.0	0.1	6.0
Moody's industrials:						
12 Net earnings per share	8.45	9.60	8.50	19.0	1.3	7.1
13 Price-earnings ratio (A)	6.8	18.0	22.6	14.0	12.8	-2.5
14 (B)				18.0		
15 (C)				22.0		2.0
16 Average price (A)	57.83	173.20	192.5	266.0	14.2	4.4
17 (B)				342.0‡		7.0
18 (C)				418.0		9.2
19 Dividend yield	6.3	3.6	3.1	2.7§		
20 Aaa Bond yield	2.6	4.4	4.3	4.8		

SOURCE: John W. Kendrick, "Investment Implications of Long-Run Economic Trends," *Financial Analysts Journal*, September–October 1961, p. 32.

*Seasonally adjusted at annual rates; preliminary estimates.
†Not available.
‡This figure is equivalent to approximately 1200 on the Dow-Jones Industrial Average.
§The dividend yield is computed using the (C) price projection on line 18.

The final estimate of GNP in constant dollars in Table 2-1 was $762 billion in 1970, compared to $503.2 billion in 1960. The estimate was a result of these assumptions: average increase of labor time applied in government sector at 1.3 percent per year and in private sector at 1.5 percent, and also a 3 percent annual increase in labor productivity in the private sector.

Method of Long-Term Financial Projection

After the economic forecast is completed, a conversion into financial projection can be developed by further assuming and quantifying a few more factors:

1. Rates of change in price indexes for the private and the public sectors.
2. The percentage of GNP to be carried into corporate profits.
3. Level of the corporate tax rate.
4. Range of price-earnings ratios applicable to a general market index, such as Standard & Poor's "425" Industrials, and also converting the after-tax corporate profits figure into per-share earnings of the general market index.

Table 2-2 shows the procedure as well as assumptions by Professor Kendrick in converting his long-term economic projections into a financial forecast on corporate profits and stock market averages in the decade to 1970.

EVALUATION OF KENDRICK'S LONG-TERM FORECASTS

The evaluation of Kendrick's long-term economic and financial forecasts at this point is a little difficult for two reasons. First, 1970 was not yet over at the time of this writing, and secondly, what is more important is the fact that Kendrick assumed 1970 to be a year of high economic activity, whereas actually it turned out to be a recession year. However, some brief comments may still be useful.

Economic Projections

For purpose of convenient comparison, the adjoining table shows what Kendrick forecasted a decade ago for 1970 and the current estimates for 1970.

	Assumptions and Projections by Kendrick	Actual Results and Current Estimates*
Rate of unemployment in 1970, percent	4	5–6
Average annual rate of inflation during 1960–1970, percent	2.3	2.7–2.9
Real GNP in 1970 over that in 1960 762.0/503.2, percent	151	147–150
GNP in billions of current dollars	950	975–990

*It was assumed that the real GNP in 1970 will be probably at the same level as in 1969. Rate of inflation is estimated at about 5 percent for 1970.

As can be seen from the table, Kendrick did remarkably well in his long-term economic projections.

Financial Projections

A similar table is prepared below for ready comparison between Kendrick's financial forecasts and actual results and current estimates for 1970.

	Projections by Kendrick for 1970	Actual Results or Current Estimates for 1970
Corporate profits before taxes, billions	81.0	91–93*
Corporate profits after taxes, billions	41.0	50–51*
Moody's Industrials (Index of 125 Industrial stocks):		
Net earnings per share	$19.00	16.50[†]
Price-earnings ratio		P/E range:
(A) 14		1/1–7/17/70 14–18.3[‡]
(B) 18		Actual 7/17/70 15.2
(C) 22		
Average price		Price range:
(A) 266		1/1–7/17/70 231.10–302.85
(B) 342		Actual price 7/17/70 251.65
(C) 418		
Dividend yield	2.7%	Actual 7/17/70 3.85
Aaa bond yield	4.8%	Actual range: 1/1–7/17/70 7.57–8.25

*Estimated by the Standard & Poor's Corp.
[†]Estimated by Moody's.
[‡]P/E range in 1969 was 16.8–18.7; in 1968, 16.3–19.5.

As mentioned above, Kendrick had assumed the year 1970 would be of high economic activity. He further assumed a yield of 4.8 percent for Aaa bonds. On the magnitude of price-earnings ratios, he did not choose a specific figure for 1970. However, the implication was that he was thinking of a price-earnings ratio of about 18 for the year. Therefore the resultant average price for Moody's industrials index would be about 342 in 1970. The actual price for this index on July 17, 1970 was 251.65, about 90 points lower than that forecasted by Kendrick.

Unfortunately, Kendrick did not indicate anywhere in his article what would seem to be a proper price-earnings ratio for Moody's industrials index in 1970 if the year happened to be a recession year, except for remarking in one passage that the increase in price-earnings ratio in a recession year is normal. Therefore, instead of conjecturing what Kendrick would have forecast in a recession year, let us turn to the explanation of the difference between the forecast price of 342 (P/E 18) and the actual July 17 price of 251.65, about 1/3 off the mark. The explanation of the difference seems to be accounted for by three factors: First, the actual interest rate in 1970 was much higher than assumed. The yield on Aaa bonds from January to July 1970 ranged from a low of 7.57 percent to a high of 8.25 percent, about 3 to 3½ percent higher than assumed by Kendrick.

	Forecast	Actual
Aaa bond yield, percent	4.8	7½–8¼ (3 to 3½% higher)
Earnings per share,		
Moody's industrials	19	16.50 (about 13% lower)
Price-earnings ratio		
Moody's industrials	18	15.20 (15% lower)

The second factor was the fact that currently estimated earnings of $16.50 for Moody's Industrials are about 13 percent lower than the forecast figure of $19. The third factor is the difference in the level of P/E between actual and forecast. The actual P/E on July 17, 1970 was 15.2, about 15 percent lower than the forecast level of 18.

To conclude our evaluation, a few points should probably be noted. First, while a good long-term economic forecast is not easy, a good financial forecast would be even more difficult. Second, the estimate of earnings per share for a small sample, such as Moody's 125 industrial stocks, is subject to greater error than the forecast of a large aggregate such as corporate profits for all U.S. corporations. Third, a financial forecast requires an assumption on the level of interest rate or bond yield. As shown in Kendrick's forecast, a long-term forecast of interest rate level is subject to a large degree of error, because a basic secular change in level may occur.

Finally, the most difficult and speculative part in a financial forecast is the projection of future price-earnings level. This ratio is highly volatile. In the past the price-earnings ratio for the Dow Jones 30 Industrials has fallen as low as 7 during 1948-49 and reached as high as 24 in the last half of 1961. For all of these reasons, financial and investment analysts oftentimes find their jobs more vexing than do the economic analysts.

SHORT-TERM ECONOMIC FORECAST

Stock prices in the long run are determined primarily by earnings. However, in the short run the psychology of investors plays a part no less important than actual earnings. The cyclical expansion and contraction of general business affects not only earning power of corporations but more importantly the attitudes of investors toward equities in general. Consequently, violent fluctuations in security prices are usually associated with cyclical turns in general business, though the timing is not the same. Because investors as a class are trying to anticipate what will be the near-term outlook of general business, stock prices are found usually leading the turning points of general business. Because of the close relationship between stock prices and the cyclical phase of general business, investors of all kinds, irrespective of their objectives and practices, are all keenly interested in the short-term economic forecast.

Of course most individual investors are unable to make their own forecast because of lack of training and experience, and therefore have to depend on the opinions of others—mostly economists employed by public and private institutions. Economists use a variety of concepts and techniques in attempting to forecast near-term business. In the following section four useful techniques are discussed.

1. Economic indicators.
2. Diffusion index.
3. Business and consumer surveys.
4. National income and product accounts.

SHORT-TERM FORECAST ON BASIS OF ECONOMIC INDICATORS

The National Bureau of Economic Research (NBER) is famous for its pioneering and comprehensive statistical studies of business cycles. In 1938 the NBER published its first list of business cycle indicators, as compiled by Wesley C. Mitchell and Arthur F. Burns. The list was later expanded and modified in 1950 and again in 1960. The most recent revision was made in 1966.[3] The current full list includes 88 series which are classified into 36 series of leading indicators, 25 series of roughly coincident indicators, 11 series of lagging indicators, and 16 other series unclassified by timing. The names of the 36 leading indicators with their current data are shown in Table 2-3. What is best known is their summary list, which currently consists of 12 leading indicators, 7 coincident indicators, and 6 lagging indicators—a total of 25 series. Their names and numerical ratings are shown in Table 2-4.

The system of numerical ratings was recently introduced. It was designed to help analysts in their evaluation of the current behavior of each indicator. The rating system evaluates each indicator from 0 to 100 in accordance with six major criteria: (1) economic significance of the indicator in business-cycle analysis, (2) statistical adequacy of the series in terms of reporting system, (3) historical conformity of the indicator to business cycles, (4) cyclical timing record of the indicator in relation to cyclical turning points, (5) smoothness of the series, and (6) promptness of publication of the data.

The usefulness of the NBER's statistical indicators is well recognized by government officials, business decision makers, and students of the business

[3]Geoffrey H. Moore and Julius Shiskin, *Indicators of Business Expansions and Contractions* (New York: National Bureau of Economic Research), 1967.

cycle. The statistical indicators provide not only a perspective of the historical relationship of timing between the cyclical turning points of general business and some key segments of the economy, but also a logical framework of business-cycle analysis plus valuable relationships among many key factors themselves. Reference to the current level of these indicates the current state of general business and its key components. However, the future course of the economy is affected by many imponderables. The indicators cannot normally anticipate wars, strikes, unusual weather, drastic changes in monetary or fiscal policies which may seriously affect the course of the economy. As is the case with any tool, if they are placed in the hands of experienced users, they should facilitate immensely the forecast of near-term business developments.

SHORT-TERM FORECAST ON BASIS OF DIFFUSION INDEX

The national aggregates such as GNP, personal income, corporate profits, and industrial production are extremely important statistics in indicating the current state of economic activity. However, they cover up the wide variation in the fortunes of individual firms, individual industries, and markets. The internal diversity of experience, however, is no less important than the overall average in affecting the future course of the economy. "Diffusion indexes represent an attempt to reveal and forecast the business cycle by measuring the ebb and flow of tides in the diversity of experience that underlines the cycle."[4]

The diffusion index is a statistical series indicating the percentage of items in a group which is rising at any given time. By nature, it resembles rates of change of the aggregate to which it applies. The diffusion index tends to change direction ahead of the aggregate. When the diffusion index starts to descend from a high level, the aggregate will continue to ascend. Conversely, when the diffusion index begins its rise from a low level, the aggregate will continue its decline. Only after the diffusion index rises to the 50 percent line will the aggregate cease to decrease.

As a tool in the forecast of short-term business developments, the diffusion index is either related to a group of NBER's indicators or a given economic process or factor of importance such as rising profits reported by corporations in manufacturing. The Bureau of the Census makes available in Business Cycle Developments its current compilation of diffusion indexes. They are all related to individual economic series. As shown in Figures 2-2 and 2-3, there are seven diffusion indexes relating to leading indicators and four diffusion indexes relating to coincident indicators.

To provide a current forecast, a summary is necessary of all the components in a diffusion index, or alternatively all the individual diffusion indexes. The

---

4 Albert T. Sommers, "Diffusion Indexes," in William F. Butler and Robert A. Kavesh, (eds.), *How Business Economists Forecast* (Englewood Cliffs, N.J.: Prentice-Hall, Inc., 1966).

TABLE 2-3
Summary of Recent Data and Current Changes for Leading Indicators

Series Title	Unit of Measure	Basic Data† 1968	1969	3d Q 1969	4th Q 1969	1st Q 1970	Feb. 1970	Mar. 1970	Apr. 1970	Percent Change Feb. to Mar. 1970	Mar. to Apr. 1970	3d Q to 4th Q 1969	4th Q 1969 to 1st Q 1970	Series Number
B1. Employment and Unemployment														
Marginal Employment Adjustments:														
*1. Average workweek, prod. workers, mfg.	Hours	40.7	40.6	40.7	40.6	40.1	39.9	40.2	40.0	0.8	- 0.5	-0.2	-1.2	1
4. Nonagri. placements, all industries	Ann. rate, thous.	5,716	5,149	5,136	4,728	4,420	4,332	4,284	NA	-1.1	NA	-7.9	-6.5	4
2. Accession rate, manufacturing‡	Per 100 employ.	4.6	4.7	4.7	4.6	4.2	4.3	4.0	NA	-0.3	NA	-0.1	-0.4	2
*5. Avg. weekly initial claims, State unemployment insurance (inverted§)	Thousands	194	194	197	208	248	250	263	326	-5.2	-24.0	-5.6	-19.2	5
3. Layoff rate, manufacturing (inverted§)‡	Per 100 employ.	1.2	1.2	1.2	1.3	1.7	1.7	1.8	NA	-0.1	NA	-0.1	-0.4	3
B3. Fixed Capital Investment														
Formation of Business Enterprises:														
*12. Index of net business formation	1957-59 = 100	117.8	123.6	124.0	122.4	120.2	121.7	117.1	NA	-3.8	NA	-1.3	-1.8	12
13. New business incorporations	Ann. rate, thous.	233.2	273.2	278.6	278.0	265.6	279.0	253.1	NA	-9.3	NA	-0.2	-4.5	13
New Investment Commitments:														
*6. New orders, durable goods industries	Ann. rate, bil. dol.	334.5	367.0	374.8	373.2	348.8	355.9	343.6	346.9	-3.5	1.0	-0.4	-6.5	6
8. Construction contracts, total value	1957-59 = 100	176	194	190	197	209	215	208	203	-3.3	- 2.4	3.7	6.1	8
*10. Contracts and orders, plant, equipment	Ann. rate, bil. dol.	85.0	95.7	96.0	97.2	99.5	102.6	91.2	98.9	-11.1	8.4	1.2	2.4	10
11. New capital appropriations, manufacturing	....do....	24.8	30.0	31.8	30.4	25.9	...	...	...	...	...	-4.4	-14.8	11
24. New orders, mach. and equip. industries	....do....	69.7	78.8	79.8	78.6	76.0	79.2	71.8	72.7	-9.3	1.3	-1.5	-3.3	24
9. Construction contracts, commercial and industrial buildings	Ann. rate, mil. sq. ft. floor space	793	905	858	925	948	971	805	768	-17.1	- 4.6	7.8	2.5	9
7. Private nonfarm housing starts	Ann. rate, thous.	1,484	1,464	1,410	1,328	1,232	1,267	1,364	1,164	6.0	-14.7	-5.8	-7.2	7
*29. New bldg. permits, private housing	1957-59 = 100	112.9	109.7	102.3	100.6	90.5	95.0	91.8	104.4	-3.4	13.7	-1.7	-10.0	29

Table 2-3 (Continued)

Series Title	Unit of Measure	Basic Data†								Percent Change				Series Number
		1968	1969	3d Q 1969	4th Q 1969	1st Q 1970	Feb. 1970	Mar. 1970	Apr. 1970	Feb. to Mar. 1970	Mar. to Apr. 1970	3d Q to 4th Q 1969	4th Q 1969 to 1st Q 1970	
B4. Inventories and Inventory Investments														
Inventory Investment and Purchasing:														
245. Change in business inventories, all industries.‡	Ann. rate, billion dollars	7.3	8.0	10.7	7.7	0.8	...	...	...	...	...	-3.0	-6.9	245
*31. Change in book value, manufacturing and trade inventories‡	. . . . do. . . .	10.1	12.3	13.9	13.5	3.3	11.7	1.8	NA	-9.9	NA	-0.4	-10.2	31
37. Purchased materials, percent reporting higher inventories‡	Percent.	51	50	50	53	50	50	51	45	1	-6	3	-3	37
20. Change in book value, manufacturers' inventories of materials, supplies.‡	Ann. rate, billion dollars	1.4	1.1	0.4	2.0	0.9	2.2	2.0	NA	-0.2	NA	1.6	-1.1	20
26. Buying policy, production materials, commitments 60 days or longer‡ ⑪	Percent.	64	63	62	64	60	62	56	60	-6	4	2	-4	26
32. Vendor performance, percent reporting slower deliveries‡ ⑪	. . . . do. . . .	53	65	67	64	55	58	50	52	-8	2	-3	-9	32
25. Change in unfilled orders, durable goods industries.‡	Ann. rate billion dollars	3.5	2.6	1.9	1.2	-11.8	-8.9	-13.0	-10.3	-4.1	2.7	-0.7	-13.0	25
B5. Prices, Costs, and Profits														
Sensitive Commodity Prices:														
*23. Industrial materials prices ⑪	1957-59 = 100	97.8	111.8	114.9	116.1	119.5	120.0	119.2	118.7	-0.7	-0.4	1.0	2.9	23
Stock Prices:														
*19. Stock prices, 500 common stocks ⑪	1941-43 = 10	98.7	97.8	94.5	94.3	88.7	87.2	88.6	86.0	1.6	-2.9	-0.2	-5.9	19

16

Profits and Profit Margins:

Series		Unit													Series
*16. Corporate profits, after taxes		Ann. rate, bil. dol.	49.8	50.5	49.7	49.0	46.1	...	...	...	...	...	-1.4	-5.9	16
22. Ratio, profits to income originating, corporate, all industries‡		Percent	11.4	10.7	10.4	10.2	9.6	...	...	...	...	...	-0.2	-0.6	22
15. Profits (after taxes) per dol. of sales, mfg.‡		Cents	5.1	4.8	4.8	4.5	NA	...	...	...	...	...	-0.3	NA	15
*17. Ratio, price to unit labor cost, mfg.		1957-59 = 100	99.8	99.4	99.4	98.4	98.8	99.1	98.9	99.2	-0.2	0.3	-1.0	0.4	17

B6. Money and Credit

Flows of Money and Credit:

Series		Unit													Series
98. Change in money supply and time deposits‡		Ann. rate, percent	9.0	-1.5	-6.7	0.6	2.2	-5.8	13.8	16.3	19.6	2.5	7.3	1.6	98
85. Change in money supply‡‡		do	7.0	2.4	0.0	1.2	3.8	-10.8	13.2	10.7	24.0	-2.5	1.2	2.6	85
33. Change in mortgage debt‡		Ann. rate, bil. dol.	20.1	19.9	19.5	17.6	15.0	14.5	13.7	NA	-0.8	NA	-1.9	-2.6	33
*113. Change in consumer installment debt‡		do	8.9	8.1	7.7	6.8	4.0	5.0	2.4	NA	-2.6	NA	-0.9	-2.8	113
112. Change in business loans‡		do	7.4	7.4	3.3	6.1	-3.2	5.5	-2.4	-2.1	-7.9	0.3	2.8	-9.3	112
110. Total private borrowing		do	84.1	91.9	89.7	81.8	78.8	...	...	...	...	...	-8.8	-3.7	110

Credit Difficulties:

Series		Unit													Series
14. Liabilities of business failures (inv.§)⑪		do	0.94	1.14	1.00	1.36	1.59	1.67	1.44	1.58	13.8	-9.7	-36.0	-16.9	14
39. Delinquency rate, installment loans (inverted§)‡ ‖		Percent, EOP	1.67	1.81	1.70	1.81	1.79	1.79	NA	NA	NA	NA	-0.11	0.02	39

SOURCE: Table 1 "Summary of Recent Data and Current Changes for Principal Indicators" in *Business Conditions Digest*, May 1970, pp. 6–7.
NOTE: Series are seasonally adjusted except for those indicated by ⑪, which appear to contain no seasonal movement. *Series included in the 1966 NBER "short list" of indicators. NA = not available. a = anticipated. EOP = end of period.
†In many cases, data shown here are rounded to fewer digits or are in different units than those shown in the tables in part II. Where available, annual figures are the figures published by the source agencies or they are rounded from published figures; otherwise they (and the quarterly figures for monthly series) are averages or totals of the data as shown in part II.
‡Differences rather than percent changes are shown for this series.
§Inverted series. Since this series tends to move counter to movements in general business activity, signs of the changes are reversed.
‖End-of-period series. The annual figures (and quarterly figures for monthly series) are the last figures for the period.

TABLE 2-4
Short List of Indicators: Scores and Timing Characteristics

Classification and Series Title (1)	First Business Cycle Turn Covered (2)	Average Score (3)	Scores, Six Criteria						Timing at Peaks and Troughs				
			Economic Significance (4)	Statistical Adequacy (5)	Conformity (6)	Timing (7)	Smoothness (8)	Currency (9)	Business Cycle Turns Covered (10)	Leads (11)	Rough Coincidences* (12)	Lags (13)	Median Lead (−) or Lag (+) in Months (14)
Leading indicators (12 series)													
1. Avg. workweek, prod. workers, mfg.	1921	66	50	65	81	66	60	80	19	13	4(2)	2	−5
30. Nonagri. placements, BES	1945	68	75	63	63	58	80	80	10	8	4(0)	1	−3
38. Index of net business formation	1945	68	75	58	81	67	80	40	10	8	3(1)	0	−7
6. New orders, dur. goods indus.	1920	78	75	72	88	84	60	80	20	16	7(1)	0	−4
10. Contracts and orders, plant and equipment	1948	64	75	63	92	50	40	40	8	7	2(0)	1	−6
29. New building permits, private housing units	1918	67	50	60	76	80	60	80	22	17	5(1)	1	−6
31. Change in book value, mfg. and trade inventories	1945	65	75	67	77	78	20	40	10	9	2(1)	0	−8
23. Industrial materials prices	1919	67	50	72	79	44	80	100	21	13	9(4)	2	−2
19. Stock prices, 500 common stocks	1873	81	75	74	77	87	80	100	44	33	14(2)	5	−4
16. Corporate profits after taxes, Q	1920	68	75	70	79	76	60	25	20	13	11(4)	2	−2
17. Ratio, price to unit labor cost, mfg.	1919	69	50	67	84	72	60	80	21	17	10(1)	3	−3
113. Change in consumer instalment debt	1929	63	50	79	77	60	60	40	14	11	4(0)	1	−10

Roughly coincident indicators (7 series)													
41. Employees in nonagri. establishments	1929	81	75	61	90	87	100	80	14	6	12(6)	2	0
43. Unemployment rate, total (inv.)	1929	75	75	63	96	60	80	80	14	4	8(3)	6	0
50. GNP in constant dollars, expenditure estimate, Q	1921	73	75	75	91	58	80	50	17	7	9(3)	3	−2
47. Industrial production	1919	72	75	63	94	38	100	80	21	9	13(9)	3	0
52. Personal income	1921	74	75	73	89	43	100	80	19	10	12(2)	5	−1
816. Mfg. and trade sales	1948	71	75	68	70	80	80	40	8	4	6(4)	0	0
54. Sales of retail stores	1919	69	75	77	89	12	80	100	21	5	7(1)	6	0
Lagging indicators (6 series)													
502. Unempl. rate, persons unempl. 15+ weeks (inv.)	1948	69	50	63	98	52	80	80	8	1	5(1)	6	+2
61. Bus. expend., plant and equip., Q	1918	86	75	77	96	94	100	80	20	2	16(5)	13	+1
71. Book value, mfg. and trade inventories	1945	71	75	67	75	66	100	40	10	2	7(0)	8	+2
62. Labor cost per unit of output, mfg.	1919	68	50	70	83	56	80	80	21	0	1(0)	14	+8
72. Comm. and indus. loans outstanding	1937	57	50	47	67	20	100	100	12	1	6(0)	7	+2
67. Bank rates, short-term bus. loans, Q	1919	60	50	55	82	47	80	50	21	2	5(1)	15	+5

SOURCE: Geoffrey H. Moore and Julius Shiskin, *Indicators of Business Expansions and Contractions*, (New York: National Bureau of Economic Research), 1967, p. 68.

*Rough coincidences include exact coincidences (shown in parentheses) and leads and lags of 3 months or less. Leads (lags) include leads (lags) of 1 month or more. The total number of timing comparisons, which can be less than the number of business cycle turns covered by the series, is the sum of the leads, exact coincidences, and lags. Leads and lags of quarterly series are expressed in terms of months.

Figure 2-2
Diffusion Indexes

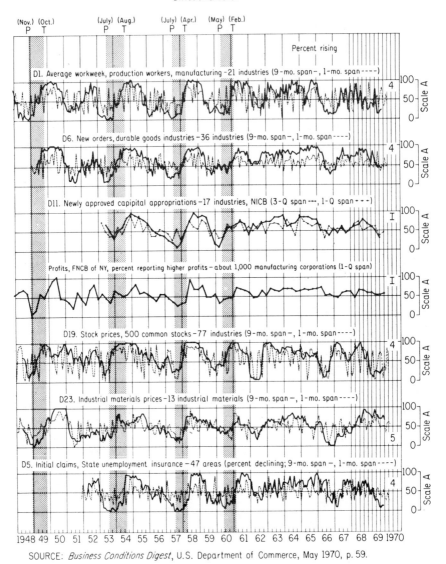

SOURCE: *Business Conditions Digest*, U.S. Department of Commerce, May 1970, p. 59.

widely used technique is a weighted average or "duration of run" index. Under this method, each series is weighted by the number of months during which it has been rising. The weights of all the component series will be first added and then divided by the number of the component series. The resulting figure is the "duration of run" index, indicating the summarized view of the current forecast.

Figure 2-3
Diffusion Indexes

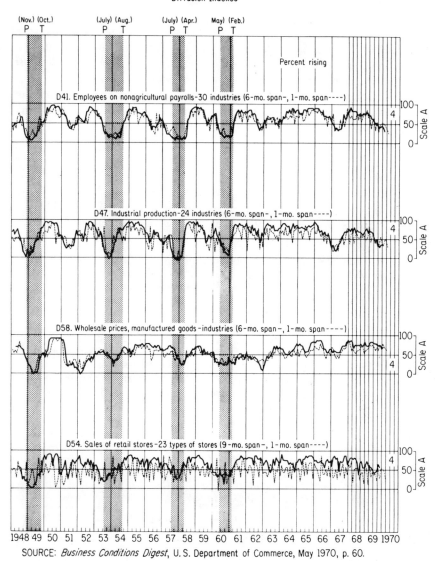

SOURCE: *Business Conditions Digest*, U. S. Department of Commerce, May 1970, p. 60.

The usefulness of diffusion index as a supplementary tool in near-term business forecast is well acknowledged by most students of business cycle. However, as a statistical tool it suffers the same limitations as economic indicators. Besides occasionally flashing invalid signals, the diffusion indexes cannot anticipate impending events such as major strikes or changes in governmental policies.

SHORT-TERM FORECAST ON BASIS OF BUSINESS AND CONSUMER SURVEYS

In recent years more emphasis has been placed on surveys of plans and intentions of business decision makers and consumers in the formulation of short-term business forecast. Of course, business and consumer plans for investments and purchases in the near future can be modified or, occasionally, completely abandoned or reversed. But experience in the postwar years indicates that by and large the plans of business units and consumers as revealed in various surveys in most cases compare quite closely to actual expenditures in subsequent periods.[5]

The more important and also more successful surveys of expectations in recent years have been capital expenditures by businesses and purchases of durables by consumers. The results from surveys on inventory intentions by business and on plans of home building have, however, been less successful. The major types of surveys of anticipatory data and the agencies which are conducting these surveys are[6]

1. Plant and equipment. Commerce-SEC and McGraw-Hill capital budgets; National Industrial Conference Board surveys of capital appropriations; McGraw-Hill survey of order expectations by machinery producers; *Fortune* surveys of order expectations by machinery producers and building activity by construction contractors; other private surveys, such as the *Electrical World*, Edison Electric Institute, and American Gas Association.
2. Sales expectations and inventory plans. Commerce Department and *Fortune* surveys for manufacturing and nonmanufacturing; McGraw-Hill surveys of annual sales expectations; Dun & Bradstreet surveys; *Fortune* "business mood" survey; National Association of Purchasing Agents surveys.
3. Consumer surveys. Census Bureau, University of Michigan Survey Research Center, and Sindlinger-NICB surveys.
4. Home building: *Fortune* and National Association of Home Builders surveys of builders; consumer surveys in (3) above.
5. Foreign activity. Commerce Department and McGraw-Hill surveys of capital expenditures abroad; NICB foreign capital appropriations; McGraw-Hill exports sales expectations.

The usefulness and limitation of the survey approach to short-term business forecast is well explained by Morris Cohen in these words:

> Surveys do provide forecasting inputs, sensitive tools for short-term forecasting. They cannot be simply used for a once-a-year forecast which is then placed in the desk drawer for twelve months. Rather, surveys are useful in economic projections that are constantly under

[5]Morris Cohen, "Surveys and Forecasting," in William F. Butler and Robert A. Kavesh, (eds.), *How Business Economists Forecast* (Englewood Cliffs, N.J.: Prentice-Hall, Inc., 1966), pp. 55–85.
[6]Cohen, *op. cit.*, p. 60.

review, preferably on a quarterly basis. What is required is an hypothesis for the operation of the economy which is then tested by various survey results and other factors and information. The hypothesis must be consistent with survey results, and when the two differ, the hypothesis is subject to change. The human element of judgement still must play the most important part of all. Surveys can sometimes yield conflicting results, and at times, surveys covering the same field can point to opposite conclusions. All this means that intentions are only one set of tools that the forecaster must use, along with other tools and considerations. Despite these disclaimers and limitations, foreshadowing surveys of businessmen and consumers represent a most important body of economic intelligence for business forecasting. Those who ignore such findings do so at their peril.[7]

SHORT-TERM FORECAST ON BASIS OF NATIONAL INCOME AND PRODUCT ACCOUNTS

Possibly the most widely used technique of short-term forecast today employs as framework the national income and product accounts. There are many advantages to this approach. Gross national product represents the market value of goods and services currently produced or, alternatively, the sum of expenditures by consumers, government, business, and the net difference between exports and imports. Detailed figures for each component of GNP for many years are available. Through regression analysis valuable historical relationships can be found among the different components and subcomponents of GNP. Additionally, the current data of each component or subcomponent of GNP can be used as a starting point in the estimates for the next period. Under this approach, the forecaster can weigh diverse elements and make up a final judgment as to the probable size and timing of a particular component of GNP. Specifically, he will examine

(a) The factors that are supposed to affect most the type of expenditure under consideration according to theories of business cycles.
(b) The historical relationship between the type of expenditure under consideration and other economic series.
(c) Probable future developments such as governmental policies and institutional changes which will likely affect the item under consideration.

In other words, this approach is flexible enough to allow the incorporation of results from other forecasting methods mentioned above and, more importantly, the full play of the role of judgment of the forecaster.

The forecasting process, which is followed by many forecasters and is highly recommended, consists of several steps:

1. To list the assumptions under which the economy is expected to operate

[7]*Ibid.*, p. 85.

in the forthcoming period. The assumptions usually relate to war or peace, major strikes, taxes, relationship between the government and the business community, and so forth.

2. To estimate individually the major components of GNP and then sum them up, yielding the forecast of GNP. The major components follow.

   (a) Government expenditures on goods and services, excluding transfer payments

      Federal nondefense expenditures
      Federal defense expenditures
      State and local government expenditures

   (b) Gross private-domestic investment

      Nonresidential structures
      Producers' durable equipment
      Residential structures
      Changes in business inventories

   (c) Personal consumption expenditures

      Durable goods
      Nondurable goods
      Services

   (d) Net exports of goods and services

3. To estimate independently GNP on basis of assumptions relating to

   Civilian labor force
   Length of work week
   Unemployment rate
   Increase of productivity per man hour
   Increase in general price level

4. To reconcile the estimates from (2) and (3) above to arrive at a final estimate of GNP.

Among the components of GNP there are four areas that are most difficult to forecast. They represent postponable expenditures by business and consumers.

   Capital spending on plant and equipment
   Residential construction
   Changes in business inventories
   Consumer purchases of durable goods

Capital spending on plant and equipment depends on a variety of factors, including corporate cash flow (retained earnings plus depreciation allowance), rate of capacity utilization in manufacturing, profit margins, and increase in labor cost. It is difficult to find consistent relationships over time between capital spending and other factors, especially in the short run. Analysts therefore lean quite heavily on spending anticipations of business from surveys by McGraw-Hill, Department of Commerce, Securities and Exchange Commission, and National Industrial Conference Board.

The forecast of residential construction is complicated by the fact that the residential housing cycle differs importantly from the cycles of the general economy. On the demand side, residential construction depends primarily on rate of family formation and disposable income. Availability and cost of credit, together with changes in regulations respecting government financing, on the other hand, dominate the supply side. The figures on contract awards of residential construction by F. W. Dodge and the results from some housing surveys are often refered to for indications.

The forecast of changes in business inventory is often considered to be the least successful part in short-term business forecasting. Lack of current data on inventories and quick changes in inventory policy by business are cited by two leading business analysts as the most vexing problems in the area.[8] The forecaster in developing his forecast would have to examine a number of factors for indications. Some of the important factors are

(a) The prospective demand in major industries.
(b) The extent of price increase expected and its possible influence on inventory policy of business.
(c) The pattern of inventory/sales ratio in the past.
(d) Projections by businessmen about their own stocks as revealed by surveys.

Careful consideration of these factors does not automatically guarentee good results. However, it is hoped that gross miscalculation may be thereby avoided.

The purchases of consumer durable goods in the past were found quite responsive to the rate of gain of personal income as well as to its absolute level. Automobiles, appliances, and furniture represent 90 percent of the total expenditures on durables. The forecast of new car sales is by far the most important one because of its relative size as well as its volatility.

Unfortunately, economic forecasting at the current stage of development is still no less an art than science. A good forecaster needs to have a good command of theoretical knowledge about business cycles as well as methods and techniques in statistical analysis. Moreover, he should be endowed with the ability to exercise good judgments in most of his estimates and projections. The work of the economic forecaster is very complex and challenging, but never dull. Because of the complexity in making up a forecast, investment analysts usually do not make up forecasts themselves but lean more or less on the professional economists inside and outside their organization for advice and "enlightening." However, in order to appreciate fully the implications of economic forecasts by others, the investment analysts should be thoroughly versed in the techniques of

[8]*Business Outlook—1968*, Studies in Business Economics, No. 99, National Industrial Conference Board, p. 51.

TABLE 2-5
Forecast of 1971 GNP by Standard & Poor's Corporation

KEY PATTERNS IN THE ECONOMY

(In billions of dollars unless otherwise stated)	Actual 3Q '70 (annual rate)	Estimated % Changes 1970	Estimated % Changes 1971	1970 as reported I	1970 II	1970 III	1970 IV	1971 S&P estimates I	1971 II	1971 III	1971 IV
Basic Data											
Gross national product	990.9	4.9	8.1	959.5	971.1	985.5	990.9	1021.0	1049.0	1063.0	1090.0
Deflated GNP	721.3	-0.4	2.8	723.8	724.9	727.4	721.3	735.1	745.1	745.0	753.4
Corporate pretax profits	80.2	-9.8	10.0	82.6	82.0	84.4	80.2	86.0	91.0	91.0	95.0
Corporate after tax profits	43.7	-8.5	10.1	44.6	43.9	45.4	43.7	46.4	49.1	48.6	51.3
Unemployment rate (%)	5.8			4.2	4.8	5.2	5.8	5.8	5.4	5.2	4.8
Corporate bond yields (%)				8.95	9.44	9.06		Rising Trend			
Consumer sentiment (index)	72.4			78.1	75.4	77.1	72.4	Rising Trend			
Quarter-to-Quarter % Changes (annual rates)											
Gross national product	990.9	4.9	8.1	3.3	4.9	6.1	2.2	12.8	11.4	5.4	10.6
Inflation factor (1958=100)	137.39	5.3	5.1	6.4	4.3	4.6	5.7	4.5	5.5	5.5	5.7
Deflated GNP	721.3	-0.4	2.8	-2.9	0.6	1.4	-3.3	7.9	5.6	0	4.6
FRB production index	162.6	-3.0	2.6	-2.7	-3.1	-0.4	-12.8	15.6	12.4	-2.4	7.1
Disposable personal income	696.9	8.4	7.0	9.3	11.5	5.7	2.3	8.3	9.3	6.8	7.8

Dynamic Spending Sectors				Quarter-to-Quarter Changes (billions of dollars)							
Inventory change.	4.1			-5.6	1.5	2.4	-1.4	3.9	3.0	-3.0	2.0
Residential construction . .	32.0	-7.2	24.9	-1.3	-0.7	0.8	2.8	3.0	2.0	1.0	0.5
Consumer durables	85.4	-0.7	6.5	-1.7	2.8	-0.7	-5.8	5.0	5.1	-0.5	5.0
Business capital spending . .	101.4	3.3	6.8	0	0.2	0.8	-2.2	3.1	3.5	3.0	4.0
Highly cyclical expenditures†	222.9	-2.0	11.7	-8.7	3.9	3.3	-6.6	15.0	13.6	0.5	12.5
Mildly cyclical expenditures‡	396.5	8.1	8.1	10.0	5.1	6.9	8.3	8.2	8.3	8.0	8.0
Other expenditures	371.5	6.1	5.8	6.7	2.7	4.2	3.6	6.9	6.1	5.5	6.5

Sensitive Indicators		Quarter-to-Quarter % Changes (annual rates)							
Money supply	213.7	5.9	5.8	6.1	3.2	7.0	5.5	5.0	5.0
Highly cyclical expenditures†	222.9	-15.9	7.2	5.9	-11.0	29.7	24.9	0.8	21.3
Productivity (1957-59=100)	136.1*	-2.9	3.9	4.8	Average about 3.0%				

SOURCE: "Trends and Projections," *Industry Survey*, Standard & Poor's Corporation, Feb. 7, 1970.

*Third quarter value.

†Highly cyclical expenditures include consumer durables, residential construction, inventory change, and business capital spending.

‡Mildly cyclical expenditures include consumer nondurables and state and local government spending. Other expenditures include consumer services, the federal government, and net exports.

TABLE 2-6
Projections of Gross National Product*

Source and Date	Projections (billions of dollars)						
	Quarterly					Annual	
	Actual '70 IV	'71 I	'71 II	'71 III	'71 IV	Actual 1970	1971
ASA/NBER Survey of Regular Forecasters, January 1971	991 (2.2%) 721 (−3.3%)	1014 (9.7%) 733 (6.6%)	1033 (7.7%) 741 (4.4%)	1051 (7.2%) 748 (3.8%)	1069 (7.0%) 755 (3.8%)	977 (4.9%) 724 (−0.4%)	1043 (6.8%) 745 (2.9%)
Wharton Econometric Model, January 1971	991 (2.2%) 721 (−3.3%)	1024 (13.8%) 740 (10.8%)	1041 (6.9%) 745 (2.7%)	1052 (4.4%) 743 (−0.8%)	1084 (12.6%) 759 (8.4%)	977 (4.9%) 724 (−0.4%)	1050 (7.5%) 747 (3.1%)
Michigan Econometric Model, November 1970	991 (2.2%) 721 (−3.3%)	1013 (9.4%) 735 (8.0%)	1035 (8.7%) 743 (4.3%)	1053 (7.2%) 752 (4.7%)	1070 (6.4%) 758 (3.4%)	977 (4.9%) 724 (−0.4%)	1043 (6.7%) 747 (3.1%)
GNP/Money Supply Relationship, January 1971	991 (2.2%) 721 (−3.3%)	1015 (10.0%) 733 (6.4%)	1029 (6.0%) 736 (1.7%)	1052 (9.0%) 744 (4.7%)	1068 (6.3%) 748 (2.3%)	977 (4.9%) 724 (−0.4%)	1041 (6.6%) 740 (2.2%)
MKE Associates, January 1971	991 (2.2%) 721 (−3.3%)	1022 (13.2%) 737 (9.0%)	1042 (8.1%) 745 (4.4%)	1053 (4.3%) 746 (0.5%)	1073 (7.8%) 754 (4.4%)	977 (4.9%) 724 (−0.4%)	1048 (7.3%) 745 (2.9%)
Data Resources Inc., January 1971	991 (2.2%) 721 (−3.3%)	1019 (11.7%) 735 (7.8%)	1043 (9.7%) 747 (6.8%)	1054 (4.6%) 748 (0.4%)	1072 (7.1%) 755 (4.1%)	977 (4.9%) 724 (−0.4%)	1047 (7.2%) 746 (3.1%)
GNP/Leading Indicators Relationship, November 1970						977 (4.9%) 724 (−0.4%)	n.a.

SOURCE: *Conference Board Statistical Bulletin*, National Industrial Conference Board, Inc., February 1971, p. 4.

*In each set of forecast data, the first line indicates current dollars, and the third line, 1958 based constant dollars. Percentages in parentheses are annual rates of growth from the previous period.

"ASA/NBER" projections are from a quarterly survey of economists who regularly prepare forecasts of the U.S. economy. The survey is made by the American Statistical Association and the National Bureau of Economic Research.

"Wharton" projections are from an econometric model developed by Wharton EFA, a non-profit group owned by the University of Pennsylvania.

"Michigan" projections are from an econometric model developed by the Research Seminar in Quantitative Economics at the University of Michigan, Ann Arbor.

"GNP/Money Supply" projections are obtained from the Federal Reserve of St. Louis. The basic model used is discussed in L.C. Andersen and K.M. Carlson, "A Monetarist Model for Economic Stabilization," Federal Reserve Bank of St. Louis *Review*, April 1970, pp. 7–25.

"MKE Assoc." (formerly "Philadelphia Research Assoc.") forecasts are from an econometric model developed by MKE Associates.

"Data Resources Inc." forecasts are from an econometric model developed by D.R.I.

The "GNP/Leading Indicator Relationship" projection (annual only) is based on a revised version of a regression equation relating GNP to the Census Bureau's composite index of twelve leading indicators; see Geoffrey H. Moore, "Forecasting Short-Term Economic Change," *Journal of the American Statistical Association*, March 1969, Vol. 64, pp. 1–22.

making up a forecast and sources of "raw materials." If necessary, he himself should be able to make up a forecast.[9]

Forecast of GNP for the current year 1971 by Standard & Poor's Corporation is shown in Table 2-5. Projections of GNP by various other organizations for 1971 are shown in Table 2-6.

INPUT-OUTPUT ANALYSIS

For purpose of developing forecast of industry sales, many analysts in recent years have turned to a type of interindustry analysis known as input-output analysis. The Input-Output analysis was developed by Wassily Leontief of Harvard University. He developed and published the first input-output table for the economy of the United States in an article "Quantitative Input-Output Relations in the Economic System of the United States," in *The Review of Economics and Statistics* for August 1936. The purpose of his approach is to show empirically the structure and the working of the national economy, highlighting the interdependence of the different sectors in the economy.

Following his lead, the U. S. Government has already compiled and published three input-output tables for the economy for the years 1947, 1958, and 1963. Though the input-output approach is still in its developmental stage in terms of content of information and frequency of publication as well as methods and techniques of analyzing the wealth of information therein, the approach seems to possess much potential and may in future years constitute an important tool in economic forecasts, particularly of interindustry relations.

The Input-Output Table

For purpose of illustration, a highly simplified hypothetical input-output relationship is shown in Table 2-7. The processing sector of the economy is divided into six basic industries labeled A to F. They can be agriculture, mining, manufacturing, transportation, wholesale and retail trade, and so on. In an actual table there may be 50 or more industries.[10] In addition, there is a payments sector composed of inventory changes, imports or exports, governments, private capital formation, and households. Altogether there are eleven departments for the economy into which all transactions representing production, distribution, transportation, and consumption are grouped.

---

[9]For more detailed discussions on how to make up a short-term forecast of the economy, the reader is advised to consult particularly the following: Bratt, *Business Cycles and Forecasting*, chaps. 17, 18; C. W. McMahon, *Techniques of Economic Forecasting*; and William F. Butler and Elmer C. Kavesh, *How Business Economists Forecast*, Part II. See Suggested Readings at end of chapter.

[10]The input-output table for 1958 included 82 industries in the processing sector which was further divided into 370 industries in the most recent table for 1963.

TABLE 2-7
Hypothetical Transactions Table

Outputs → / Inputs ↓	Processing Sector (1) A	(2) B	(3) C	(4) D	(5) E	(6) F	Final Demand (7) Gross Inventory Accumulation (+)	(8) Exports to Foreign Countries	(9) Government Purchases	(10) Gross Private Capital Formation	(11) Households	(12) Total Gross Output
(1) Industry A	10	15	1	2	5	6	2	5	1	3	14	64
(2) Industry B	5	4	7	1	3	8	1	6	3	4	17	59
(3) Industry C	7	2	8	1	5	3	2	3	1	3	5	40
(4) Industry D	11	1	2	8	6	4	0	0	1	2	4	39
(5) Industry E	4	0	1	14	3	2	1	2	1	3	9	40
(6) Industry F	2	6	7	6	2	6	2	4	2	1	8	46
(7) Gross inventory depletion (–)	1	2	1	0	2	1	0	1	0	0	0	8
(8) Imports	2	1	3	0	3	2	0	0	0	0	2	13
(9) Payments to government	2	3	2	2	1	2	3	2	1	2	12	32
(10) Depreciation allowances	1	2	1	0	1	0	0	0	0	0	0	5
(11) Households	19	23	7	5	9	12	1	0	8	0	1	85
(12) Total gross outlays	64	59	40	39	40	46	12	23	18	18	72	431

Industry Purchasing

Processing Sector Industry Producing — Payments Sector

SOURCE: William H. Miernyk, *The Elements of Input-Output Analysis* (New York: Random House, Inc., 1965), p. 9.
*Sales to industries and sectors along the top of the table from the industry listed in each row at the left of the table.
†Purchases from industries and sectors at the left of the table by the industry listed at the top of each column.

Each horizontal row of figures in the table shows the distribution of the output of one sector among other sectors of the economy including itself. The vertical columns show how each sector obtains its inputs from other sectors. Take industry B for example. The total output is 59 units or dollars worth of goods or services. They are distributed as follows: 4 for intraindustry consumption, 5 to A, 7 to C, 1 to D, 3 to E, 8 to F, 1 for addition to inventory, 6 for exports to foreign countries, 3 to governments, 4 for private capital formation, and 17 for consumption by households. In order to enable industry B to produce 59 units of goods, it obtains inputs from other sectors as follows: 15 from A, 4 from intraindustry firms, 2 from C, 1 from D, 6 from F, 2 from depletion of inventory, 1 from imports, 3 from government services, 2 from wear and tear of equipment, and 23 from services rendered by households.

As shown in the table, the total inputs of each industry in the processing sector must equal its total outputs. For the payments sector, however, receipts and expenditures of each department can vary. For example, the households received a total of 85 units but spent only 72 units. Of course, the total receipts of all departments in the payments sector must be the same as their total expenditures for the whole payments sector.

Possible Applications of the Input-Output Table

The possibilities for applications are not yet fully developed. They depend not only on the ingenuity of the user but also on the amount of desegregation of industries contained in the table, and on its timeliness. However, several obvious uses can be noted:

1. Some tables can be derived from the input-output table to indicate:
   (a) the amount of direct purchases required from other industries per dollar of output for each industry, and,
   (b) the total direct and indirect requirements for inputs from other sectors in order to satisfy an additional unit of final demand for any industry.
2. It is possible to estimate not only the distribution of output of one sector but probably also the type of uses the product enters into.
3. It is conceivable that the use of such an empirical table can help avoid some inconsistencies that may develop otherwise in economic projections, both long-term and short-term.
4. The input-output table can be used by individual business to evaluate market prospects for established products, to identify potential markets for new products, to spot prospective shortages in supplies, and to enable them to evaluate investment prospects in various industries.
5. It can be readily seen that the input-output tables are very helpful when the analyst is attempting to make a forecast of the total sales of an industry. He can estimate the demands from individual sectors and then

32 Analysis and Forecast of Trend of General Business

the total demand for the industry. He can also start from an assumed level of GNP for the economy and work backward to individual industries.[11]

SUGGESTED READINGS

Ahearn, Daniel S., "Investment Management and Economic Research," *Financial Analysts Journal*, January-February 1964.

Bratt, Elmer C., *Business Cycles & Forecasting*. 5th ed. Homewood, Ill.. Richard D. Irwin, Inc. 1961.

Butler, William F., and Elmer C. Kavesh, *How Business Economists Forecast*, Part II.

Dauten, Carl A., and Lloyd M. Valentine, *Business Cycles and Forecasting*. Cincinnati, Ohio: South-Western Publishing Co., 1968.

Dunlop, John T., "New Forces in the Economy," *Harvard Business Review*, March-April 1968.

Ferretti, Andrew P., "Long-Term Perspective on Stock Prices," *Financial Analysts Journal*, November-December 1962; "The Economist's Role," *Financial Analysts Journal*, January-February 1969.

Gordon, Robert A., *Business Fluctuations*. New York: Harper & Row, Publishers, 1952.

Harriman, John W., "The Economic Outlook-1968," *The Exchange*, January 1968.

Levin, Jesse, "Prophetic Leaders," *Financial Analysts Journal*, July-August 1970.

Mennis, Edmund A., "Economies and Financial Analysis," *Financial Analysts Journal*, November-December 1965; "Economies and Investment Management," *Financial Analysts Journal*, November-December 1966.

Miller, Paul F., "Economy's Next Structural Change and the Stock Markets' Direction," *Commerical and Financial Chronicle*, Feb. 22, 1968.

Samuelson, Paul A., "Economies of the Stock Market and the Investor," *Commercial and Financial Chronicle*, Oct. 26, 1967.

Wendt, Paul F., "International Development and the Determination of Investment Policy," *Financial Analysts Journal*, February 1968.

Weston, J. F., and D. K. Eiteman, "Economic Trends and Security Values—A Bleak or Bountiful Future For Investors," *Financial Analysts Journal*, January-February 1965.

Wolfe, Harry Deane, *Business Forecasting Methods*. New York: Holt, Rinehart and Winston, Inc., 1966.

[11] As to using the input-output table as model of economic forecast for the nation as a whole, opinion varies. The interested reader is asked to consult W. Leontief, *Input-Output Economics* (New York: Oxford University Press, 1966); National Bureau of Economic Research, *Input-Output Analysis: An Appraisal* (Princeton, N. J.: Princeton University Press, 1955), and the article "Input-Output Structure for 1963," *Survey of Current Business*, November 1969.

QUESTIONS AND PROBLEMS

1. Prepare a table listing data on stock prices (as measured by Standard & Poor's "425" Industrials or other popular indexes), gross national product, and industrial production. Can you find any relationships or correlation between the change in stock prices and the change in the state of the economy?
2. How may investment policies protect against cyclical risks?
3. Prepare a long-term economic projection to the year 1980 on model of what Prof. J. W. Kendrick did for 1970.
4. Obtain a forecast of GNP and national income prepared by a well-known public or private agency for the current year or next year. List their assumptions and evaluate their estimates of different components of GNP. Do you agree with their forecast? Why or why not?
5. What is your view of the current state of general business on basis of the latest information published on leading economic indicators?
6. Gather some information on several diffusion indexes of key factors from the latest issue of *Business Cycle Developments*. Evaluate them and express your opinion of the current state of general business and its possible trend.
7. Using information from *Survey of Current Business*, *Federal Reserve Bulletin*, *Business Cycle Developments*, and similar publications, identify the present position of general business in the stages of business cycle. Will business activity likely move up or down in the next six to twelve months?

3. Analysis and Forecast of Trend of Corporate Profits

DETERMINANTS OF SECURITY VALUES—LONG RUN VS. SHORT RUN

In the long run, security values are determined primarily by earnings. This is true for individual stocks as well as stock market indexes. On the basis of his study of historical data of Cowles Commission Index and Standard & Poor's "500" Index for the period 1871-58, Molodovsky reported that he found "the fundamental underlying relations of the three principal factors of the stock market. Regardless how they fluctuate historically, earnings, dividends, and prices are bound together by a real definite relationship."[1] The trend lines of prices, earnings, and dividends were found almost identical in their upward slope: 1.99 percent for prices, 2.13 percent for earnings, and 2.12 percent for dividends as revealed in Figure 3-1.

However, in the short run, security prices are notoriously volatile. They reflect not so much the underlying earning power of the corporation but rather the current earnings, the earnings expected in the period immediately beyond, and not the least the changing mood of optimism and pessimism. Nonetheless, earnings are still one of the key factors. The difference is only that the importance of changes in current earnings, both actual and prospective, is being exaggerated in the marketplace.

The diagnosis of the profits trend both in the long run and in the short run for industries and corporation is therefore, the most essential ingredient of investment success and deserves the most careful study.

AGGREGATE MEASURES OF CORPORATE PROFITS

Compilations of aggregate profits series are based on reports of corporation either issued to shareholders or submitted to the Internal Revenue Service. Ag-

[1] Nicholas Molodovsky, "Valuation of Common Stocks," *Analysts Journal*, February 1959, p. 5.

Figure 3-1

Basic Relations in the Stock Market

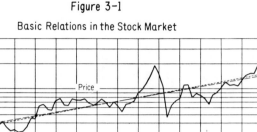

SOURCE: Nicholas Molodovsky, "Valuation of Common Stocks", *Analysts Journal*, February 1959.

gregate profit reports which are widely used by financial analysts are:

1. The Internal Revenue Service publishes annually in *Statistics of Income* compilations of profits of all corporations in the United Staes from income tax returns.
2. The Commerce Department's National Income Division prepares estimates of corporate profits and publishes seasonally adjusted quarterly figures in *Survey of Current Business*.
3. The Federal Trade Commission and Securities and Exchange Commission publish their compilations of profits of manufacturing corporations by industries and sizes in *Quarterly Financial Report for Manufacturing Corporations.*
4. The First National City Bank of New York publishes quarterly in *The Monthly Economic Letter* their compilations of profits of more than 1,000 leading manufacturing corporations.
5. The Board of Governors of the Federal Reserve System publishes in *The Federal Reserve Bulletin* its compilations of profits of about 180 large manufacturing corporations plus some public utility companies.

A comparison of these reports in terms of coverage, frequency, consistency in sample, time lag, and accounting detail and treatment is shown in the accompanying Table 3-1.[2]

[2] Edmund A. Mennis, "Forecasting Corporate Profits," in William F. Butler and Robert A. Kavesh (eds.), *How Business Economists Forecast* (Englewood Cliffs, N.J.: Prentice-

TABLE 3-1

Comparison of Detailed Reports of Corporate Profits

Basis of Reports	Internal Revenue Service	Department of Commerce	FTC-SEC	First National City Bank	Federal Reserve
	Income-Tax Returns	Income-Tax Returns	Shareholder Reports	Shareholder Reports	Shareholder Reports
Coverage	All companies	All companies	All mfg. companies	Quarterly–about 900 Annually–about 3800 leading concerns	180 large mfg. concerns; Class I railroads; utilities; Bell Telephone System
Frequency	Annually	Annually†	Quarterly	Quarterly	Quarterly
Time lag	2 years	2 years†	3–4 months	1–2 months	3 months
Industry classification	Mostly 2-digit SIC basis	2-digit SIC basis	2- to 4-digit SIC basis	Primarily 3-digit SIC basis	6 major mfg. groups; rails, utilities, banks, telephone
Consistent sample over time	No	No	No	No	Yes
Accounting detail	Income account and balance sheet	Sales, pretax, taxes, net, dividends, depreciation	Income account and balance sheet	Net income, net assets	Sales, pretax, net, dividends
Accounting treatment of:					
Cap. gains and losses, spec. reserves,	Included	Excluded	Excluded	Included	Excluded
foreign subsidiary earnings,	Excluded	Excluded	Excluded	Included	Excluded
intercorporate dividends	Dividends only Included	Excluded* Excluded	Included as reported Included	Included as reported Included	Included as reported Excluded if identified

SOURCE: Edmund A. Mennis, "Forecasting Corporate Profits," in William F. Butter and Robert A. Kavesh (eds.), *How Business Economists Forecast* (Englewood Cliffs, N.J.: Prentice-Hall, Inc., 1966), p. 469.
   * Although not shown by industry, a "Rest of the World" adjustment indicates the net effect of corporate profits and dividends received from abroad by both corporations and individuals in the United States less corporate profits and dividends paid abroad.
   † Estimates of seasonally adjusted annual rates of total corporate profits and three of the major components are also available quarterly with a two- to four-months time-lag.

CORPORATE PROFITS LEVEL IN LAST TWO DECADES

As shown in Table 3-2, the growth of GNP and national income from 1949 to 1970 was comparable at 280 percent and 270 percent respectively. However, the increase of corporate profits both before and after tax during the same period was much lower. The decline in profits relative to GNP and national income was partly due to inflated profits from low book cost in early postwar years and later changes in regulations on depreciation.

During the last decade, 1960-70, corporate profits before tax as a percentage of national income fluctuated within a range of 10.3 to 13.8 percent, while corporate profits after tax as a percentage of GNP varied between 4.6 and 6.8 percent. 1970 proved to be a disastrous year in terms of absolute level of corporate profits and their relation to GNP and national income.

RATES OF RETURN ON EQUITY, NET PROFIT MARGINS, AND TURNOVER CAPITAL

The structure of corporate profits in the last two decades can best be analyzed in terms of three concepts: rates of return on equity, net profit margins, and turnover of equity capital. Rates of return on equity is a ratio between corporate profits after tax and shareholders' equity or net worth. It indicates the percentage return the business has earned on each dollar invested by the shareholders. Net profit margin is a ratio between net profits after tax and sales. It measures how many cents per dollar of sales accrue to the shareholder in the form of profits. Turnover of capital is a ratio between sales and equity capital. It measures how fast a dollar of capital invested by shareholder can be transformed into sales. Rate of return on equity is, therefore, the product of net margin times turnover of equity capital.

Corporate profits after taxes in the last two decades, according to two different time series, are analyzed in terms of these ratios in Table 3-3. The FNCB figures for rates of return and net profit margins are higher than the FTC-SEC figures. The former indicates the profitability and profit margin of larger manufacturing corporations whereas the latter series covers all manufacturing corporation in the United States.

It is evident that the turnover of equity capital was quite stable in the postwar period, ranging from 2 to 2.5 during 1949-70 and only from 2.1 to 2.4 in the last decade. Net profit margins were, however, quite sensitive to changes in general business. In the most recent recession year 1970 it

Hall, Inc., 1966); "Aggregate Measures of Corporate Profits," *Financial Analysts Journal*, January-February 1964.

TABLE 3-2
Corporate Profits as Percent of GNP and National Income

Year	GNP	National Income	Corporate Profit Before Tax	Corporate Profit After Tax	Corp. Profit Before Tax as Percent of National Income	Corp. Profit After Tax as Percent of GNP
1949[R]	256.5	217.5	28.9	18.5	13.3	7.2
50	284.8	241.1	42.6	24.9	17.6	8.7
51	328.4	278.0	43.9	21.6	15.8	6.6
52[R]	345.5	291.4	38.9	19.6	13.4	5.7
53[R]	364.6	304.7	40.6	20.4	13.3	5.6
54[R]	364.8	303.1	38.3	20.6	12.7	5.7
55	398.0	331.0	48.6	27.0	14.7	6.8
56	419.2	350.8	48.8	27.2	13.8	6.5
57[R]	441.1	366.1	47.2	26.0	12.9	5.9
58[R]	447.3	367.8	41.4	22.3	11.3	5.0
59	483.7	400.0	52.1	28.5	13.0	5.9
60[R]	503.7	414.5	49.7	26.7	12.0	5.3
61[R]	520.1	427.3	50.3	27.2	11.8	5.2
62	560.3	457.7	55.4	31.2	12.1	5.6
63	590.5	481.9	59.4	33.1	12.3	5.6
64	632.4	518.1	66.8	38.4	12.9	6.1
65	684.9	564.3	77.8	46.5	13.8	6.8
66	749.9	620.6	84.2	49.9	13.6	6.7
67[R]	793.9	653.6	79.8	46.6	12.2	5.9
68	865.0	712.7	88.7	48.2	12.5	5.6
69	931.4	769.5	91.2	48.5	11.9	5.2
70[R,P]	976.8	801.0	82.3	44.4	10.3	4.6
1949–70						
High					17.6	8.7
Low					10.3	4.6
Percent increase	280	270	185	140		
1960–70						
High					13.8	6.8
Low					10.3	4.6
Percent increase	94	93	65	66		

SOURCE: *Economic Report of the President*, 1971.
[R] Recession.
[P] Preliminary.

reached a low of 4.0 percent for FTC-SEC and 4.6 percent for FNCB figures. In the last decade 1960-70 net profit margins fluctuated between 5.6 and 4.0 percent for FTC-SEC and between 6.4 and 4.6 percent for FNCB series. The variation in rates of return on equity capital during 1960-70 was between 13.4 and 8.9 percent for FTC-SEC and between 14.1 and 9.9 percent for FNCB figures. Consequently, it appears that the variation in rates of return is primarily a function of changes in net profit margins. The changes in turnover of capital were relatively small in the past and, therefore, of secondary importance.

TABLE 3-3

Rates of Return on Equity, Net Profit Margins, and Turnover of Equity Capital, Manufacturing, 1949–70

Year	Rates of Return on Equity		Net Profit Margins		Turnover Equity Capital FTC–SEC
	FNCB	FTC–SEC	FNCB	FTC–SEC	
1949^R	13.8	11.6	6.8	5.8	2.0
50	17.1	15.4	7.7	7.1	2.2
51	14.4	12.1	6.2	4.8	2.5
52$_R$	12.3	10.3	5.4	4.3	2.4
53^R	12.5	10.5	5.3	4.3	2.5
54^R	12.4	9.9	5.9	4.5	2.2
55	15.0	12.6	6.7	5.4	2.3
56$_R$	13.9	12.3	6.0	5.3	2.3
57^R	12.8	10.9	5.9	4.8	2.3
58^R	9.8	8.6	5.2	4.2	2.1
59$_R$	11.6	10.4	5.8	4.8	2.2
60^R	10.5	9.2	5.4	4.4	2.1
61^R	9.9	8.9	5.2	4.3	2.1
62	10.9	9.8	5.5	4.5	2.2
63	11.6	10.3	5.7	4.7	2.2
64	12.6	11.6	6.1	5.2	2.2
65	13.9	13.0	6.4	5.6	2.3
66$_R$	14.1	13.4	6.3	5.6	2.4
67^R	12.6	11.7	5.6	5.0	2.3
68	13.1	12.1	5.7	5.1	2.4
69$_{R,P}$	12.4	11.5	5.4	4.8	2.4
70^{R,P}	10.1	9.2	4.6	4.0	2.3
1949–70					
High	17.1	15.4	7.7	7.1	2.5
Low	9.8	8.6	4.6	4.0	2.0
1960–70					
High	14.1	13.4	6.4	5.6	2.4
Low	9.9	8.9	4.6	4.0	2.1

SOURCES: First National City Bank of New York; FTC–SEC; *Economic Report of the President,* 1971.

^{R}Recession.

^{P}Preliminary.

FACTORS AFFECTING PROFIT MARGINS

Barring changes in corporate income tax rates, net profit margins in manufacturing are determined basically by three factors: (1) the prices at which finished manufacturing goods are sold, (2) labor cost per unit of output, and (3) fixed cost per unit of output. Labor cost per unit of output is in turn determined by two factors: increase in wage rate per man hour, and increase in output per man hour or labor productivity. There are no current statistics on fixed cost per unit of output. However, it can be approximated by percent of industrial capacity currently unused. The higher the percent of unused industrial

TABLE 3-4

Factors Affecting Net Profit Margins, Manufacturing

Year	Net Profit Margins Mfg.*	Wholesale Price Indexes, Industrial Commodities	Labor Cost Index per Unit of Output, Mfg.	Average Gross Hourly Earnings, Mfg.	Output per Man-hour, Mfg.	Percent of Capacity, Unused, Mfg.
1949^R	5.8	75.3	2.30	1.38	60.0	19.8
50	7.1	78.0	2.24	1.44	64.4	9.6
51	4.8	86.1	2.36	1.56	65.9	6.0
52	4.3	84.1	2.50	1.65	66.2	8.7
53^R	4.3	84.8	2.55	1.74	68.3	5.8
54^R	4.5	85.0	2.56	1.78	69.5	16.5
55	5.4	86.9	2.52	1.86	73.7	10.0
56	5.3	90.8	2.68	1.95	72.9	12.3
57^R	4.8	93.3	2.76	2.05	74.4	16.4
58^R	4.2	93.6	2.84	2.11	74.4	26.0
59	4.8	95.3	2.80	2.19	78.5	18.5
60^R	4.4	95.3	2.83	2.26	79.9	19.4
61^R	4.3	94.8	2.84	2.32	81.8	21.5
62	4.5	94.8	2.76	2.39	86.6	17.9
63	4.7	94.7	2.74	2.46	90.1	16.7
64	5.2	95.2	2.68	2.53	94.5	14.3
65	5.6	96.4	2.65	2.61	98.3	11.5
66	5.6	98.5	2.72	2.72	99.9	9.5
67^R	5.0	100.0	2.83	2.83	100.0	14.7
68	5.1	102.5	2.88	3.01	104.7	15.4
69	4.8	106.0	2.98	3.19	106.9	16.3
70^{R,P}	4.0	110.0	3.10	3.36	108.1	23.4

SOURCE: *Economic Report of the President,* 1971.
*Profits after taxes per dollar of sales.
^{R}Recession.
^{P}Preliminary.

capacity, the higher should be the fixed cost per unit. In Table 3-4 net profit margins in manufacturing in the postwar period are analyzed in terms of these determining factors.

Ignoring the most recent recession year 1970, net profit margins hit the lowest level at 4.2 percent in the recession year 1958. This was caused by the fact that while the wholesale price index for finished industrial goods stayed roughly unchanged, the labor cost per unit of output increased about 3 percent, and the unused capacity jumped from 16.4 percent in 1957 to 26 percent in 1958. In the last decade, net profit margins scored the highest level of 5.6 percent in 1965 and 1966. In both years, in addition to the fact that the percent of unused capacity was substantially reduced, the wholesale price indexes of finished manufactured goods rose faster than labor cost per unit. In fact, labor cost per unit in 1965 was even lower than in 1964. This in turn was caused by labor productivity increasing faster than hourly wage rate in manufacturing.

TABLE 3-5
Average Annual Rates of Return: Net Income after Taxes as a Percent of Net Worth of Leading Manufacturing Corporations for the Years 1963-69

No. of Companies in 1968-69	Industry Groups	1963	1964	1965	1966	1967	1968	1969
13	Baking	11.0	11.3	11.9	13.9	15.7	13.4	10.2
11	Dairy products	11.2	12.2	12.5	12.4	11.8	11.7	11.0
30	Meat packing.	6.1	8.6	5.3	5.5	9.2	8.3	9.6
11	Sugar	9.6	8.1	9.5	10.5	10.2	9.3	7.2
69	Other food products	12.1	11.8	12.6	13.3	12.3	12.7	12.0
9	Soft drinks	17.9	20.1	21.1	22.3	23.3	22.7	21.5
14	Brewing	9.1	10.0	11.1	12.8	12.2	13.2	13.3
10	Distilling	7.9	8.5	9.6	10.6	10.5	10.2	9.9
9	Tobacco products	14.0	13.4	13.3	13.8	14.8	14.6	14.7
69	Textile products	7.1	8.9	11.6	11.9	8.8	9.8	8.8
88	Clothing and apparel	12.0	13.6	16.3	15.9	13.6	15.7	13.4
27	Shoes, leather, etc.	8.1	11.0	11.8	13.1	13.6	15.7	12.5
60	Rubber and allied products . .	9.9	11.4	11.8	13.0	10.8	12.7	11.1
26	Lumber and wood products .	8.1	11.5	11.5	10.9	9.4	14.1	15.3
35	Furniture and fixtures	8.1	10.4	13.0	14.2	11.9	11.3	12.0
60	Paper and allied products . . .	9.2	10.5	10.5	11.8	9.5	10.7	11.1
81	Printing and publishing	12.4	14.6	16.9	18.1	15.4	14.9	14.4
69	Chemical products	13.2	14.2	15.4	15.1	11.5	11.7	11.1
19	Paint and allied products . . .	12.0	13.6	14.1	13.9	11.6	11.5	10.4
38	Drugs and medicines	18.7	19.8	21.2	21.0	20.3	19.8	19.9
36	Soap, cosmetics	16.9	17.6	17.0	17.7	19.4	18.9	18.4
91	Petroleum prod. and refining .	11.5	11.5	11.9	12.6	12.8	13.1	12.1
15	Cement	9.3	9.8	8.8	7.0	6.5	7.5	6.7
10	Glass products	11.6	12.1	13.5	12.8	11.1	11.9	12.2
38	Other stone, clay products . . .	9.1	10.5	9.9	9.6	7.3	8.9	9.2
63	Iron and steel	7.3	9.0	9.6	9.3	7.4	8.5	7.6
56	Nonferous metals	7.1	9.2	11.8	15.4	11.4	11.1	12.5
37	Hardware and tools	14.6	16.1	17.1	19.2	17.2	16.7	15.7
48	Building, heating, plumbing equip	6.4	8.9	10.6	11.9	11.3	11.3	8.6
58	Other metal products	9.3	10.4	12.9	14.0	13.8	13.3	12.2
41	Farm, construction, materials handling equip.	9.4	13.7	14.4	14.6	10.9	8.4	10.2
43	Office, computing equip. . . .	18.0	17.9	18.7	18.4	17.8	19.0	17.5
170	Other machinery	9.7	12.3	14.4	16.0	14.7	13.5	13.1
286	Electrical equip. and electronics	10.7	11.1	14.8	16.5	15.4	14.1	12.9
17	Household appliances	12.8	14.1	15.0	14.4	14.7	14.0	13.8
11	Autos and trucks	19.6	19.9	23.4	17.8	12.0	16.6	13.8
36	Automotive parts	11.4	12.2	13.4	14.5	11.4	12.6	12.9
6	Railway equipment	7.9	11.2	12.7	14.2	11.9	8.8	9.6
51	Aircraft and space	11.7	13.1	15.4	15.5	13.4	13.9	11.2
111	Instruments, photo goods, etc.	13.4	16.6	19.2	21.7	20.3	19.2	18.8
96	Misc. manufacturing	9.5	12.3	13.5	13.0	13.2	15.2	13.5
2068	Total manufacturing	11.6	12.6	13.9	14.1	12.6	13.3	12.5

SOURCE: Economics Department, First National City Bank, New York, N.Y.

TABLE 3-6

Profit Margins: Net Income after Taxes in Cents per Sales Dollars of Leading Manufacturing Corporations for the Years 1963–69

No. of Companies in 1968-69	Industry Groups	1963	1964	1965	1966	1967	1968	1969
13	Baking	2.8	3.0	2.9	3.1	3.7	3.2	2.5
11	Dairy products	2.8	3.1	3.2	3.2	3.2	3.1	2.9
30	Meat packing	0.8	1.1	0.6	0.7	1.0	1.0	1.0
11	Sugar	3.7	3.1	3.5	3.8	3.6	3.7	2.8
69	Other food products	4.1	4.1	4.3	4.4	4.0	4.0	3.7
9	Soft drinks	6.7	6.6	7.2	7.3	7.6	7.5	7.0
14	Brewing	4.2	4.7	4.5	4.9	4.5	4.6	4.6
10	Distilling	4.0	4.2	4.5	4.7	4.7	4.4	4.1
9	Tobacco products	6.1	6.0	6.0	5.9	5.8	5.7	5.2
69	Textile products	3.0	3.4	4.5	4.7	3.6	3.7	3.3
88	Clothing and apparel	3.4	3.6	4.3	4.1	3.7	4.0	3.6
27	Shoes, leather, etc.	2.6	3.3	3.5	3.7	3.6	3.9	3.3
60	Rubber and allied products . .	3.8	4.3	4.4	4.7	4.1	4.7	4.1
26	Lumber and wood products .	4.9	6.0	5.9	5.4	4.8	6.3	6.5
35	Furniture and fixtures	3.6	4.4	5.3	5.6	4.6	4.2	4.4
60	Paper and allied products . . .	5.7	6.3	6.2	6.6	5.2	5.2	5.2
81	Printing and publishing	5.2	5.7	6.6	7.1	6.4	6.2	6.0
69	Chemical products	7.5	8.1	8.6	8.2	6.5	6.3	6.1
19	Paint and allied products . . .	5.8	5.7	5.6	5.5	4.9	4.8	4.1
38	Drugs and medicine	10.2	10.8	11.0	10.8	9.8	9.6	9.6
36	Soap, cosmetics	6.2	6.3	6.4	6.5	6.7	6.6	6.6
91	Petroleum products and refining	9.2	9.3	9.5	9.6	9.1	8.8	8.1
15	Cement	10.1	10.4	9.0	7.2	6.2	6.6	5.6
10	Glass products	6.8	7.1	7.4	7.2	6.1	6.3	6.3
38	Other stone, clay products . .	6.6	7.1	6.8	6.4	4.8	5.3	5.1
63	Iron and steel	5.2	5.9	5.9	5.8	5.0	5.3	4.6
56	Nonferrous metals	6.0	7.0	8.0	9.2	7.2	6.6	6.8
37	Hardware tools	6.5	6.9	6.7	7.0	6.7	6.3	6.0
48	Building, heating, plumbing equip.	3.0	3.6	4.2	4.5	4.1	3.8	2.7
58	Other metal products	4.0	4.2	4.9	5.2	5.1	4.9	4.4
41	Farm, construction, materials handling equip.	4.7	6.0	6.0	6.0	4.8	3.8	4.4
43	Office, computing equip. . . .	9.9	9.3	8.9	8.5	8.3	8.6	8.8
170	Other machinery	4.7	5.4	5.8	6.1	5.5	5.2	4.9
286	Electr. equip. and electronics .	3.7	3.9	4.8	4.9	4.5	4.3	4.1
17	Household appliances	5.0	5.4	5.5	5.1	4.6	4.5	4.4
11	Autos and trucks	7.3	7.4	7.8	6.5	4.9	5.8	4.9
36	Automotive parts	4.7	4.6	4.9	5.2	4.4	4.5	4.5
6	Railway equipment	4.0	5.2	5.5	5.8	5.2	4.0	4.2
51	Aircraft and space	2.3	2.7	3.2	3.0	2.7	2.8	2.5
111	Instruments, photo goods, etc.	6.8	8.1	9.3	9.9	9.0	8.6	8.5
96	Misc. manufacturing	4.3	5.3	5.4	5.1	4.3	4.5	4.1
2068	Total manufacturing	5.7	6.1	6.4	6.3	5.6	5.7	5.4

SOURCE: Economics Department, First National City Bank, New York, N. Y.

RATES OF RETURN AND PROFIT MARGINS IN INDIVIDUAL INDUSTRIES

For purposes of comparison of profitability between industries and between a company and its industry average, composite averages on rates of return and profit margins for individual industries are highly useful. The analyst can refer to these industry ratios made available by FTC-SEC and the First National City Bank. The FNCB figures are more timely and represent industry averages of larger companies for which there is greater interest from the investment community. In accompanying Tables 3-5 and 3-6, their compilations on rates of return on net worth and net profit margins for 41 industry groups since 1963 are shown. Standard & Poor's Corporation publishes in its *Industry Survey* a more detailed breakdown of industry composite data on a per-share basis. These statistics are even more valuable than the data provided by FTC-SEC and FNCB. In a later chapter on industry analysis, S&P's materials will be introduced for analysis and comparison.

LONG-TERM PERSPECTIVE OF CORPORATE PROFITS

The forecast of the level of corporate profits, say, five years or a decade from now is far more difficult than the forecast of GNP. As shown in Figure 3-2, the trend line of GNP in the postwar period was quite smooth except the year 1949. This, however, was not the case for corporate profits. As indicated and stressed before in our discussions, profit margins are very sensitive to cyclical turns and rate of change in general business. The level of profits will vary substantially, depending on whether the terminal year will be a good business, fair business, or recession year. It is probably a good practice to assume the terminal year as a fair business year. Despite the difficulty of formulating a long-term forecast of profits, it is still advisable to have one in addition to a short-term forecast in order to sharpen one's investment perspective.

The first step in a long-term forecast of profits is to develop a projection of GNP both in current and constant dollars. The next step is deciding what percentages of GNP or national income should be carried into corporate profits. The second step is likely more critical than the first one. In trying to arrive at a correct judgment of percentages of GNP to profits, the analyst should weigh carefully the factors as follows.

(a) The trends of corporate profits in the last two decades (Figure 3-3) and especially in the recent decade in terms of corporate profits before tax as a percentage of national income, corporate profits after tax to GNP, or to corporate gross product.

(b) The probable influence on corporate profits from prospective changes

Figure 3-2
Quarterly Data, Seasonally Adjusted
(Sources: OBE, FTC–SEC, author's computations)

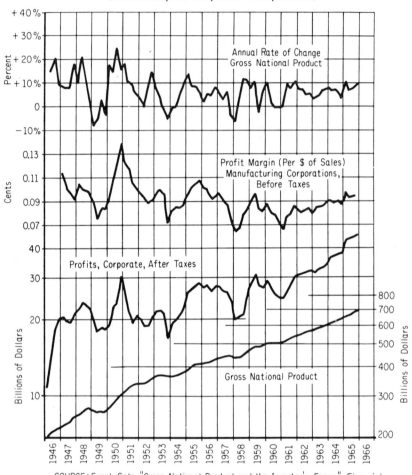

SOURCE: Frank Salz, "Gross National Product and the Investor's Focus," *Financial Analysts Journal*, July–August 1966.

in price level, depreciation regulation, income tax rates and growth of real GNP.

(c) Relative scarcity of capital vs. labor in the forthcoming period.

Admittedly, the forecasting procedure is quite complex, and the finished product represents at best an informed guess, which is all that can be hoped for.

SHORT-TERM PROFITS FORECAST

The near-term profit outlook of the economy is one of the key factors affecting security prices in the market place. It affects both investors' psychol-

Figure 3-3
Profits and Profit Margins

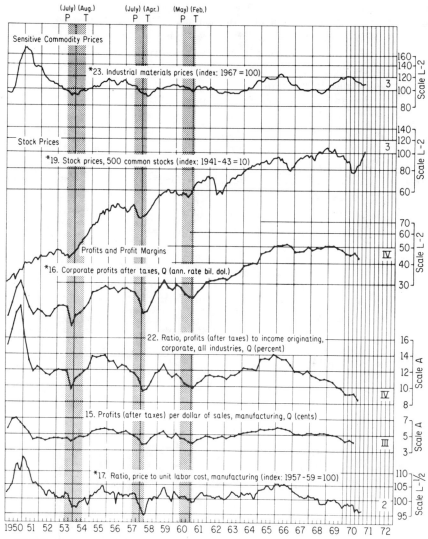

SOURCE: *Business Conditions Digest*, U. S. Department of Commerce, March 1971, p. 28.

ogy and the ability of industries and corporations to make profits. Therefore serious investors, whether interested in long-term investment or short-term trading, should make an effort to gauge the near-term outlook of corporate profits. Several logical approaches to short-term forecast of corporate profits are discussed below.

1. *"Net profit margin approach."* Since the level of corporate profits is affected primarily by changes in net profit margin as discussed before, a forecast

of near-term corporate profits should logically concentrate on this volatile factor and its determinants. As shown in Table 3-4, the factors affecting net profit margins are selling price of finished manufactured products, hourly wage rate, labor productivity, and the percent of manufacturing capacity unused. The job of the forecaster must therefore start with weighing and ascertaining the numerical value for each factor just mentioned for the forthcoming period in the light of the current stage of the business cycle and possible developments. Then he will assign a value to net profit margin. This can be done either intuitively or through the use of multiple correlation analysis. The final step is to decide a figure for GNP from which the sales of the manufacturing sector can be derived. Multiplying manufacturing sales by net profit margin yields corporate profits after tax for the manufacturing sector.

  2. *"Net corporate profits as percent of GNP through correlation analysis."* Corporate profits after tax as a percentage of GNP were found through scatter diagram to be highly correlated to either rate of utilization of manufacturing capacity or net profit margins in manufacturing. A multiple correlation analysis

TABLE 3-7

Net Corporate Profits as Percent of GNP, Rate of Utilization of Manufacturing Capacity and Net Profit Margins, Manufacturing

	Corp. Profits after Tax as Percent of GNP, Y	Rate of Utilization of Mfg. Capacity, X_1	Profits after Tax per Dollar of Sales, Mfg., X_2
1948	8.8	89.7	7.0
9	7.2	80.2	5.8
50	8.7	90.4	7.1
1	6.6	94.0	4.8
2	5.7	91.3	4.3
3	5.6	94.2	4.3
4	5.7	83.5	4.5
5	6.8	90.0	5.4
6	6.5	87.7	5.3
7	5.9	83.6	4.8
8	5.0	74.0	4.2
9	5.9	81.5	4.8
60	5.3	80.6	4.4
1	5.2	78.5	4.3
2	5.6	82.1	4.5
3	5.6	83.3	4.7
4	6.1	85.7	5.2
5	6.6	88.5	5.6
6	6.6	90.5	5.6
7	6.0	85.1	4.9

SOURCE: FTC–SEC; FRB.

$$Y = -1.867 + 0.028X_1 + 1.128X_2$$

Standard error ±0.201

$$R^2 = .98$$

is therefore run on the data of the two factors from 1948 to 1967. The resultant equation was:

$$Y = -1.867 + 0.028X_1 + 1.128X_2$$

where Y = corporate profits after tax as a percentage of GNP
X_1 = rate of utilization of manufacturing capacity
X_2 = profits after tax per dollar of sales, manufacturing

The standard error was 0.201 and the coefficient of determination (R^2) was 98 percent. (Table 3-7.) The first step the forecaster should take is to select the numerical values for X_1 and X_2 in the coming period. There are current monthly data available for these two factors. Reviewing the data of these two factors during different phases of business cycles in the past and judging the stage of business cycle that the current condition of general business is in, the forecaster should have a fair chance of achieving a good forecast for the two factors. The second step is to assign a numerical value for GNP in next period. Multiplying GNP estimate by the computed Y yields the level of net corporate profits for manufacturing.

3. *Projection of GNP components approach."* Under this approach the forecaster will estimate the numerical values for GNP, capital consumption allowances and indirect business taxes to arrive at a figure for national income for the next period. As shown in Table 3-2, corporate profit before tax as a percentage of national income in the last decade varied from a low of 10.3 percent in 1970 to a high of 13.8 percent in 1965. The forecaster, on the basis of these ratios, should proceed to estimate a most probable percent for next period in the light of anticipated business developments and government policies. Multiplying the national income estimate by the estimated percent of national income going to corporate profits will yield the total amount of corporate profits before tax for the economy.

SUGGESTED READINGS

Andersen, Theodore A., "Trends in Profit Sensitivity," *Journal of Finance*, December 1963.

Cottle, Sidney, "Corporate Earnings: A Record of Contrast and Changes," *Financial Analysts Journal*, November–December 1965.

Cottle, Sidney, and Whitman, "Twenty Years of Corporate Earnings," *Harvard Business Review*, May–June 1958.

Cragg, J. G. and B. G. Malkiel, "The Consensus and Accuracy of some Predictions of the Growth of Corporate Earnings," *Journal of Finance*, March 1968.

Fiedler, Edgar R., "Keeping Posted on Profits," *Financial Analysts Journal*, May–June 1964.

Gorman, John A., "Commerce Department Corporate Profit Measures," *Financial Analysts Journal*, May–June 1965.

Lewis, Robert E., "Four Decades of Shareholder Profits Data," *Financial Analysts Journal*, July–August 1964.

Mennis, Edmund A., "Corporate Profits and the Financial Analyst," *Financial Analysts Journal*, November–December 1964; "New Tools for Profits Analysis," *Financial Analysts Journal*, January–February 1969.

Norby, W. C., and H. E. Neil, Jr., "Dynamic Factors in Corporate Profits," *Financial Analysts Journal*, July–August 1962.

Osborn, Richard C., *Corporate Profits: War and Postwar.* Urbana, Ill.: University of Illinois Press, 1954.

Stigler, George J., *Capital and Rates of Return in Manufacturing Industries.* Washington, D. C.; National Bureau of Economic Research, 1963.

Stockwell, Eleanor J., "Federal Reserve Corporate Profits Series," *Financial Analysts Journal*, September–October 1965.

Widmann, E. R., and P. F. Miller, "Economic Stability and Profit Cyclicality," *Financial Analysts Journal*, January–February 1965.

QUESTIONS AND PROBLEMS

1. "Corporate earnings always follow the direction of sales. As sales increase, corporate profits increase and vice versa." Do you agree with the statement? Why or why not?
2. Prepare a table showing rates of return on equity, net profit margins, and turnover of equity capital for all manufacturing corporations in the United States in the past ten years.
3. What factors were responsible for the poor showing of corporate profits after taxes during 1967-69? Prepare a table of statistics to substantiate your arguments.
4. What is the outlook of corporate profits in the current year or next twelve months? Why? Substantiate your arguments with tables of latest information or relevant factors.
5. Prepare a short-term profits forecast using the multiple correlation technique.
6. Prepare a short-term profits forecast using the projection of GNP components approach.

4. Analysis and Forecast of Trend of Interest Rates

IMPORTANCE OF INTEREST RATE FORECAST

There are good reasons why investors should make an effort to forecast the trend and level of interest rates in the near future, especially in the next twelve months. First, as discussed in Chapter 1, the price of outstanding federal bonds and high-grade corporate bonds will vary inversely with future changes in interest rates. Prices of these bonds will fall as interest rates go up, and vice versa. Second, some sectors of the economy, such as construction and spending by state and local governments, are very sensitive to changes in interest rates. Their change in spending could in turn affect the course of the economy. Third, changes in interest rates may be partly influenced by deliberate actions on the part of the Federal Reserve authorities, thereby indicating the direction of monetary policy. Fourth, interest is a cost of borrowing and a reward for saving. Changes in interest rates will affect the relative attractiveness of saving and spending in general. Fifth, there is a general relationship between the tempo of general business and changes in interest rates. The change in the latter could indicate to some extent the condition in the former, and vice versa. Finally, the equity market will be affected by relative attractiveness between bonds and stocks, and by all other factors mentioned above.

STRUCTURE OF INTEREST RATES

Interest is the price paid for the use of funds on loan for a period of time, expressed most commonly as a percent of principal for a period of one year. At a given moment of time there is not a single interest rate but a host of interest rates. Differences in rates arise from differences in a variety of factors: degree of risk of default, duration of loan, marketability, repayment terms, tax treatment, and servicing costs. Table 4-1 shows some important interest rates from 1929 to 1970 on U.S. government short-term and long-term securities, high-grade corporate bonds, municipal bonds, short-term bank loans, commercial paper, bor-

TABLE 4-1
Bond Yields and Interest Rates, 1929-70
(Percent per annum)

Year or Month	U.S. Government Securities				Corporate Bonds (Moody's)		High Grade Municipal Bonds (Standard & Poor's)	Average Rate on Short-Term Bank Loans to Business—Selected Cities	Prime Commercial paper, 4-6 Months	Federal Reserve Bank Discount Rate	FHA New Home Mortgage Yields‖
	3-Month Treasury Bills*	9-12 Month Issues†	3-5 Year Issues‡	Taxable Bonds§	Aaa	Baa					
1929	(#)	—	—	—	4.73	5.90	4.27	(**)	5.85	5.17	—
1930	(#)	—	—	—	4.55	5.90	4.07	(**)	3.59	3.04	—
1931	1.402	—	—	—	4.58	7.62	4.01	(**)	2.64	2.12	—
1932	.879	—	2.66	—	5.01	9.30	4.65	(**)	2.73	2.82	—
1933	.515	—	2.12	—	4.49	7.76	4.71	(**)	1.73	2.56	—
1934	.256	—	—	—	4.00	6.32	4.03	(**)	1.02	1.54	—
1935	.137	—	1.29	—	3.60	5.75	3.40	(**)	.75	1.50	—
1936	.143	—	1.11	—	3.24	4.77	3.07	(**)	.75	1.50	—
1937	.447	—	1.40	—	3.26	5.03	3.10	(**)	.94	1.33	—
1938	.053	—	.83	—	3.19	5.80	2.91	(**)	.81	1.00	—
1939	.023	—	.59	—	3.01	4.96	2.76	2.1	.59	1.00	—
1940	.014	—	.50	—	2.84	4.75	2.50	2.1	.56	1.00	—
1941	.103	—	.73	—	2.77	4.33	2.10	2.0	.53	1.00††	—
1942	.326	—	1.46	2.46	2.83	4.28	2.36	2.2	.66	1.00††	—
1943	.373	0.75	1.34	2.47	2.73	3.91	2.06	2.6	.69	1.00††	—
1944	.375	.79	1.33	2.48	2.72	3.61	1.86	2.4	.73	1.00††	—
1945	.375	.81	1.18	2.37	2.62	3.29	1.67	2.2	.75	1.00††	—
1946	.375	.82	1.16	2.19	2.53	3.05	1.64	2.1	.81	1.00††	—
1947	.594	.88	1.32	2.25	2.61	3.24	2.01	2.1	1.03	1.00	—
1948	1.040	1.14	1.62	2.44	2.82	3.47	2.40	2.5	1.44	1.34	—
1949	1.102	1.14	1.43	2.31	2.66	3.42	2.21	2.68	1.49	1.50	4.34

1950	1.218	1.26	1.50	2.32	2.62	3.24	1.98	2.69	1.45	1.59	4.17
1951	1.552	1.73	1.93	2.57	2.86	3.41	2.00	3.11	2.16	1.75	4.21
1952	1.766	1.81	2.13	2.68	2.96	3.52	2.19	3.49	2.33	1.75	4.29
1953	1.931	2.07	2.56	2.94	3.20	3.74	2.72	3.69	2.52	1.99	4.61
1954	.953	.92	1.82	2.55	2.90	3.51	2.37	3.61	1.58	1.60	4.62
1955	1.753	1.89	2.50	2.84	3.06	3.53	2.53	3.70	2.18	1.89	4.64
1956	2.658	2.83	3.12	3.08	3.36	3.88	2.93	4.20	3.31	2.77	4.79
1957	3.267	3.53	3.62	3.47	3.89	4.71	3.60	4.62	3.81	3.12	5.42
1958	1.839	2.09	2.90	3.43	3.79	4.73	3.56	4.34	2.46	2.15	5.49
1959	3.405	4.11	4.33	4.08	4.38	5.05	3.95	5.00‡‡	3.97	3.36	5.71
1960	2.928	3.55	3.99	4.02	4.41	5.19	3.73	5.16	3.85	3.53	6.18
1961	2.378	2.91	3.60	3.90	4.35	5.08	3.46	4.97	2.97	3.00	5.80
1962	2.778	3.02	3.57	3.95	4.33	5.02	3.18	5.00	3.26	3.00	5.61
1963	3.157	3.28	3.72	4.00	4.26	4.86	3.23	5.01	3.55	3.23	5.47
1964	3.549	3.76	4.06	4.15	4.40	4.83	3.22	4.99	3.97	3.55	5.45
1965	3.954	4.09	4.22	4.21	4.49	4.87	3.27	5.06	4.38	4.04	5.46
1966	4.881	5.17	5.16	4.65	5.13	5.67	3.82	6.00§§	5.55	4.50	6.29
1967	4.321	4.84	5.07	4.85	5.51	6.23	3.98	6.00§§	5.10	4.19	6.55
1968	5.339	5.62	5.59	5.26	6.18	6.94	4.51	6.68	5.90	5.17	7.13
1969	6.677	7.06	6.85	6.12	7.03	7.81	5.81	8.21	7.83	5.87	8.19
1970	6.458	6.90	7.37	6.58	8.04	9.11	6.51	8.48	7.72	5.95	9.05
1968: Jan	5.081	5.39	5.53	5.18	6.17	6.84	4.34	—	5.60	4.50	6.81
Feb	4.969	5.37	5.59	5.16	6.10	6.80	4.39	6.36	5.50	4.50	6.81
Mar	5.144	5.55	5.77	5.39	6.11	6.85	4.56	—	5.64	4.66	6.78
Apr	5.365	5.63	5.69	5.28	6.21	6.97	4.41	—	5.81	5.20	6.83
May	5.621	6.06	5.95	5.40	6.27	7.03	4.56	6.84	6.18	5.50	6.94
June	5.544	6.01	5.71	5.23	6.28	7.07	4.56	—	6.25	5.50	—
July	5.382	5.68	5.44	5.09	6.24	6.98	4.36	—	6.19	5.50	7.52
Aug	5.095	5.41	5.32	5.04	6.02	6.82	4.31	6.89	5.88	5.48	7.42
Sept	5.202	5.40	5.30	5.09	5.97	6.79	4.47	—	5.82	5.25	7.35
Oct	5.334	5.44	5.42	5.24	6.09	6.84	4.56	—	5.80	5.25	7.28
Nov	5.492	5.56	5.47	5.36	6.19	7.01	4.68	6.61	5.92	5.25	7.29
Dec	5.916	6.00	5.99	5.66	6.45	7.23	4.91	—	6.17	5.26	7.36

TABLE 4-1 (*Continued*)

Year or Month	U.S. Government Securities				Corporate Bonds (Moody's)		High Grade Municipal Bonds (Standard & Poor's)	Average Rate on Short-Term Bank Loans to Business— Selected Cities	Prime Commercial paper, 4-6 Months	Federal Reserve Bank Discount Rate	FHA New Home Mortgage Yields‖
	3-Month Treasury Bills*	9-12 Month Issues†	3-5 Year Issues‡	Taxable Bonds§	Aaa	Baa					
1969: Jan	6.177	6.26	6.04	5.74	6.59	7.32	4.95	—	6.53	5.50	7.50
Feb	6.156	6.21	6.16	5.86	6.66	7.30	5.10	7.32	6.62	5.50	—
Mar	6.080	6.22	6.33	6.05	6.85	7.51	5.34	—	6.82	5.50	7.99
Apr	6.150	6.11	6.15	5.84	6.89	7.54	5.29	—	7.04	5.95	8.05
May	6.077	6.26	6.33	5.85	6.79	7.52	5.47	7.86	7.35	6.00	8.06
June	6.493	7.07	6.64	6.05	6.98	7.70	5.83	—	8.23	6.00	8.06
July	7.004	7.59	7.02	6.07	7.08	7.84	5.84	—	8.65	6.00	8.35
Aug	7.007	7.51	7.08	6.02	6.97	7.86	6.07	8.82	8.33	6.00	8.36
Sept	7.129	7.76	7.58	6.32	7.14	8.05	6.35	—	8.48	6.00	8.36
Oct	7.040	7.63	7.47	6.27	7.33	8.22	6.21	—	8.56	6.00	8.40
Nov	7.193	7.94	7.57	6.52	7.35	8.25	6.37	8.83	8.46	6.00	8.48
Dec	7.720	8.34	7.98	6.81	7.72	8.65	6.91	—	8.84	6.00	8.48
1970: Jan	7.914	8.22	8.14	6.86	7.91	8.86	6.80	—	8.78	6.00	8.62
Feb	7.164	7.60	7.80	6.44	7.93	8.78	6.57	8.86	8.55	6.00	—
Mar	6.710	6.88	7.20	6.39	7.84	8.63	6.14	—	8.33	6.00	9.29
Apr	6.480	6.96	7.49	6.53	7.83	8.70	6.55	8.49	8.06	6.00	9.20
May	7.035	7.69	7.97	6.94	8.11	8.98	7.02	—	8.23	6.00	9.10
June	6.742	7.50	7.86	6.99	8.48	9.25	7.06	—	8.21	6.00	9.11
July	6.468	7.00	7.58	6.57	8.44	9.40	6.69	—	8.29	6.00	9.16
Aug	6.412	6.92	7.56	6.75	8.13	9.44	6.33	8.50	7.90	6.00	9.11
Sept	6.244	6.68	7.24	6.63	8.09	9.39	6.45	—	7.32	6.00	9.07
Oct	5.927	6.34	7.06	6.59	8.03	9.33	6.55	—	6.85	6.00	9.01
Nov	5.288	5.52	6.37	6.24	8.05	9.38	6.20	8.07	6.30	5.85	8.97
Dec	4.860	4.94	5.86	5.97	7.64	9.12	5.71	—	5.73	5.52	8.90

SOURCE: *Economic Report of the President*, 1971, pp. 264-265.

ORIGINAL SOURCES: Treasury Department, Board of Governors of the Federal Reserve System, Moody's Investors Service, Standard & Poor's Corporation, and Federal Housing Administration.

NOTES: Yields and rates computed for New York City except for short-term bank loans.

*Rate on new issues within period. Issues were tax exempt prior to March 1, 1941, and fully taxable thereafter. For the period 1934-37, series includes issues with maturities of more than 3 months.

†Certificates of indebtedness and selected note and bond issues (fully taxable).

‡Selected note and bond issues. Issues were partially tax exempt prior to 1941, and fully taxable thereafter.

§First issued in 1941. Series includes bonds which are neither due nor callable before a given number of years as follows: April 1953 to date, 10 years; April 1952-March 1953, 12 years; October 1941-March 1952, 15 years.

‖Data for first of the month, based on the maximum permissible interest rate (8 percent beginning December 2, 1970). Through July 1961, computed on 25-year mortgages paid in 12 years and thereafter, 30-year mortgages prepaid in 15 years.

#Treasury bills were first issued in December 1929 and were issued irregularly in 1930.

**Not available on same basis as for 1939 and subsequent years.

††From October 30, 1942, to April 24, 1946, a preferential rate of 0.50 percent was in effect for advances secured by Government securities maturing in 1 year or less.

‡‡Beginning 1959, series revised to exclude loans to nonbank financial institutions.

§§Beginning February 1967, series revised to incorporate changes in coverage, in the sample of reporting banks, and in the reporting period (shifted to the middle month of the quarter).

rowing from Federal Reserve banks, and home mortgages. However, in analytical expositions economists often speak of "the" interest rate or the "basic" interest rate. When these terms are used, they are usually referring to the yields on taxable federal government securities for which there is no risk of default. Specifically, the "basic" interest rate often refers to the yield on 90-day Treasury bills for the short-term and yield on Treasury bonds for the long-term as shown in Figure 4-1.

Figure 4-1
Money Market Interest Rates

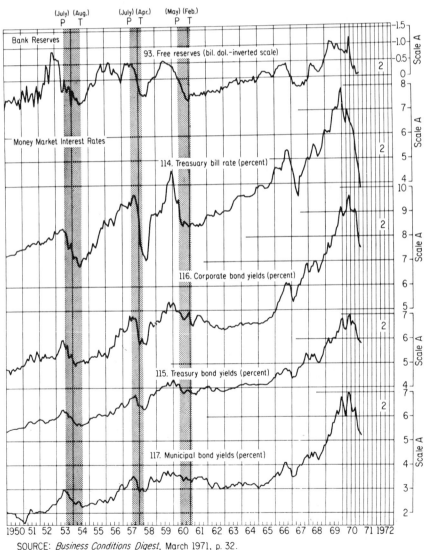

SOURCE: *Business Conditions Digest*, March 1971, p. 32.

The spread in yields between short- and long-term maturities for a given type of security does not stay the same over time. It widens or narrows depending on uncertainties at the moment and expectations of investors. The pattern of yields on short- and long-term maturities for a given type of issue is usually expressed by a "yield curve." Figure 4-2 shows yield curves in U.S. government securities on three dates, in May 1963, May 1966, and May 1967.

Figure 4-2

Yields on U.S. Government Securities

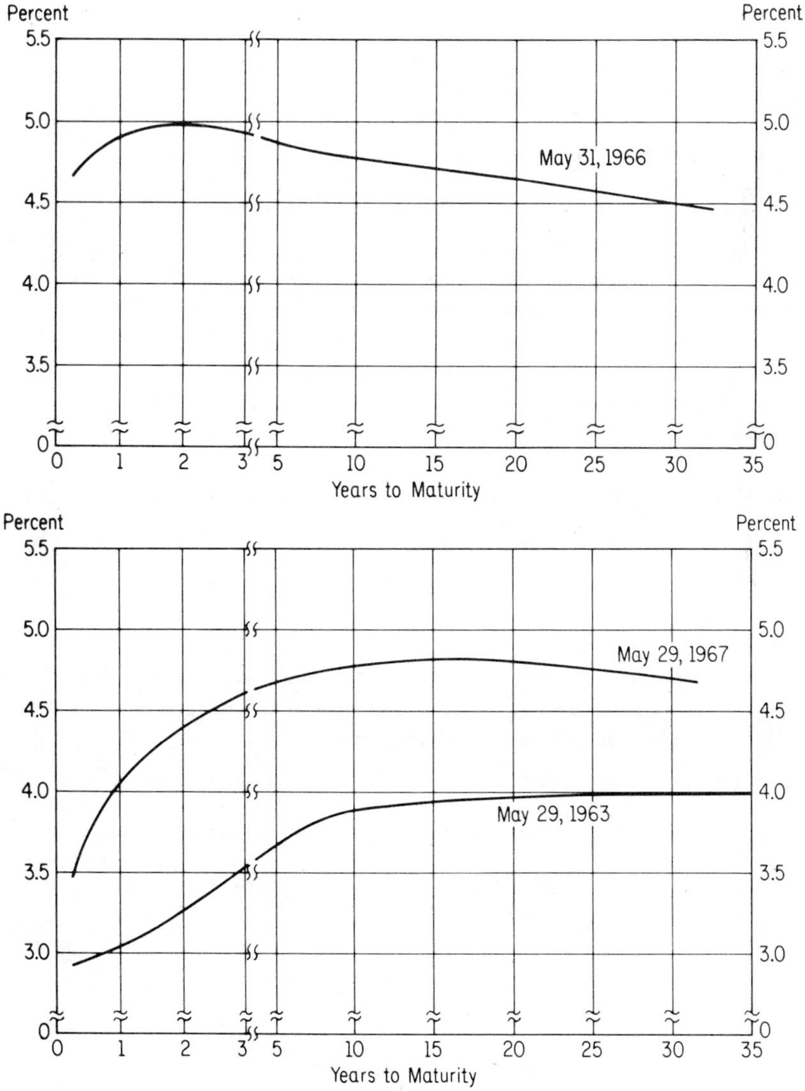

SOURCE: *Review*, Federal Reserve Bank of St. Louis, June 1967.

Although yield curves can take various shapes—sloping upward, downward, or flat—the most common pattern of a yield curve is sloping upward, indicating higher yields on longer maturities than on shorter-term maturities. The explanation for this phenomenon lies in the fact that investors in longer maturities will have to bear greater risks than short-term investors from changes either in interest rates and/or in financial ability of the issuer of the security. The yield curves on U.S. government securities on May 29,1963 and May 1967 in the lower half of Figure 4-2 show the common upsweeping pattern of yield curve. However, the two yield curves differed in two respects. First, the slope of the 1967 curve was steeper than the 1963 curve. In another word, the yields on 1–3 year maturities rose much faster in 1967 than in 1963. Secondly, the level of yield was much higher in 1967 than in 1963 for both short and long term maturities.

The yield curve on U.S. government securities on May 31, 1966, on the other hand, showed a different pattern, rising at first and then sloping downward. This kind of curve is sometimes referred to as "humpback" yield curve. The curve had a marked hump in the intermediate-term range. The short-term yields in this case were slightly above long-term rates, but the yield on two-year maturities was the highest on the curve, about half a percentage point higher than short-term yields. The explanation for this kind of pattern in the yield curve may be that the conditions at the time (May 31, 1966) were such that lenders and borrowers were expecting a further rise in short-term rates, but at the same time they might have believed that the short-term rates would average much lower in the longer period.

TRENDS AND CYCLICAL VARIATIONS OF INTEREST RATES

The pattern of fluctuations in interest rates can be best examined in terms of three different types of factors: (1) seasonal, (2) cyclical,   d (3) secular trend.

Seasonal Variation

Examination of monthly data of interest rates in the past revealed that while seasonal factors had strong influences on short-term rates, they had negligible effects on long-term rates. Conard reports:

> To review briefly, short-term rates showed clear and convincing evidence of a seasonal pattern from 1951 through 1960, though both the causes and the seasonals themselves have largely faded since that time. While these seasonals existed, their amplitude was substantial, running from about 90 percent to 110 percent of their average for the year. Their timing was quite consistent over the decade, and among the three series studied (Treasury bills, bankers' acceptances, and commercial paper) highs were in December and lows in June or July. In partial contrast to this record, long-terms revealed less convincing evidence of a clear seasonal. Their seasonal amplitude was much lower than in the case of shorts, and what seasonal did appear shifted over time.[1]

[1] Joseph W. Conard, *The Behavior of Interest Rates* (New York: National Bureau of Economic Research, 1966), pp. 53–54.

Secular Trends

The level of interest rates on high-grade corporate bonds since the beginning of this century has been dominated by several secular trends as can be seen from Figure 4-3. Their time periods, upward or downward movements, and dominant factors are as shown in the accompanying table.

Period	Direction of Secular Trend	Dominant Factors
1900–20	Up	War financing.
1921–28	Down	
1932–50	Down	Depression and pegging of interest rates during war.
1951–70	Up	After-effects of war financing. Treasury–Federal Reserve "accord."

Figure 4-3
Long- and Short-Term Interest Rates

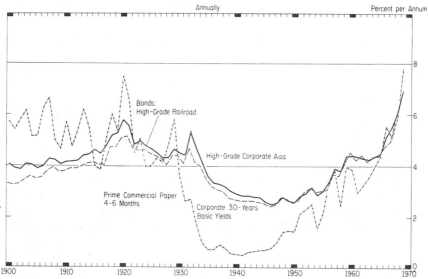

SOURCE: *Historical Chart Book*, Federal Reserve System, 1970, p. 23.
NOTE: Refer to Figure 4-1 for further rise in interest rates followed by substantial decline in 1970.

The explanations of these secular trends lies in the happening of extraordinary events. The upward sweeps of interest rates were caused mainly by inflationary war financing. The sharp and long decline of interest rates in the 1930's reflected the extremely depressed state of the economy. The secular upward trend of interest rates since 1951 covers, however, three dissimilar subperiods: (1) 1951–59, (2) 1960–65, and (3) 1966–70.

In the first period, the yield on corporate Aaa bonds rose from 2.62 percent in 1950 to 4.38 percent in 1959. The dominant factors were the after-effects of war financing and the fact that the Federal Reserve was no longer required to support the government bond market since the famous Treasury–Federal Reserve "accord" in March 1951. In the period from 1960 to 1965, the yield on corporate Aaa bonds stabilized around a level from 4¼ to 4½ percent. This period was characterized by relative equilibrium between supply and demand for funds. The fact that the federal government did not incur a substantial deficit and the price level was relatively stable during the period largely accounted for the relative equilibrium between supply and demand of funds, and therefore the stability of interest rates.

In the most recent period from 1965 to 1970, the yield on corporate Aaa bonds rose steadily from 4.49 percent in 1965 to a peak of 8.48 percent in June 1970 after which it began to decline. By December 1970, the yield was 7.64 percent, almost one percentage point lower than at peak. This steep rise in interest rate had aroused a great deal of concern by both the general public and the business community and was caused by a combination of factors. First, as shown in Table 4-1A, the huge demand for funds by the U.S. Government and its agencies in 1967 and 1968 because of the Vietnam war was probably the foremost factor for the rapid rise in interest rate. Secondly, the rapid rising in the price level since 1965 created an inflation psychology for business firms and individuals alike, which in turn cut down the flow of savings to savings institutions and at the same time bolstered demand for funds from larger programs for capital and equipment expenditures by business firms.

Thirdly, even before the emergence of huge federal deficit in 1967 and 1968, the yield on corporate Aaa bonds went up more than half a point from 4.49 percent in 1965 to 5.13 percent in 1966. This indicates that the increase in demand for funds from various sectors of the economy exceeded the increase in available savings. Finally, the overly expansionary monetary policy pursued by the Federal Reserve during 1967–68 followed by an overly restrictive monetary policy in 1969 had a great deal to do with the steep rise in interest rates in the past few years. The supply of money during 1967–68 increased at about 7½ percent per annum. This overly expansionary monetary policy probably contributed to the problem of inflation and helped create an inflation psychology and the imbalance in the supply and demand for funds in the credit and capital markets. During 1969, the Federal Reserve, being worried by the accelerating inflationary pressures in the economy, adopted a progressively more restrictive credit policy. This policy, in retrospect, seems overly restrictive. Money supply increased about 2½ percent in the first half of 1969, but in the second half of 1969 there was only half a percent increase in money supply. While the demand for funds from the private sector remained strong in 1969, this overly restrictive monetary policy helped bring about unprecedented high level of interest rates.

TABLE 4-1A
Sources and Uses of Funds, 1963–70

	1963	1964	1965	1966	1967	1968	1969	1970 (est.)
USES (FUNDS RAISED)								
Real estate mortgages	25.7	25.8	25.7	21.3	22.9	27.4	27.8	25.1
Corporate securities	3.6	5.4	5.4	11.4	17.0	12.0	15.4	27.8
State and local government securities	6.1	6.0	7.6	6.4	7.9	10.2	8.9	12.7
Foreign securities	1.0	.7	1.0	.7	1.3	1.7	1.5	.7
Term bank loans	2.5	2.7	4.6	2.4	2.6	4.0	5.5	.1
Total investment funds (long-term)	39.0	40.7	44.3	42.2	51.7	55.3	59.1	66.4
Short-term funds.	17.6	22.2	28.1	24.0	23.5	36.6	38.7	24.7
U.S. Government and Agency Securities.	.7	3.4	−1.9	−.4	7.7	8.9	−8.3	6.5
Total Uses	57.3	66.3	70.5	65.8	82.9	100.8	89.5	97.6
SOURCES (FUNDS SUPPLIED)								
Savings institutions: life and casualty insurance companies, pension funds, etc. .	14.4	15.7	17.7	18.8	20.4	21.3	22.1	22.6
Savings institutions: savings banks, savings and loan associations, etc.	17.6	16.3	14.6	7.8	15.0	16.1	14.5	18.7
Mutual funds	.8	1.0	1.9	2.5	1.0	2.4	3.4	1.6
Total from savings institutions	32.7	32.9	34.2	29.1	36.4	39.7	39.9	42.9
Commercial banks	17.7	21.9	26.7	18.1	38.5	37.3	15.0	29.7
Business corporations	10.3	10.4	11.6	9.4	6.6	23.4	27.3	7.4
Government and agencies (federal, state, and local)	.7	.8	4.3	6.7	5.4	7.0	9.0	5.1
Other investment groups	1.1	1.1	.2	−1.2	2.7	1.8	.3	10.1
Residual: individuals and others	−1.0	3.7	−1.0	11.7	−4.1	−1.7	19.9	11.0
Total gross sources	61.5	70.9	76.1	73.8	85.6	107.6	111.3	106.2
Less: funds raised by financial intermediaries	4.2	4.5	5.6	7.9	2.6	6.7	21.9	8.6
Total net sources	57.3	66.3	70.5	65.8	82.9	100.8	89.5	97.6
Personal savings	19.9	26.2	28.4	32.5	40.4	40.4	37.6	50.0
Federal government surplus or deficit (−) in fiscal years . . .	−4.8	−5.9	−1.6	−3.8	−8.7	−25.1	3.2	−2.8
Consumer price index	91.7	92.9	94.5	97.2	100.0	104.2	109.8	116.1
Total money supply (currency and demand deposits) at year end in billions	153.6	160.5	168.0	171.7	183.1	197.4	203.6	214.6

SOURCE: *The Investment Outlook for 1971*, Bankers Trust Company, N.Y., and *Economic Report of the President*, February 1971.

Cyclical Variation

The cyclical influence on interest rates was clearly noticeable in Figure 4-1 for the postwar period. For the longer perspective, Sidney Homer prepared the data for Figure 4-4 to show the pattern of fluctuation of high-grade bond prices during the 15 industrial production cycles in this century. From peak to trough, except the 6th, 7th, and 9th cycles, bond prices were all gradually increasing. To express it in reverse, the interest rates on bonds decreased from peak to trough in general business. From trough to peak, bond prices first increased and then declined with only one exception, the 9th cycle. In other words, the interest rates on bonds continued to decline in the initial stage of the recovery and then began to increase with the economy gathering strength. However, the timing of changes

Figure 4-4

Cyclical Patterns of High-Grade Corporate Bond Price Fluctuations During
Industrial Production Cycles

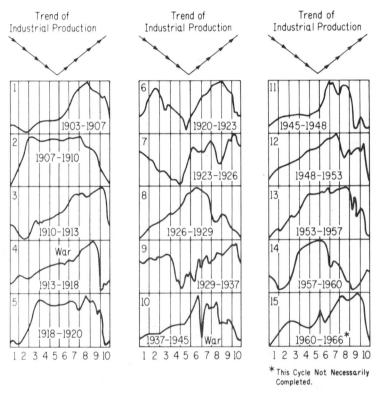

* This Cycle Not Necessarily Completed.

Inverted yields of prime 30-year corporate bonds adjusted to eliminate secular yield trend and charted so that yield range within each cycle appears identical.

Plotted to coincide with major trends in industrial production. The first half of each chart covers a downtrend in industrial production from cyclical peak to trough in 5 equal time segments, and the second half covers the succeeding uptrend in industrial production from trough to the next peak, also in 5 equal time segments.

SOURCE: "Interest Rate Forecasting Techniques and Outlook," Sidney Homer, *Commercial and Financial Chronicle*, June 30, 1966.

of interest rates in both direction and magnitude were never uniform during these cycles. Conard reported similar findings by Kessel and Cagan on cyclical behavior of interest rates in these words:

> First, between 1885 and 1913, interest rate cycles were far from being synchronous with business cycles, but the two moved closer together after World War I and much closer yet after World War II. During the thirties, however, interest rates were less synchronous with business cycles than during the twenties. Second, as generally observed, short-term rates on governments move much more widely over the cycle than do longs.[2]

INFLUENCE OF FEDERAL RESERVE POLICY ON SHORT- AND LONG-TERM INTEREST RATES

The Federal Reserve System, the central bank of the United States is responsible for monetary policy. Its objectives are basically threefold:

(a) To moderate ups and downs of business cycle and to promote sustainable economic growth of the nation.

(b) To maintain price stability and to reduce tendencies toward inflation.

(c) To maintain external equilibrium in terms of balance of payments and the value of dollar.

To achieve these objectives, the Federal Reserve System relies on its control of *cost* and *availability* of credit to commercial banks. By affecting the ability of the commercial banking system to extend credit to borrowers, the Federal Reserve System can achieve its aim of accelerating or decelerating the spending and investment in the economy. The immediate impact of tightening credit by the Federal Reserve System is reflected on short-term rates in the money market. The changes there will be gradually transmitted to the long term sector through adjustments by investors in maturities of their portfolio. However, economists are by no means unanimous about the extent and importance of the effects of monetary policy on interest rates. The difference in view is explained by Professor Robinson in these words:

> The interest-rate effects of monetary policy, combined with the natural forces of saving supply and investment demand are, of course, a central feature of money and capital market concern. The exact nature of Federal Reserve influence on rates is uncertain. Those of a traditional bent are inclined to view this influence as minor and transitory. They view the "real" forces as dominant. But modern economic thought gives more weight to monetary factors in the determination of interest rates, and therefore attaches more long-run significance to central bank policy than do the traditionalists.[3]

[2] Conard, *op. cit.*, p. 69.
[3] Roland I. Robinson, *Money and Capital Markets* (New York: McGraw-Hill Book Company, 1964), p. 119.

FORECAST OF TREND OF INTEREST RATES BY SUPPLY AND DEMAND ANALYSIS

Interest rates, the prices paid for the use of funds owned by others are determined by forces underlying their supply and demand, as are other prices in a free-enterprise economy. The most logical approach to the forecast of trend of interest rates should therefore include an estimate of demand for funds by various sectors, on the one hand, and the supply of funds from different sources on the other hand. The actual procedure of a forecast can be broken down into several steps:

1. To enumerate the basic assumptions. The basic assumptions specify the kind of external environment under which the economy is expected to function in the coming period. They relate to peace or war, tax changes, major strikes, and monetary policy.
2. To provide an economic projection for the economy in the form of GNP and its components.
3. On basis of (1) and (2) above,
   (a) To estimate demand for funds from business, federal government, state and local governments, home financing, consumer credit, and foreigners.
   (b) To estimate supply of funds from savings (contractual, and noncontractual), commercial banks' credit, business corporations, government agencies, and foreigners.
   (c) To calculate the difference between 3(a) and 3(b) above which calls for financing by individuals and others.
4. (a) To interpret the implications on interest rates of the total picture of financial requirements and resources and particularly the amounts to be contributed by commercial banks and individuals.
   (b) To reassess the probable course of Federal Reserve policy in the light of above estimates and to make final judgment as to possible *movements* and *levels* of interest rates.

FINANCIAL FORECAST FOR 1971

For purpose of illustration and reference, an actual financial forecast for 1971 by the Bankers Trust Company is summarized below.

The Bankers Trust Company of New York publishes in early spring of each year a highly regarded pamphlet entitled "The Investment Outlook." It sets forth the views of the bank on demands and sources of funds in various sectors of the economy and their implications for interest-rate movements, plus some thirty tables of statistics and estimates on uses and sources of funds for the economy and its various sectors and institutions.

To begin their forecast for 1971, they listed a number of specific assumptions. Several assumptions relate to the government sector, while others represent economic projections. We, therefore, summarize these assumptions below under two headings: basic assumptions of the government sector and economic projections.

Basic assumptions of the government sector:

1. In order to stimulate the economy, the Administration has budgeted for another sizable Federal deficit in the fiscal year beginning next July. A realistic expectation would be for a deficit in the next fiscal year about as large as the $18.6 billion now officially estimated for fiscal 1971.

2. The likehood of a less-than-vigorous business recovery would seem to rule out any shift to a restrictive credit policy for some time to come, and the Federal Reserve will presumably also be deterred from adopting a much easier credit stance for fear of adding to inflationary pressures. We have assumed a 6 per cent increase in the money stock for 1971.

Economic projections:

1. Spending by business on plant and equipment gives every indication of remaining sluggish through most of this year. Capital spending by business this year will probably be little different from last year's approximately $80^1/$_2$ billion.

2. One of the major areas of strength in the economy this year is expected to be residential building and construction by state and local governments, both of which are now benefiting from the greatly improved availability and lower cost of funds. Housing starts are projected as totalling close to 1.8 billion units, an increase of 25 per cent over last year.

3. Consumer spending on durable goods is also expected to rise noticeably this year, with purchases of autos and home appliances leading the parade. Consumers are expected to step up their spending gradually over the course of the year.

4. For 1971 as a whole, the gross national product is projected at $1045 billion, and the growth in output in real terms is estimated at $2^1/_2$–3 percent. The rate of inflation in 1971—using the GNP price deflator as the measure—is expected to average around $4^1/_4$ per cent, compared with $5^1/_4$ per cent last year. The unemployment rate will probably average above $5^1/_2$ per cent for the year as a whole.[4]

ESTIMATES OF DEMAND FOR AND SOURCES OF FUNDS

The estimates of demand for and sources of funds for the whole economy for the year 1971 with historical data up to 1963 are shown in Table 4-2. A detailed breakdown of the uses and sources of investment (long-term) funds is shown in Table 4-3. The estimates of demand for funds in 1971 are

[4] *The Investment Outlook for 1971,* Economic Department, Bankers Trust Company, New York, February 1971, pp. 2–4.

Demand for Funds   Billions

Real estate mortgages 32.1
Corporate securities
   Bonds 17.3
   Stocks 7.2   24.5
Term bank loans to business 2.8
U. S. Government and agency securities 10.6
State and local government securities 13.7
Foreign securities 1.2
Short-term securities and credit to business 31.1
   Total demand for funds in 1971 . . . .   116.0

   The estimates of sources of funds for 1971:

Estimates of Sources of Funds

Savings institutions
   Life insurance companies 8.7
   Private noninsured pension funds 6.5
   State and local government retirement funds 6.1
   Fire and casualty insurance companies 3.4
   Savings and loan associations 14.5
   Mutual savings banks 6.3
   Credit unions 2.1
   Mutual funds 2.2
     Total from savings institutions 49.8
Commercial banks
   Time and savings deposits 33.0
   Demand deposits and other sources 5.4
     Total from commercial banks 38.4
Business corporations 14.1
Federal, state and local governments and agencies 4.8
Residual: to be supplied by individuals and other investor groups 14.9
   Total gross sources 122.0
Less: funds raised by financial intermediaries 6.0
   Total supply of funds 116.0

TABLE 4-2

Summary of Financing—Total Funds

(Billions of Dollars)

	1963	1964	1965	1966	1967	1968	1969	1970 (est.)	1971 (proj.)
USES (FUNDS RAISED)									
Investment funds	39.0	40.7	44.3	42.2	51.7	55.3	59.1	66.4	74.3
Short-term funds	17.6	22.2	28.1	24.0	23.5	36.6	38.7	24.7	31.1
U.S. Government and budget agency securities, publicly held.	.7	3.4	-1.9	-.4	7.7	8.9	-8.3	6.5	10.6
Total uses	57.3	66.3	70.5	65.8	82.9	100.8	89.5	97.6	116.0

TABLE 4-2 (*Continued*)

	1963	1964	1965	1966	1967	1968	1969	1970 (est.)	1971 (proj.)
SOURCES (FUNDS SUPPLIED)									
Savings institutions—contractual-type									
Life insurance companies	6.6	7.4	8.3	8.1	8.5	8.7	8.6	8.8	8.7
Private noninsured pension funds	4.1	4.4	5.2	5.4	5.3	5.9	6.2	5.8	6.5
State and local government retirement funds	2.4	2.8	3.3	3.8	4.5	4.1	5.0	5.1	6.1
Fire and casualty insurance companies	1.3	1.1	.9	1.6	2.2	2.5	2.3	2.9	3.4
Total	14.4	15.7	17.7	18.8	20.4	21.3	22.1	22.6	24.7
Savings institutions—deposit-type									
Savings and loan associations	13.3	11.1	9.6	4.2	9.2	10.2	9.8	12.6	14.5
Mutual savings banks . .	3.6	4.3	3.9	2.6	5.1	4.5	2.8	4.3	6.3
Credit unions	.7	.9	1.1	1.0	.8	1.5	1.8	1.8	2.1
Total	17.6	16.3	14.6	7.8	15.0	16.1	14.5	18.7	22.9
Mutual funds.	.8	1.0	1.9	2.5	1.0	2.4	3.4	1.6	2.2
Total savings institutions	32.7	32.9	34.2	29.1	36.4	39.7	39.9	42.9	49.8
Commercial banks.	17.7	21.9	26.7	18.1	38.5	37.3	15.0	29.7	38.4
Nonfinancial corporations	6.0	6.5	6.5	7.0	6.0	18.1	18.5	4.7	8.6
Financial corporations . .	4.3	3.9	5.1	2.4	.6	5.3	8.8	2.7	5.5
Government									
U.S. Government	−.3	.2	.2	1.4	1.1	1.4	1.1	.8	.9
Federally sponsored agencies	−.2	.6	1.4	3.2	2.5	2.5	5.3	5.5	3.3
State and local general funds	1.1	.1	2.6	2.1	1.8	3.2	2.6	−1.2	.6
Federal Reserve banks .	.1	−.1	.1	−	−	−.1	−	−	−
Total	.7	.8	4.3	6.7	5.4	7.0	9.0	5.1	4.8
Other investor groups . . .									
Noncorporate business .	.3	.3	.4	.6	.6	.6	.5	.6	.6
Foreign investors	.8	.8	−.2	−1.8	2.1	1.2	−.2	9.5	7.6
Total	1.1	1.1	.2	−1.2	2.7	1.8	.3	10.1	8.2
Residual: Individuals and others	−1.0	3.7	−1.0	11.7	−4.1	−1.7	19.9	11.0	6.7
Total gross sources .	61.5	70.9	76.1	73.8	85.6	107.6	111.3	106.2	122.0
Less: Funds raised by financial intermediaries									
Investment funds	1.7	2.6	2.6	.9	1.3	1.1	2.7	2.3	3.5
Short-term funds	1.0	1.5	1.0	3.4	1.8	2.5	8.8	−2.4	.1
Federally sponsored credit agency securities, publicly held	1.5	.4	2.0	3.6	−.5	3.1	10.4	8.7	2.4
Total	4.2	4.5	5.6	7.9	2.6	6.7	21.9	8.6	6.0
Total net resources .	57.3	66.3	70.5	65.8	82.9	100.8	89.5	97.6	116.0

SOURCE: *The Investment Outlook for 1971*, Bankers Trust Company, New York, February 1971.
    *Includes affiliates.

TABLE 4-3
Summary of Financing—Investment Funds
(Billions of dollars)

	1963	1964	1965	1966	1967	1968	1969	1970 (est.)	1971 (proj.)
USES (FUNDS RAISED)									
Real estate mortgages	25.7	25.8	25.7	21.3	22.9	27.4	27.8	25.1	32.1
Corporate securities									
Bonds	3.9	4.0	5.4	10.2	14.7	12.9	12.0	21.7	17.3
Stocks	−.3	1.4	—	1.2	2.3	−.9	3.4	6.1	7.2
Total	3.6	5.4	5.4	11.4	17.0	12.0	15.4	27.8	24.5
State and local									
government securities	6.1	6.0	7.6	6.4	7.9	10.2	8.9	12.7	13.7
Foreign securities	1.0	.7	1.0	.7	1.3	1.7	1.5	.7	1.2
Term loans									
Commercial banks. . .	2.5	2.7	4.5	2.3	2.5	3.9	5.4	—	2.7
Banks for cooperatives	—	—	.1	.1	.1	.1	.1	.1	.1
Total	2.5	2.7	4.6	2.4	2.6	4.0	5.5	.1	2.8
Total uses	39.0	40.7	44.3	42.2	51.7	55.3	59.1	66.4	74.3
SOURCES (FUNDS SUPPLIED)									
Savings institutions— contractual-type									
Life insurance companies	6.5	7.2	8.2	6.8	7.7	7.8	5.6	6.0	7.3
Private noninsured pension									
funds	4.0	4.4	5.2	5.8	5.6	5.4	6.1	5.4	6.1
State and local govern- ment retirement									
funds	2.0	2.3	2.9	3.7	4.5	4.0	5.1	5.5	6.0
Fire and casualty									
insurance companies	1.1	.9	.7	1.3	3.0	2.6	2.6	2.8	3.3
Total	13.6	14.9	17.0	17.7	20.8	19.8	19.4	19.7	22.7
Savings institutions— deposit-type									
Savings and loan									
associations	12.2	10.4	9.0	3.8	7.5	9.4	9.5	10.4	14.4
Mutual savings banks .	3.7	4.2	4.1	3.0	5.4	4.4	3.1	3.9	5.8
Credit unions	—	.1	.1	.1	−.1	.2	.2	.2	.2
Total	15.9	14.7	13.1	6.8	12.9	14.0	12.9	14.5	20.4
Mutual funds	.8	1.1	1.6	1.4	1.5	1.9	2.7	1.8	2.2
Total savings institutions	30.3	30.6	31.7	25.8	35.2	35.7	34.9	36.0	45.3
Commercial banks . . .	12.6	10.9	15.1	8.9	16.3	19.5	11.2	13.8	19.5
Nonfinancial corporations	.2	.2	.5	1.0	−.4	.4	2.3	−2.0	.5
Financial corporations .	.8	.4	.5	−.6	.4	.7	1.9	1.4	1.4
Government									
U.S. Government . . .	−.3	.2	.2	1.4	1.1	1.4	1.1	.8	.9
Federally sponsored									
agencies	−.5	.4	1.2	2.7	1.9	2.3	4.6	4.8	2.5
State and local general									
funds	.5	.5	.4	.7	1.2	1.2	.8	.6	.6
Total	−.3	1.1	1.8	4.8	4.2	4.9	6.5	6.2	4.0
Foreign investors	.2	−.2	−.6	−.2	.5	2.0	1.3	.3	1.0
Residual: Individuals									
and others	−3.1	.3	−2.1	3.4	−3.2	−6.8	3.7	13.0	6.1
Total gross sources	40.7	43.3	46.9	43.1	53.0	56.4	61.8	68.7	77.8

TABLE 4-3 (*Continued*)

	1963	1964	1965	1966	1967	1968	1969	1970 (est.)	1971 (proj.)
Less: Investment funds raised by financial intermediaries									
Bonds	1.6	2.6	2.7	.9	1.3	1.1	1.8	1.7	3.2
Stocks	.1	–	-.1	–	–	–	.9	.6	.3
Total	1.7	2.6	2.6	.9	1.3	1.1	2.7	2.3	3.5
Total net sources .	39.0	40.7	44.3	42.2	51.7	55.3	59.1	66.4	74.3

SOURCE: *The Investment Outlook for 1971*, Bankers Trust Company, New York, February 1971.

IMPLICATIONS FOR INTEREST RATES

In the evaluation of the implications of the above estimates of demand for and supply of funds, several items should receive special attention. One item is the excess of commercial bank credit over and above their increase in time and savings deposits. If this item is large relative to expected growth of GNP and the experience in previous years, pressures on the supply side are indicated. The figures for this item since 1963 are shown in the accompanying table.

Year	Commercial Banks' Credit (billions)	Increase in Time and Savings Deposits	Excess of Commercial Banks' Credit over Time and Savings Deposits
1963	19.4	14.3	5.1
1964	22.4	14.5	7.9
1965	29.1	20.0	9.1
1966	16.8	13.3	3.5
1967	36.4	23.8	12.6
1968	39.7	20.6	19.1
1969	16.9	–9.7	26.6
1970 (est.)	30.8	36.0	–5.2
1971 (proj.)	40.0	33.0	7.0

Another item is the residual which calls for financing by individuals and other investors. If this item as shown below for the years 1963-1970 is relatively large, there will be strong tendency toward material increases in interest rates and yields on securities in order to induce residual lenders and buyers to enter into the market in volume as shown in the next table.

Together with the evaluation of these two strategic items, a qualitative judgment should be made respecting the probable course of policy the Federal Reserve is most likely to pursue in the following period.

The Bankers Trust Company interpreted their own 1971 estimates of de-

Year	Funds to be Supplied by the Residual Group—Individuals and Other Investors
1963	−1.0
1964	3.7
1965	−1.0
1966	11.7
1967	−4.1
1968	−1.7
1969	19.9
1970 (est.)	11.0
1971 (proj.)	6.7

mand for and supply of funds on interest rates movements in these words:

The shift in the credit climate and the downward swing in both money market rates and bond yields over the past several months are without parallel in recent years. The slide in interest rates, moreover, has proceeded in the face of emerging signs of a pickup in economic activity and continuing strong inflationary pressures. It is therefore not surprising that opinions differ greatly as to the outlook for interest rates, particularly corporate bond yields, during the balance of 1971; few believe, however, in view of economic developments and prospects, that money market rates can hold at their current low levels.

... our analysis of the credit markets suggests that, even without a vigorous business recovery, total demands for credit will show a sizable increase in 1971, with nearly all important sectors of the financial markets displaying a bigger appetite for funds this year than in 1970.

... a large volume of bonds will still have to be placed with individuals and other noninstitutional investors, and some fairly attractive yields will be required to induce these investors to add to their holdings.

No doubt a major factor in determining the trend of long-term interest rates in the period ahead will be the behavior of wages and prices and their impact on investor sentiment. . . . Currently, the Administration's emphasis on stimulating the economy is being interpreted by many investment officers as being inflationary. Against this background, and considering that only limited progress is in prospect toward curbing the wage-cost-price spiral, it would not be surprising if interest rates begin to firm at some point in 1971.[5]

FEDERAL RESERVE POLICY AND LEVELS OF INTEREST RATES IN 1969–70

In 1969 and 1970 we witnessed that both short-term and long-term interest rates rose to unprecedented high levels, and then turned down precipitously. As shown in Table 4-4, the yield on 3-month treasury bills rose from 4.32 percent

[5] *The Investment Outlook for 1971*, Bankers Trust Company, New York, February 1971, p. 7.

in 1967 to an all time high of 7.72 percent in December 1969. In the first quarter of 1970, it began to turn downward. At the end of the year 1970, the yield was at 4.86 percent, about three percentage points lower than a year ago. The yield on corporate Aaa bonds rose from 5.51 percent in 1967 to an all time high of 8.48 percent in June 1970 and then began to decline. By the end of the year 1970 the yield was around 7.64 percent.

TABLE 4-4
Selected Interest Rates, 1965–70

Year	3-Month Treasury Bills	Prime Commerical Paper (4-6 months)	Corporate Aaa Bonds
1965	3.95	4.38	4.49
1966	4.88	5.55	5.13
1967	4.32	5.10	5.51
1968	5.34	5.90	6.18
1969 March	6.08	6.82	6.85
June	6.49	8.23	6.98
Sept.	7.13	8.48	7.14
Dec.	7.72^H	8.84^H	7.72
1970 March	6.71	8.33	7.84
June	6.74	8.21	8.48^H
Sept.	6.24	7.32	8.09
Dec.	4.86	5.73	7.64

SOURCE: *Economic Report of the President,* February 1971.
^{H} Highest.

The sequence of rapid rise of interest rates to historical levels and then followed by abrupt decline as happened in 1969–70 was not too common in terms of past experience. It should be worthwhile to examine in detail some of the major contributing factors, including the role played by Federal Reserve policy.

Federal Reserve Policy

To combat increasing inflationary pressures in the economy the Federal Reserve Board adopted a progressively greater restrictive credit policy during 1969. As shown in Table 4-5, the money supply (currency and demand deposits) increased at an average annual rate of about $7\frac{1}{2}$ percent from December 1966 to December 1968. During the first half of 1969 money supply rose about $2\frac{1}{2}$ percent, but in the second half of 1969 money supply increased only half a percent. The progressively restrictive credit policy was also reflected in the total amount of reserves available to member banks of the Federal Reserve System. During the first three quarters of 1969 total reserves actually decreased slightly from $27.22 billion in December 1968 to $26.97 billion in September 1969, whereas the rate of growth of reserves in the previous two years from December 1966 to December 1968 was about 14 percent.

As can be seen from the figures on money supply in Table 4-5, the turn-around of Federal Reserve policy began in the first quarter of 1970 when the

TABLE 4-5
Money Supply, Member Bank Reserves, and
Member Bank Free Reserves, 1965–70

Year	Money Supply Seasonally Adjusted (billions)	Rate of Increase of Money Supply (percent)	Member Bank Reserves (billions)	Member Bank Free Reserves (Excess reserves less borrowings) (millions)
1965 Dec.	168.0		22.72	−2
1966 Dec.	171.7 ⎫		23.83	−165
1967 Dec.	183.1 ⎭ 7%		25.26	107
1968 Dec.	197.4 ⎬ 8%		27.22	−310
1969 March	200.1 ⎫		26.75	−701
June	202.4 ⎭ 2½%		27.32	−1064
Sept.	202.8 ⎫		26.97	−831
Dec.	203.6 ⎭ ½%		28.03	−829
1970 March	206.6 ⎫		27.47	−781
June	209.6 ⎪		27.57	−701
Sept.	212.8 ⎬ 5½%		28.83	−335
Dec.	214.6 ⎭		29.23	−77

SOURCE: *Economic Report of the President*, February 1971.

real output of the economy began to decline and the rate of unemployment began to rise above the 4 percent level. However, the Federal Reserve did not take an aggressive stand to ease monetary conditions until the third quarter of 1970 because as of June 1970 member bank free reserves were still at a high negative figure (−$701 million).

Demand for Funds

The supply of funds, assuming a neutral Federal Reserve policy, is historically more stable than the demand for funds. Hence, the explanation of a persistent rise or fall in interest rates lies mostly in the fluctuation of demand for funds in the credit markets besides the role played by the prevailing Federal Reserve policy. The magnitude and intensity of the demand for funds by different sectors of the economy is reflected to some extent by the amounts actually raised in the credit markets. Table 4-6 shows the amounts of funds actually raised by nonfinancial sectors in the credit markets from 1966 to 1970.

Because of a budget surplus, the federal government changed from a heavy borrower in 1968 to a net lender in 1969. However, the combined demand from all other nonfinancial sectors was very strong. In the face of rapidly rising high interest rates, they raised a total of $94.1 billions of funds in 1969 against $83.5 billions in 1968, an increase of about 13 percent. Corporations issued $4.8 billions worth of equity shares in 1969 against a net reduction in shares of $0.7 billion in 1968. The reason for the substantial increase in corporate demand for funds was due to their high level of capital expenditures for plant and equipment which in turn was influenced by continued inflationary expectations. So the high level of demand for funds in 1969 coupled with unusually restrictive

TABLE 4-6

Funds Raised in Credit Markets by Nonfinancial Sectors, 1966–70

	1966	1967	1968	1969	1970
Total funds raised by nonfinancial sectors	68.5	83.5	96.6	90.4	95.4
U.S. Government and agencies.	3.5	13.0	13.4	−3.6	12.7
All other nonfinancial sectors	65.0	70.5	83.5	94.1	82.7
Corporate equity shares	.9	2.4	−.7	4.8	6.6
State and local government securities.	5.7	8.7	9.6	8.1	11.8
Corporate and foreign bonds.	11.0	15.9	14.0	13.1	22.4
Mortgages	22.3	22.0	27.3	27.9	24.6
Bank loans not elsewhere classified . .	10.3	9.6	13.4	15.7	.7
Consumer credit	7.2	4.6	11.1	9.3	4.3
Open market paper	1.0	2.1	1.6	3.3	3.8
Other	6.5	5.2	7.2	11.9	8.4

SOURCE: *Federal Reserve Bulletin*, April 1971, p. A70.

credit policy of the Federal Reserve pushed the already high level of interest rates in 1968 to an unprecedented level by the end of 1969.

However, the increase of real output of the economy came to a halt in the third quarter, 1969. Beginning from the fourth quarter and continuing throughout the whole year of 1970, the economy turned gradually downward, reflecting the impact of restrictive monetary policy and substantial cuts in defense spending. As shown in Table 4-6, the nonfinancial sectors, except the U.S. Government and agencies, raised a total of $82.7 billions in 1970 compared to $94.1 billions in 1969, a decline of about 12 percent. The demand by business for bank loans and the demand for funds by consumers were particularly weak. In the meantime, as mentioned above, the Federal Reserve began to take steps in easing the monetary conditions by increasing money supply at about 5 percent annual rate in the first quarter of 1970. It took even more aggressive stand to ease credit conditions after middle of the year. The reversal of monetary policy from restraint to ease plus dampened demand for funds from the private sector brought about a turnaround in interest rates. The yield on 3-month treasury bills dropped about 3 percentage points to 4.86 in December 1970. However, the long-term interest rates did not decline until after middle of 1970, and even then only moderately.

In summary, it is clear that the Federal Reserve plays a critical role in influencing the level and direction of movements of interest rates. The Federal Reserve achieves this result through influencing the cost and amount of credit available to commercial banks, and through affecting the general course of the economy. However, other factors such as extent of actual inflation and the degree of expectation of continued inflation are no less important in influencing the flow of savings and the demand for funds, and therefore the level and movements of interest rates.

SUGGESTED READINGS

Fisher, Douglas, *Money and Banking*. Homewood, Ill.: Richard D. Irwin, Inc., 1971.

Freund, W. C., and E. D. Zinbarg, "Application of Flow of Funds to Interest-Rate Forecasting," *Journal of Finance*, May 1963.

Harriss, C. Lowell, *Money and Banking*, Allyn and Bacon, Inc., Boston, 1965.

Homer, Sidney, "The Impact of Corporate Pension Funds on Equity and Bond Markets," *Commercial & Financial Chronicle*, Feb. 23, 1967; "Interest Rate Forecasting Techniques and Outlook," *Commercial & Financial Chronicle*, June 30, 1966.

"Interest Rates in Capital Markets," *Federal Reserve Bulletin*, August 1965.

Kaufman, Henry, "Pressures on Capital and Money Markets to Increase in 1968,"*Commercial & Financial Chronicle*, Oct. 5, 1967; "The Interest Rate Outlook for Short and Long Issues," *Commercial & Financial Chronicle*, Jan. 19, 1967.

Ketchum, M. D., and H. R. Bartell, Jr., *Conference on Savings and Residential Financing, 1966 Proceedings*, Washington, D.C.: U.S. Savings & Loan League, 1967.

"Money Supply and the Market," *Outlook*, Standard & Poor's Corporation, Jan. 1, 1968.

O'Leary, James J., "The Outlook for Interest Rates and the Economy in Year Ahead," *Commercial & Financial Chronicle*, Dec. 22, 1966; "The Economic and Investment Outlook," *Financial Analysts Journal*, January–February 1966.

Palmer, Michael, "Money Supply, Portfolio Adjustments and Stock Prices," *Financial Analysts Journal*, July–August 1970.

Poole, Alan C., "Relationship of Money Market to Stock Market and the Economy," *Commercial & Financial Chronicle*, Sept. 8, 1966.

Sprinkel, Beryl W., *Money and Markets, A Monetarist View*. Homewood, Ill.: Richard D. Irwin, Inc., 1971.

———, *Money and Stock Prices*. Homewood, Ill.: Richard D. Irwin, Inc., 1964.

QUESTIONS AND PROBLEMS

1. Why should purchasers of equities be concerned with the analysis and forecast of interest rates?
2. Discuss the role of the Federal Reserve System in influencing the level and trend of interest rates.
3. What is a yield curve? Of what use is it to an analyst?
4. Prepare a table showing the changes in both long-term and short-term interest rates and their relation to stock prices and bond prices in the last five years. Discuss the implications of your table.
5. Discuss the changes of interest rates in relation to different stages of the most recent two business cycles.

6. Obtain a financial forecast for the current year or next year from the Bankers Trust Company of New York. Evaluate their forecast.
7. Gather enough relevant materials or information in key factors and discuss outlook of interest rates in the next six to twelve months.
8. What is the individual investor in bonds to do at this juncture of time in order to protect himself from interest-rate risks?

5. Industry Analysis

CHANGING IMPORTANCE OF INDUSTRIES

A growing economy is characterized not only by its absolute growth in output but also by changing composition of the economy and relative importance of industries. In a growing economy, new products, new processes, and new industries are continuously introduced to displace partly or wholly the older products, processes, and industries. The changing growth rates and fortunes of American industries in the past forty years or more are shown in Figures 5-1, and 5-2 and in Table 5-1. The growth rates of Federal Reserve production indexes for major industry groups from 1923-26 to 1948-53 are compared with those from 1948-53 to 1960-65 in Figure 5-1. Figure 5-2 compares growth rates for the same groups between 1948-53 to 1957-60 and 1957-60 to 1960-65. Chemicals, rubber and plastics, electrical machinery, furniture, instruments, and transportation equipment were above all industry average in both postwar periods. Table 5-1 shows the growth rates at five-year intervals of some thirty industries for a period of forty years or more.

ADVANTAGES OF FASTER-GROWING INDUSTRIES

In a growing economy, most industries will participate. However, some industries may grow at lower rates than the economy. The faster-growing industries naturally enjoy some advantages over slower-growing industries. For one thing, the demand is increasing rapidly, assuring sales outlook of the many firms in the fast-growing industry. If there is no fierce price competition, profit margin will be either maintained or even improved, thus creating larger profits for the firm in the industry. Besides, firms with rapidly expanding demand can easily absorb the rising costs from depreciation, labor, materials, and taxes. The late Professor Grodinsky, a famous exponent of the industry approach to investment, discussed the favorable implications of fast-growing demand in these words.

Changing trends of demand underlie long-term investment values. In-

Figure 5-1

Regional and Industry Trends. Growth Rates of Federal Reserve
Production Indexes for Major Industry Groups

(1923-26 to 1948-53 compared with 1948-53 to 1960-65)

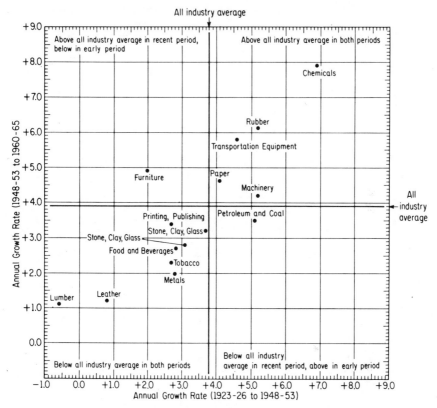

Industry titles are shortened. See series C268 to C306 in appendix 2 for sources and in appedix 3 for basic
data. Primary metals and fabricated metal products groups were combined for 1948 to 1965, and iron
and steel and nonferrous metals and products groups, for 1923 to 1953 to obtain comparibility. Also
combined were textile mill products and apparel groups and nonelectrical and electrical machinery groups
for 1948 to 1953 to correspond with the textile products group and machinery group for 1923 to 1953.
The manufactured food products and alcoholic beverages groups were combined for 1923 to 1953 to
correspond with the food and beverage manufactures group for 1948-1965.

SOURCE: *Long-Term Economic Growth 1860-1965,* U.S. Department of Commerce, p. 85.

creasing production lays the foundation for increasing profits. The rise
in sales dilutes the increasing overhead, and overhead is a constantly
rising factor in American industry. Capital equipment necessary to reduce labor costs carries a fixed overhead, such as interest, maintenance,
depreciation, and salaries for skilled and professional personnel. Social
security funds and appropriations to special welfare insurance funds are
on the increase. The break-even point, the point in the percentage of
capacity operation of a plant at which, at a given price and cost structure, the company covers its expenses, steadily increases. For an indus-

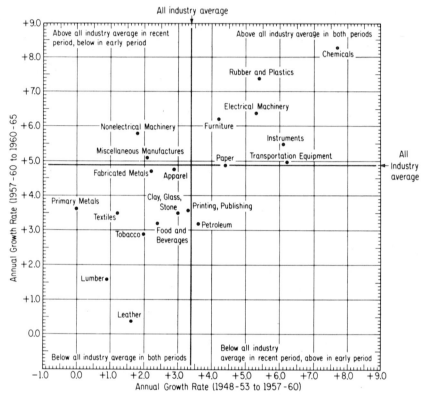

Figure 5-2
Regional and Industry Trends. Growth Rates of Federal Reserve
Production Indexes for Major Industry Groups
(1948-53 to 1957-60 compared with 1957-60 to 1960-65)

Industry titles are shortened. See series C268 to C306 in appendix 2 for sources and in appendix 3 for basic data.

SOURCE: *Long-Term Economic Growth 1860-1965*, U.S. Department of Commerce, p. 86.

try to operate at a profit under such conditions, it is essential that the demand increase, so that plants can operate at a higher percentage of their capacity.[1]

CLASSIFICATION OF THE ECONOMY INTO INDUSTRIES

Industries are usually classified into several broad categories such as industrials, railroads, financial, and public utilities. The New York Stock Exchange has classified all listed companies into four major categories: industrials, transportation, utilities, and finance and real estate. The category of industrials is

[1] Julius Grodinsky, *Investments*, (New York; 1953), The Ronald Press Co., pp. 53-54.

TABLE 5-1
Percentage Rate of Change at Stated Intervals

Industry and Beginning Year	1870	1880	1890	1900	1910	1915	1920	1925	1930	1935	1940	1945	1950	1955	1960
Aluminum production (1891)				19.83	16.38	14.89	13.53	12.30	11.18	10.16	9.23	8.39	7.63	6.93	6.30
Asphalt production (1916)							8.91	8.35	7.83	7.34	6.88	6.45	6.04	5.66	5.31
Bituminous coal production (1870)	17.65	10.89	6.72	4.15	2.56	2.01	1.58	1.24	0.98	0.77	0.60	0.47	0.37	0.29	0.23
Butter, margarine prod. (1909)					2.06	1.78	1.54	1.33	1.15	1.00	0.86	0.75	0.64	0.56	0.48
Cigarette consumption (1915)						14.79	12.21	10.08	8.33	6.87	5.68	4.69	3.87	3.20	2.64
Copper consumption (1885)			8.38	6.54	5.11	4.52	3.99	3.53	3.12	2.75	2.43	2.15	1.90	1.68	1.48
Corn production (1866)	4.79	3.41	2.42	1.73	1.23	1.04	0.87	0.74	0.62	0.52	0.44	0.37	0.31	0.27	0.22
Cotton consumption (1870)	6.64	5.27	4.19	3.33	2.64	2.36	2.10	1.87	1.67	1.49	1.33	1.18	1.05	0.94	0.84
Electric energy production (1902)					10.82	9.99	9.22	8.51	7.85	7.25	6.69	6.17	5.70	5.26	4.86
Energy fuel production (1900)				4.29	3.43	3.07	2.74	2.45	2.19	1.96	1.75	1.56	1.40	1.25	1.12
Fiber (man-made) cons. (1911)						31.35	25.25	20.34	16.38	13.20	10.63	8.56	6.89	5.55	4.47
Gross physical output (1889)			4.33	3.98	3.67	3.52	3.37	3.24	3.11	2.98	2.86	2.74	2.63	2.53	2.42
Lead consumption (1919)							5.43	3.69	2.50	1.70	1.15	0.78	0.53	0.36	0.24
Life insurance in force (1880)		9.16	8.74	8.35	7.97	7.78	7.61	7.43	7.26	7.09	6.93	6.77	6.62	6.46	6.32
Margarine production (1909)					4.85	4.29	3.79	3.35	2.96	2.61	2.31	2.04	1.80	1.59	1.41
Margarine (late period) (1940)											15.42	10.01	6.50	4.22	2.74
Motor-fuel demand (1918)							8.02	7.44	6.90	6.41	5.95	5.52	5.12	4.75	4.41
Motor-vehicle registrations (1901)					33.48	23.98	17.18	12.31	8.82	6.32	4.53	3.24	2.32	1.66	1.19
Natural gas production (1895)				8.83	8.06	7.71	7.36	7.04	6.73	6.43	6.14	5.87	5.61	5.36	5.12
Paper, paperboard cons. (1899)				5.68	5.32	5.14	4.97	4.81	4.65	4.49	4.35	4.20	4.06	3.93	3.80
Petroleum consumption (1916)							7.62	6.73	5.95	5.26	4.65	4.10	3.63	3.20	2.83
Phosphate rock sold (1870)	12.46	10.36	8.60	7.15	5.94	5.41	4.93	4.50	4.10	3.74	3.41	3.11	2.83	2.58	2.35
Pig iron production (1870)	11.87	8.90	6.67	5.00	3.75	3.25	2.81	2.43	2.11	1.82	1.58	1.37	1.18	1.03	0.89
Portland cement production (1890)			49.15	25.25	12.97	9.30	6.67	4.78	3.43	2.46	1.76	1.26	0.90	0.65	0.46
Potato production (1866)	3.93	3.03	2.33	1.79	1.38	1.21	1.06	0.93	0.81	0.71	0.63	0.55	0.48	0.42	0.37
Railway ton-miles (1870)	13.61	9.95	7.28	5.33	3.90	3.33	2.85	2.44	2.09	1.78	1.53	1.31	1.12	0.95	0.82
Rolled iron, steel prod. (1865)	12.05	9.44	7.40	5.80	4.54	4.02	3.56	3.15	2.79	2.47	2.19	1.93	1.71	1.52	1.34
Rubber consumption (1919)							6.36	6.06	5.77	5.50	5.24	4.99	4.76	4.53	4.32
Soybean production (1919)							38.84	30.10	23.33	18.08	14.01	10.86	8.42	6.52	5.06
Steel ingot production (1870)	22.06	16.00	11.61	8.42	6.11	5.21	4.43	3.78	3.22	2.74	2.33	1.99	1.69	1.44	1.23
Sulphur production (1900)				33.09	19.62	15.11	11.63	8.96	6.90	5.31	4.09	3.15	2.43	1.87	1.44
Tangible capital input (1889)			4.28	3.55	2.95	2.69	2.45	2.23	2.03	1.85	1.69	1.54	1.40	1.28	1.16
Wheat production (1866)	4.45	3.35	2.52	1.90	1.43	1.24	1.08	0.93	0.81	0.70	0.61	0.53	0.46	0.40	0.35

SOURCE: J. Frank Gaston, *Growth Patterns in Industry: A Reexamination*, Washington, D.C.: National Industrial Conference Board, 1961, p. 14.

subdivided into 20 industry groups. The accompanying table shows the distribution of 1,273 listed companies among these industry groups and the relative importance of each group in terms of market value at the end of 1968.

Listed Common Stocks at the End of 1968
(By industry)

Group	Number of Companies	Number of Shares (millions)	Market Value (millions)	Percent
Industrials	954	9,040	$523,214	78.4
Aircraft.	22	229	10,425	1.6
Amusement	18	115	5,686	0.9
Automotive	39	606	36,593	5.3
Building.	43	191	9,052	1.4
Chemicals (incl. glass). . . .	72	984	62,255	9.3
Drugs, cosmetics.	38	492	30,296	4.5
Electronics, electrical	94	909	80,798	12.1
Foods, commodities.	82	681	30,147	4.5
Furniture, office equip.. . . .	17	102	11,847	1.8
Leather, shoes	14	51	2,444	0.4
Machinery, metals	160	915	42,458	6.4
Mining.	44	443	19,567	2.9
Paper, publishing	47	372	18,552	2.8
Petroleum, natural gas . . .	50	1,455	97,219	14.6
Retail trade.	78	707	31,243	4.7
Rubber	13	123	6,347	0.9
Steel.	37	283	11,116	1.7
Textiles	45	165	6,564	1.0
Tobacco	10	102	4,472	0.7
Other	31	114	6,135	0.9
Transportation.	85	512	22,688	3.4
Utilities	147	2,593	95,276	14.2
Finance, real estate	87	650	26,628	4.0
Grand total	1,273	12,795	$667,806	100.0

SOURCE: *Fact Book 1969*, New York Stock Exchange.

The Value Line Investment Survey, on the other hand, classified some 1,400 stocks under their review into 65 industries. They are

Aerospace
Agricultural equip.
Air transport
Aluminum
Auto truck
Auto parts
Baking
Bank

Brewing
Building
Chemical
Coal and uranium
Conglomerates
Copper
Department Store
Distilling

Drugs
Electric utility
Electrical equipment/Electronics
Fasteners
Finance
Food processing
Furniture
Gold mining
Grocery
Household products
Insurance (fire and casualty)
Insurance (life)
Investment trust
Machinery
Machine tools
Mail order
Meat packing
Metal fabricating
Milling and vegetable oil
Natural gas
Nonferrous mining and metals
Office equip./computer
Packaging and container
Paper
Personal services

Petroleum
Precision instruments
Publishing and advertising
Railroad
Railroad equipment
Real estate
Recreation
Retail–special lines
Savings and loan associations
Shipping and shipbuilding
Shoes
Silver
Soft drinks
Specialty stores
Steel
Sugar
Telecommunications
Textiles
Tire and rubber
Tobacco
Toiletries/cosmetics
Toys and school supplies
Truck and bus lines
Variety stores

As shown in Table 5-2, the Standard & Poor's Corporation classified their selected 500 companies into three major groups: industrials (425), rails (20), and utilities (55) plus some supplementary groups for banks, insurance companies, and investment companies. The industrials is subclassified into some 80 industry groups. Other organizations, including Moody's and the Securities Exchange Commission, have their own industry classifications.

For purposes of industry analysis, the most useful classification is Standard & Poor's. The reasons are several: First, there is a price index for each industry group. Second, quarterly earnings, unadjusted and seasonally adjusted, and dividends are available to relate to the price index of each industry group. Third, composite industry data on a per-share basis like sales, operating income, depreciation, taxes, earnings, dividends, book value, working capital, and capital expenditures are published regularly in their *Industry Survey* for each industry group, with data going back to 1957.

Besides classification of industry by nature of products, industries are often classified or grouped together in terms of secular growth and cyclical stability. They are usually grouped under four categories:

TABLE 5-2
Stocks in the S & P "500" Price Index
Indexes of the Individual Groups Shown Below Are Published Each Week in *The Outlook*

— 425 INDUSTRIALS —

AEROSPACE—Boeing; General Dynamics; Grumman: Lockheed; Martin Marietta; McDonnell Douglas; No. Amer. Rockwell; United Aircraft.

‡AIR FREIGHT—Emery Air Freight; Flying Tiger Corp.; Seaboard World Airlines.

AIR TRANSPORT—American; Delta; Eastern; Natl. Airlines; Pan Amer.; T. W. A.; U A L Inc.

ALUMINUM—Alcan Aluminium; Aluminum Co. of Amer.; Kaiser Aluminum; Reynolds Metals.

‡ATOMIC ENERGY—EG&G; United Nuclear; Utah Construction & Mining.

AUTOMOBILE—Amer. Motors; Chrysler; Ford; Gen. Motors.

AUTO PARTS & ACCESS.—Budd Co.; Champion Spark Plug; Dana; ESB Inc.; Eaton; Fed.-Mogul; Gould Inc.; Kelsey-Hayes; Lib.-Owens-Ford.

AUTO TRUCKS & PARTS—Cummins Engine; Fruehauf; White.

BEVERAGES (BREWERS)—Falstaff; Rheingold; Schaefer (F&M); Schlitz.

BEVERAGES (DISTILLERS)—Dist. Corp.; Heublein Inc.; Natl. Dist.; Walker.

BEVERAGES (SOFT DRINKS)—Coca-Cola; Coca-Cola Btlg. of N.Y.; Dr Pepper; PepsiCo Inc.; Royal Crown Cola.

BUILDING MATERIALS (AIR CONDITIONING) — Carrier; Copeland; Fedders; Trane.

BUILDING MATERIALS (CEMENT) — Alpha; Gen. Port.; Lehigh; Lone Star; Marquette; Penn-Dixie.

BUILDING MATERIALS (HEATING & PLUMBING)—Amer. Standard; Crane; Walworth.

BUILD. MAT. (ROOFING & WALLBOARD)—Flintkote; Jim Walter Corp.; Johns-Manv.; Masonite; Natl. Gypsum; U. S. Gypsum.

CHEMICALS — Air Reduct.; Allied; Amer. Cyan.; Chemetron; Dow; du Pont; GAF Corp.; Hercules; Monsanto; Olin; Union Carbide.

COAL (BITUMINOUS)—Eastern Gas & Fuel; No. Amer. Coal; Pittston.

CONFECTIONERY—Hershey; Peter Paul; Wrigley.

‡CONGLOMERATES—Bangor Punta; City Investing; Gulf & Western; Kidde (Walter); Ling-Temco-Vought; Teledyne; Textron; United Brands; U. S. Industries.

CONTAINERS (METAL & GLASS)—Amer. Can; Contl. Can; Crown Cork; Natl. Can; Owens-Ill.

CONTAINERS (PAPER)—Brown; Diamond Intl., Federal; Fibreboard; Hoerner Waldorf; Maryland Cup.

COPPER—Anaconda; Copper Range; Inspir. Cons.; Kennecott; Newmont Mining; Phelps Dodge.

COSMETICS — Alberto-Culver; Avon; Chesebrough-Pond's; Max Factor "A"; Helene Curtis; Faberge Inc.; Revlon.

DRUGS—Abbott; Amer. Home; Lilly (Eli); Bristol-Myers; Merck; Pfizer; Richardson-Merrell; Schering-Plough; Searle (G. D.); Sterling; Warner-Lambert.

ELECTRICAL EQUIPMENT—Cutler-Hammer; Emerson Electric; I-T-E Imperial Corp.; McGraw-Edison; Square D.

ELECTRICAL-ELECTRONICS MAJOR COS.—Gen. Elec.; Intl. Tel & Tel.; Litton; RCA; Sperry Rand; Texas Instruments; Westinghouse Elec.

ELECTRICAL HOUSEHOLD APPLIANCES — Maytag; Sunbeam; Whirlpool.

ELECTRONICS—AMP Inc.; Beckman; Gen. Instrument; Raytheon; Tektronix; Varian Associates.

FINANCE—C.I.T.; Heller (Walter E.) International; Talcott National.

FINANCE (SMALL LOANS)—Amer. Invest.; Beneficial; Credithrift Financial Corp., Dial Fin.; Family Fin.; Household; Liberty Loan.

FOODS (BISCUIT BAKERS)—Keebler; Nabisco.

FOODS (BREAD & CAKE BAKERS)—Amer. Baker; Gen. Host; Ward.

FOODS (CANNED FOODS)—Camp. Soup; Del Monte; Green Giant; Heinz; Libby; Stokely-Van Camp.

FOODS (CORN REFINERS)—CPC Intl.; Staley (A.E.).

FOODS (DAIRY PRODUCTS)—Beatrice Foods; Borden; Kraftco Corp.; Pet, Inc.

FOODS (MEAT PACKING)—Cudahy; Iowa Beef Processors; Mayer (Oscar) & Co.; Swift.

FOODS (PACKAGED)—Gen. Foods; Gen. Mills; Gerber Prod.; Kellogg Co.; Quaker Oats; Stand. Brands.

FOREST PRODUCTS—Boise Cascade; Evans Products; Georgia-Pacific; Potlatch Forests; U. S. Plywood-Champion; Weyerhaeuser.

GOLD MINING—Amer. So. African Inv.; Campbell Red Lake; Dome; Homestake.

HOME FURNISHINGS—Kroehler; Mohasco; Roper; Simmons Co.

HOTEL-MOTEL—Hilton Hotels; Holiday Inns; Sonesta Intl.

LEAD & ZINC—Amer. Zinc; Hudson Bay; St. Joe Minerals.

‡LEISURE TIME—Brunswick; Chris-Craft; Handleman; Outboard Marine; Questor; Tandy; Wilson Sporting Goods.

MACHINE TOOLS—Acme Cleveland; Brown & Sharpe; Cincinnati Milacron; Giddings & Lewis; Monarch Machine Tool; Warner & Swasey.

MACHINERY (AGRICULTURAL)—Deere; Intl. Harvester; Massey Ferguson.

MACHINERY (CONSTRUCTION & MATERIALS HANDLING)—Bucyrus-Erie; Cater. Trac.; Clark Equip.; Koehring Co.; Rex Chainbelt.

MACHINERY (INDUSTRIAL)—Amer. Chain & Cable; Briggs & Stratton; Chic. Pneumatic Tool; Cooper Industries; Gardner-Denver; Ingersoll-Rand.

MACHINERY & SERVICES (OIL WELL)—Baker Oil Tools; Dresser; Halliburton; Murphy (G. W.); Schlumberger N.V.

MACHINERY (SPECIALTY)—AMF Inc.; Ex-Cell-O; Joy Manufacturing; Leesona Corp.; USM Corp.

MACHINERY (STEAM GENERATING)—Babcock & Wilcox; Comb. Engineer.; Foster Wheeler.

METAL FABRICATING—Essex Intl.; Gen. Cable; Howmet; Revere; Scovill; U. S. Smelting, Refining & Mining.

METALS MISC.—Amer. Metal Climax; Amer. Smelt.; Cerro Corp.; Engelhard Min. & Chem.; Intl. Nickel.

MISCELLANEOUS—AT&T; Armstrong Cork; Bendix; Borg-Warner; Corning Glass; Eastman Kodak; FMC; Gillette; Grace (W. R.); Honeywell Inc.; NL Industries; Minnesota Mining; Otis Elevator; Owens-Corning; PPG Industries; Polaroid; Ralston Purina; Sherwin-Williams; Singer; TRW; Timken.

‡MOBILE HOMES—Champion Homes; Fleetwood Enterprises; Philips Industries; Skyline.

MOTION PICTURES—Columbia; MCA; Metro-Goldwyn-Mayer; Twentieth Century-Fox.

OFFICE & BUSINESS EQUIPMENT—Addressograph; Burroughs; Control Data; Intl. Bus. Mach.; Natl. Cash Reg.; Pitney-Bowes; SCM Corp; Xerox Corp.

OFFSHORE DRILLING—Global Marine; Santa Fe International; Sedco.

OIL (CRUDE PRODUCERS)—Amerada Hess Corp.; Gen. Amer.; Louisiana Land & Exploration; Superior Oil.

OIL (INTEGRATED-DOMESTIC)—Atl. Richfield; Cities Ser.; Contl. Oil; Getty Oil; Phillips; Shell; S. O. Ind.; Sun Oil; Union Oil.

OIL (INTEGRATED-INTERNATIONAL)—Gulf; Mobil Oil; Royal Dutch; S. O. Calif.; S. O. N.J.; Texaco.

PAPER—Crown Zell; International; Kimb.-Clark; Mead; St. Regis; Scott; Union Camp; Westvaco.

‡POLLUTION CONTROL—American Air Filter; Culligan; Research Cottrell; Zurn Industries.

PUBLISHING—Crowell-Collier; Grolier Inc.; Harcourt Brace & World; McGraw-Hill; Meredith; Scott Foresman; Time Inc.; Times Mirror.

RADIO-TV BROADCASTERS—American; Capital Cities; Columbia Broad.; Cox Broadcasting; Metromedia; Taft.

RADIO-TV MANUFACTURERS — Admiral; Magnavox; Motorola; Zenith.

RAILROAD EQUIPMENT—ACF Ind.; Amsted Indus.; Gen. Sig.; Gen. Steel Indus.; Pullman; Stanray.

REAL ESTATE—GAC; General Development; Kaufman & Broad; Tishman Realty; Uris Buildings.

RESTAURANTS—Howard Johnson; Kentucky Fried Chicken; Marriott; McDonald's Corp.

RETAIL STORES (DEPT. STORES)—Allied Stores; Associated; Federated; Gimbel; Macy; Marshall Field; May Dept.; Mercantile; Penney.

RETAIL STORES (FOOD CHAINS)—Acme Markets; First Natl.; Food Fair; Grand Union; Great A. & P.; Jewel Companies; Kroger; Safeway; Winn-Dixie.

RETAIL STORES (MAIL ORDER & GENERAL CHAINS)—Gamble-Skogmo; Marcor Inc.; Sears.

‡RETAIL STORES (DISCOUNT STORES) — Arlan's; Interstate; King's; Vornado.

RETAIL STORES (VARIETY)—Grant; Kresge; McCrory Corp.; Murphy (G. C.); Newberry; Woolworth.

SAVINGS & LOAN ASSN.—Fin. Fed.; First Charter; Great West. Fin.; Imperial Corp. of Amer.; United Financial.

SHOES—Brown; Genesco; Interco; Melville.

SOAPS—Clorox; Colgate-Palmolive; Procter & Gamble; Purex; Unilever N.V.

STEEL—Armco; Beth.; CF&I Steel; Inland; Lykes-Youngstown; National; Republic; U.S. Steel; Wheeling Pittsburgh.

SUGAR (BEET REFINERS)—Amalgamated Sugar; Amer. Crystal; Great Western; Holly.

SUGAR (CANE REFINERS)—Amstar Corp.; Su-Crest.

SULPHUR—Freeport; Pan Amer. Sulphur; Texas Gulf.

TEXTILES (APPAREL MFRS.)—Bobbie Brooks; Cluett, Peabody; Hanes Corp.; Jonathan Logan; Kayser; Manhattan Industries; Munsingwear.

TEXTILE PRODUCTS—Burlington; Cone Mills; Dan River; Lowenstein; Reeves; Springs Mills; Stevens.

TEXTILES (SYNTHETIC FIBERS) — Akzona Inc.: Celanese.

TIRES & RUBBER GOODS—Firestone; Goodrich; Goodyear; Uniroyal.

TOBACCO (CIGARETTES)—Amer. Brands Inc.; Liggett & Myers; Philip Morris; Reynolds.

‡TOYS—Mattel; Milton Bradley; Tonka.

‡TRUCKERS: Assoc. Trans; Cons. Freight; Cooper-Jarrett; McLean Truck; Pac. Inter. Exp.; Roadway; Spector; T.I.M.E.-DC; Transcon Lines; Yellow Freight System.

VENDING MACHINES—ARA Services; Macke; Servomation; UMC Industries; Vendo Co.

— RAILROADS —

Burlington Northern Inc.; Canadian Pacific; C. & O.; Chic. Milw. St. P. & P.; Chic., R. I. & Pac.; Ill. Cent. Industries; Kans. City So. Industries; Louis. & Nash.; Norf. & West.; Penn Central Co.; Reading Co.; Rio Grande Inds.; St. Louis-S.F.; Santa Fe Industries; Seaboard Coast Line; Soo Line Railroad; So. Pac.; So. Rwy.; Union Pac.; Western Pac.

— PUBLIC UTILITIES —

ELECTRIC POWER—Allegheny Pwr.; Amer. El. Pwr.; Balt. G. & E.; Boston Edison; Cent. & So. West. Corp.; Cinci. G. & E.; Cleve. Elec.; Comm. Ed.; Con. Ed.; Consumers Pwr.; Dayton P. & L.; Delmarva P. & L.; Detroit Ed.; Duquesne Lt.; Fla. Pwr. Corp.; Gen. Pub. Util.; Idaho Pwr.; Ill. Pwr.; Indianapolis P. & L.; Middle So. Util.; New Eng. Elec. Sys.; N. Y. State E. & G.; Niagara Mohawk; No. States Pwr.; Ohio Ed.; Pac. G. & E.; Phila. Elec.; Pub. Serv. of Colo.; Pub. Serv. E. & G.; So. Calif. Ed.; Southern Co.; Texas Utils.; Union Elec.; Va. E. & P.; Wisc. El. Pwr.

NATURAL GAS DISTRIBUTORS—Amer. Natural; Bklyn. Union; Columbia; Consolidated Natural; Equitable; Laclede; Lone Star; Okla. Natural; Pac. Light; Peoples; Wash. Gas Lt.

NATURAL GAS PIPE LINES—El Paso Nat.; Miss. River Corp.; Northern Natural; Panhandle Eastern; So. Natural; Texas East. Trans.; Texas Gas Trans.

TELEPHONE—*AT&T; General Tel. & El.; Rochester Telephone.

- SUPPLEMENTARY GROUPS -

BANKS (NEW YORK CITY)—Bank of N.Y.; Bankers Trust New York; Charter New York; Chase Manhattan; Chemical; First Natl. City; Manufacturers-Hanover; Morgan (J. P.) & Co.; United States Trust.

BANKS (OUTSIDE NEW YORK CITY)—BankAmerica; Cleveland Trust; Conill Corp.; Crocker Natl.; First Chic. Corp.; First Natl. Bost.; First Penn.; First Union Inc.; Mercantile Bancorporation; Natl. Bank Det.; Natl. City of Cleve.; PNB Corp.; Pitt. Natl.; Republic Natl. Dallas; Security Pacific National Bank; Wells Fargo.

LIFE INSURANCE—Amer. National; BMA Corp.; Franklin; Jefferson Pilot; Liberty Corp.; Lincoln National; N.L.T. Corp.; Republic National Life; Richmond; Southwestern; Transamerica.

MULTI-LINE INSURANCE—Aetna Life & Cas.; American General; CNA Financial; Connecticut General; Travelers.

PROPERTY-LIABILITY INSURANCE—Chubb Corp.; Continental Corp.; Crum & Forster; Gov't Empl.; Hanover; INA Corp.; St. Paul; Safeco Corp.; Security Corp.; U.S. Fidelity & Gty.

INVESTMENT COMPANIES—Adams; Dominick Fund; Gen. Amer.; Lehman; Madison; Niagara Share; Surveyor Fund; Tri-Cont.; U. S. & For. Sec.

PREFERRED STOCKS—Amer. Can $1¾; Atlantic Rich. $3¾; Consol. Ed. $5; du Pont $4½; Duquesne Lt. $2; Gen. Motors $3¾; Pac. G. & E. $1½; Pac. T. & T. $6; USM Corp. $1½; Union Pac. $0.40.

HIGH-GRADE COMMON—Amer. Home Prod.; AT&T; Campbell Soup; Cleve. Elec.; Commonw. Edison; Eastman Kodak; Gen. Elec.; Gen. Foods; Gen. Motors; Goodyear T. & R.; Kimberly-Clark; Kraftco Corp.; Morgan, J. P.; Natl. Cash Reg.; Otis Elev.; Owens-Illinois; Penney; Phila. Elec.; Procter & Gamble; Reynolds Inds.; Sears, Roebuck; So. Cal. Edison; Std. Oil of N. J.; Texaco; U. S. Gypsum.

LOW-PRICED COMMON — Allis-Chalmers; American Motors; Apeco; Assoc. Transport; Atlas Corp.; Bell Intercontinental; Brunswick; Chemway; Cowles Communications; Falstaff; Gen. Refractories; Glen Alden; Ideal Basic; Lehigh Valley Indus.; Libby, McNeill; Martin Marietta; Natl. Tea; Publicker; Technical Material; Welbilt.

‡Not included in 425 Industrials.
*Not included in utility composite.

CHANGES SINCE April 5, 1971 (+) added to group (—) deleted from group. Low-Priced Common (+) Allis-Chalmers (—) Transitron.

SOURCE: *The Outlook*, Standard & Poor's Corporation.

(a) *Growth industry*—the growth of the industry is expected to persist and to exceed the average of the economy.

(b) *Cyclical industry*—the industry is expected to move closely with the economy and to fluctuate cyclically.

(c) *Defensive industry*—the industry is expected to grow steadily with the economy, but to decline less than the average in a cyclical downturn.

(d) *Declining industry*—the industry is expected either to decline absolutely or to grow less than the average of the economy.

In Table 5-3 industries are grouped together in terms of different growth prospects by Professor Leo Barnes.

STAGES OF INDUSTRY DEVELOPMENT

The development of each industry, according to some economic theorists, can be likened to the life cycle of individuals.[2] There are four stages to the standard life cycle of industries.

1. Pioneering stage
2. Fast-growing stage
3. Maturity and stabilization stage
4. Relative decline or eclipse stage

The pioneering stage represents the first phase of a new industry. The technology or the product is relatively new and still to be perfected. Demand expands rapidly. Opportunities of making big profits are great. Many venturesome capitalists enter into industry and organize their own firms. As a rule, competition is keen and mortality rates are high.

The second or fast-growth stage arrives when the chaotic growth and competition is over, leaving only a number of surviving large corporations dominating the industry. However, the demand is still growing faster than the economy. This is the stage of orderly, rapid growth.

During the third stage of maturity and stabilization, the industry is fully developed and grows roughly at the same pace as the whole economy.

Eventually, the industry will grow old due to inroads from new products, new industries, changes in social habits, new technology, and changes in demand. In good times the industry will grow less than the economy, and in times of recession the industry will suffer sharp declines in demand. However, the industry may continue to exist for many years.

Evaluation of the Industry Life-Cycle Theory

Several comments on the theory and its investment implications are offered below. First, the general description of the stages of development of industries

[2] Edward S. Mead and Julius Grodinsky, *The Ebb & Flow of Investment Values* (New York: Appleton-Century-Crofts, 1939); Grodinsky, op. cit., Chapters 3, 4, and 5.

TABLE 5-3

Growth Panorama of United States Business

GROWTH INDUSTRIES OF TOMORROW

FAST FUTURE GROWTH		MODERATE FUTURE GROWTH	
Comparatively Stable		**Comparatively Stable**	
Atomic power	Boron	Aerosol packaging	Nickel
Batteries, rechargeable	Cesium	Containers, metal	Office and business equipment
Cosmetics	Cobalt	Dairy products	Paper and pulp
Cryogenics	Community antenna TV	Electric utilities	Paper containers
Desalination of water	Credit services	Factors	Photographic supplies
Electronic data processing	Dry cleaning machines	Food chains	Plywood
Electronics and molectronics	Drugs, ethical	Frozen foods	Polyester fibers
Facsimile communications	Epoxy resins	Insurance	Prefabricated housing
Fluidics	Fish protein	Leather substitutes	Printing and publishing
Food irradiation	Fluorine	Musical instruments	Savings and loan assns.
Fuel cells	Germanium	Mutual fund management	Shell houses
Infrared devices	Helicopters	Pet foods and products	Synthetic fibers
Laser and maser applications	Helium	Petroleum	Tape recording
Liquefied (LP) gas	Hydrofoil ships	Radio broadcasting (FM)	Travel
Med., dent. and hosp. sup.	Leasing, auto, truck, etc.	Sewing patterns	Trucking
Microwave equipment	Lithium	Soft drinks	Uranium
Oceanography	Missiles	Telephones	Vanadium
Photosynthesis	Monorail transportation	Television broadcasting and motion pictures	
Plastic packaging	"New town" development	Toys	**Very Cyclical**
Satellite communication	Nuclear-powered ships		Building supplies
Solar energy	Nursing homes	**Moderately Cyclical**	Cement
Teaching machines	Photoprinting	Aircraft manufacturers	Construction
Textbooks	Polyethylene	Air transports and freight	Construction machinery
Thermoelectricity	Polypropylene	Aluminum	Copper
Water purification	Polyurethanes	Bowling equipment	Electrical appliances
	Powdered metals	Chemicals, basic	Electrical equipment
Moderately Cyclical	School supplies	Detergents	Floor covering (hard)
Air conditioning	Scientific instruments	Fertilizers	Foam rubber
Anti-missile defense	Semiconductors		Heating and plumbing
	Silicon and silicon plastics		Machine tools
	Smog and air control		Machinery, industrial
	Space and rocket equipt.		Materials handling eqpt.

Argon
Auto tape cartridges
Automatic vending
Automation
Autos (electric)
Beryllium
Boats and supplies

Swimming pools
Tantalum
Television, color
Tellurium
Titanium
Ultrasonics
Water meters
Zirconium and hafnium

Garages, automatic
Gardening equipment
Glass fibers and plastics
Magnesium
Manganese
Molybdenum

Mercury mining
Truck trailers
Trucks

MATURE INDUSTRIES

AVERAGE GROWTH

Comparatively Stable

Banks
Baking
Chewing gum
Confectionery
Drugs, proprietary
Drugstores
Finance companies
Glass containers
Morticians' supplies
Radio broadcasting (AM)
Tobacco, cigars and cigarettes
Toilet preparations
Variety chains

Moderately Cyclical

Advertising
Apparel chains
Apparel manufacturers
Autos (gasoline)
Coal (bituminous)
Corn refiners
Distillers and liquor
Flour millers
Gold mining
Hotels
Mail order
Meat packing
Movie theaters
Munitions

Paints and varnishes
Real estate
Restaurants
Shoes
Shopping centers
Small loan companies
Soaps and cleansers
Textiles
Tires
Transportation, urban

Very Cyclical

Agricultural equipment
Auto parts
Busses

Carpets and rugs
Furniture
Jewelry
Lead
Rail equipment
Rayon and acetate
Shelters, fallout
Shipbuilding
Shipping
Silverware
Steel and iron
Sugar
Vegetables
Watches

SOURCE: Leo Barnes, *Your Investments*, 16th ed. (Englewood Cliffs, N.J.: Prentice-Hall, Inc., 1968), p. 47.

by the life-cycle theory fits quite well to the past experience of many industries. Second, several investment implications of the theory are well worth attention by investors.

(a) The risk in the pioneering stage is too high. Speculators may find it exciting and profitable, but investors should stay away.
(b) The investors should look for opportunities in an industry when the industry enters into the second stage of fast growth.
(c) Industry selection should receive prior consideration in investment decisions.

Third, the theory offers a general description of industry life cycle. Individual industries have varied substantially from the norm in the stage of developments as portrayed by the theory. What can be most safely said of the development of industries is the common trend toward *retardation in growth rates* as shown in Table 5-1. Most industries mature and decline relatively, but do not die as individuals. Not a few industries after reaching the mature stage often go through a long period of alternate prosperity and recession. In retrospect it is often easy to define the stages a mature industry has gone through, but it is not an easy matter to identify the current stage of many industries. Finally, while the life-cycle theory offers valuable investment implications as mentioned above, it can cause financial losses to the unwary believer of this industry approach to investment. Even during the stage of fast growth, the actual performance will vary substantially among the surviving corporations. Moreover, not infrequently prices of the shares of these corporations can be bid up much too high because of impressive record and bright prospect of demand. Purchases at such high levels of prices can easily turn into substantial losses for a long period of time, and there is a good possibility that the investor may be disillusioned and sell out during the interval.[3]

STRUCTURE AND OPERATIONAL CHARACTERISTICS OF THE INDUSTRY

Each industry has its own unique characteristics. A careful review of these unique features should always form an important part in an industry study. The analysis of an industry usually covers several important areas.

(a) The structure and the state of competition in the industry.
(b) The nature and prospect of demand for the products and services of the industry.
(c) Cost conditions and profitability.
(d) Technology and research.
(e) Immediate and long-run outlook of sales and profits.

[3] Stanley S.C. Huang, "Study of the Performance of Rapid Growth Stocks," *Financial Analysts Journal*, January-February 1965.

(a) *Structure of Industry and State of Competition.* A study of the structure of an industry should cover these aspects:

1. The number of firms in the industry.
2. The size of each major firm in terms of sales and assets.
3. The concentration ratios for the largest few firms in the industry—measuring the extent of output accounted for by several large firms.
4. How stable are the concentration ratios over a longer period of time?
5. Subdivision of the industry—for example, the steel industry can be classified into major integrated firms, smaller integrated firms, stainless steel, other specialty steel firms, ore producers, merchant pig iron, and refractories.
6. Trend toward merger and diversification outside of the industry.

In respect to state of competition, the analysis should include these questions:

1. What are the price policies of the firms? Do they compete in price? Do they follow "the leader" in announcing price changes?
2. Are products of the industry relatively homogeneous in nature or highly differentiated?
3. Do firms compete actively in offering supplementary services and in advertising?
4. With which domestic industries is the industry in competition? How are the products of the industry compared with substitutes in terms of quality, price, appearance, and other features?
5. What is the state of competition with foreign producers in domestic and foreign markets? Is the industry losing or gaining in the competition with foreign producers?

(b) *Nature and Prospect of Demand for the Industry.* The pertinent questions to be raised in the inquiry of the nature and prospect of demand for the industry are

1. Which classification does this industry fall into: growth, cyclical, defensive, or relative decline industry?
2. What are the major markets by customers? What is the distribution of markets by geographical areas including foreign demand?
3. What are the determinants of demand?
4. What factors will likely affect the demand from each major group of customers?
5. What is the immediate and long-run outlook of demand, taking into consideration both the secular and cyclical prospects of general business?

(c) *Cost Considerations and Profitability.* The "intrinsic value" or normal worth of a security is determined by the profitability, current and prospective, which it represents. Fast-growing demand for an industry does not automatically guarantee higher profits for the industry as a whole or individual companies in the industry. Profitability depends no less on cost control and state of competition than on growth in demand. The cost factors and concepts which the analyst should examine in an industry study are

1. Distribution of costs for the industry among wages, raw materials, and overhead.
2. The rate of increase of labor cost per hour and labor productivity.
3. Rate of increase of prices for finished products.
4. Extent and control of excess capacity.
5. Requirement for new capital expenditures to maintain productive efficiency and keep up competition with producers outside of the industry.
6. Turnover of invested capital.

To measure profitability, the ratios listed below should be computed, compared over time, and analyzed for indications of cause of changes.

1. Gross profit margin, which relates gross income (sales less cost of goods sold) to sales to indicate profitability at manufacturing level.
2. Net profit margin, which relates income before income taxes to sales.
3. Rate of return on equity, which relates net income after income taxes to stockholders' equity.
4. Rate of return on total capital which relates net income after income taxes plus interest charges to total capital invested including loans from creditors.

(d) *Technology and Research.* Changes in technology often have important impacts on the prospects of an industry. Advances in technology can either broaden and accelerate the growth of an already fast-growing industry or rejuvenate an industry that is on the decline. As far as information is available, the analyst should try to anwer a few pertinent questions as follows:

1. Is the technology of the industry relatively stable and mature? Or is it still in a stage of rapid change?
2. Are there any important technological changes on the horizon? And what will be their effects?
3. What percent of sales growth of the industry can be attributed to introduction of new products?
4. What has been the relationship between capital expenditures and sales?
5. What percent of industry sales has been spent on research and development?

(e) *Immediate and Longer-Run Outlook of Sales and Profits for the Industry.* Finally, the analyst should assess the findings on the various factors mentioned above and translate them into two basic statistics for two time periods.

They are

1. Estimate of rate of growth of sales for the industry
   (a) in the year ahead
   (b) in the next three to five years
2. Estimate of rate of growth of profits after tax
   (a) in the year ahead
   (b) in the next three to five years

For short-term investors, the year-ahead figures for sales and profits growth are likely given more weight, whereas the longer-run oriented investors would profitably treat the three to five-year estimates as no less important than the year-ahead estimates.

If the analyst has compiled estimates of growth for the whole economy for the two time periods, a comparison should be made between the industry and the economy to see how much better or worse will be the relative position of the industry in the year ahead and in three to five years hence.

YARDSTICK OF MANAGEMENT PERFORMANCE OF INDIVIDUAL FIRMS AND INDUSTRIES

Comparative study of corporations and industries lies in the center of investment analysis and management. *Forbes* magazine rates every year the record of performance of major firms in major industries of the United States. In their *Twenty-Second Annual Report on American Industry* issued January 1, 1970, *Forbes* rated nearly 600 major firms in 25 industry groups by two yardsticks as follows:

1. Degree of Profitability
   (a) Five-year return on equity
   (b) Latest 12-month return on equity
   (c) Five-year return on total capital
2. Rate of Growth
   (a) Five-year annual sales growth
   (b) Five-year earnings per share growth (The five-year compound growth rate is measured by figures in latest 12 months vs. a three-year average in the base period 1963-65.)

In addition, each firm is ranked twice, (1) within the 600 firms and (2) within its own industry.

The first yardstick measures how profitable the corporation or industry has been in terms of net earnings per dollar of equity, and per dollar of invested capital which includes both equity and long-term debt. A comparison of return on equity in the past 12 months as against five-year average will show whether there is improvement or deterioration in profitability. The second yardstick

TABLE 5-4A
Yardsticks of Management Performance of Major Firms in the Household and Personal Products Industry

How They Rank:	A—Among All Companies									B—In Own Industry					
	Profitability						5-Year Return on Total Capital			Growth					
	5-Year Return on Equity			Latest 12 Month Return on Equity						5-Year Annual Sales Growth			5-Year Annual Earnings Per Share Growth		
Company	Rank A	B	Percent	Rank A	B	Percent	Rank A	B	Percent	Rank A	B	Percent	Rank A	B	Percent
Avon Products	2	(1)	42.5	1	(1)	39.7	1	(1)	39.6	128	(5)	15.6	81	(5)	15.5
Gillette	6	(2)	35.2	8	(2)	28.2	3	(3)	31.2	182	(10)	13.2	265	(17)	7.8
Smith Kline & French	11	(3)	31.5	18	(5)	26.1	2	(2)	31.5	411	(23)	6.9	450	(26)	1.3
Merck	16	(4)	28.6	16	(4)	26.6	6	(4)	28.1	124	(4)	15.9	116	(6)	13.5
Amer. Home Products	19	(5)	27.4	12	(3)	27.4	7	(5)	27.4	238	(13)	11.4	186	(9)	10.3
Sterling Drug	27	(6)	25.3	30	(8)	23.3	16	(7)	22.1	206	(12)	12.2	223	(13)	9.3
Bristol-Myers	31	(7)	24.6	27	(6)	24.2	18	(8)	21.6	149	(7)	14.8	121	(7)	13.2
Warner-Lambert	41	(8)	22.8	48	(9)	20.7	30	(9)	20.2	96	(2)	18.1	182	(8)	10.5
Lilly, Eli	44	(9)	22.7	28	(7)	24.0	15	(6)	22.1	170	(8)	13.9	59	(2)	18.5
Revlon	91	(10)	18.5	85	(12)	17.4	65	(13)	16.1	386	(21)	7.5	210	(12)	9.8
Pfizer, Charles	92	(11)	18.4	92	(13)	17.0	59	(11)	16.5	263	(17)	10.8	277	(18)	7.5
Reynolds Tobacco	98	(12)	18.0	105	(15)	16.4	56	(10)	16.8	487	(28)	5.3	411	(22)	3.4
Philip Morris	106	(13)	17.5	59	(10)	19.3	201	(23)	11.5	241	(14)	11.3	62	(3)	18.2
Procter & Gamble	112	(14)	17.3	74	(11)	18.1	84	(16)	15.0	362	(20)	8.0	203	(11)	10.0
Upjohn	128	(15)	16.4	150	(19)	14.7	60	(12)	16.4	251	(16)	11.1	416	(23)	3.1
Purex	138	(16)	16.1	111	(16)	16.2	107	(19)	14.1	118	(3)	16.1	228	(14)	9.1
Abbott Laboratories	145	(17)	15.9	127	(18)	15.6	92	(18)	14.6	194	(11)	12.5	258	(16)	8.1
American Hosp. Supply	151	(18)	15.8	255	(23)	12.4	91	(17)	14.6	74	(1)	19.7	52	(1)	19.0
Johnson & Johnson	154	(19)	15.6	96	(14)	16.9	78	(14)	15.3	277	(18)	10.3	70	(4)	17.6
Richardson-Merrell	168	(20)	15.3	112	(17)	16.2	80	(15)	15.2	176	(9)	13.5	190	(10)	10.2
American Cyanamid	215	(21)	14.0	224	(21)	13.3	165	(21)	12.2	429	(25)	6.6	435	(25)	2.3
American Brands	238	(22)	13.5	210	(20)	13.5	189	(22)	11.7	129	(6)	15.5	323	(19)	6.1
Parke, Davis	262	(23)	13.0	374	(25)	9.9	152	(20)	12.5	465	(27)	5.6	520	(29)	-5.2
Colgate-Palmolive	298	(24)	12.4	249	(22)	12.6	251	(24)	10.4	392	(22)	7.3	236	(15)	8.8
Scott Paper	315	(25)	12.0	290	(24)	11.6	265	(25)	10.1	243	(15)	11.3	433	(24)	2.4
Kimberly-Clark	424	(26)	9.7	378	(26)	9.7	364	(26)	8.1	425	(24)	6.7	372	(21)	4.5
General Cigar	476	(27)	8.3	434	(27)	8.5	507	(29)	5.1	333	(19)	8.6	366	(20)	4.6
Havatampa Cigar	486	(28)	7.9	467	(29)	7.7	388	(27)	7.7	495	(29)	5.0	463	(27)	0.1
Liggett & Myers	492	(29)	7.8	449	(28)	8.2	390	(28)	7.7	454	(26)	6.0	466	(28)	-0.2
Industry median			16.4			16.4			15.2			11.3			8.8

SOURCE: *Forbes Twenty-Second Annual Report on American Industry*, Jan. 1, 1970, p. 116.

TABLE 5-4B
Yardsticks of Management Performance of 25 Major Industry Groups

Yardsticks of Management Performance: Industry Medians

Industry	Profitability						Growth			
	5-Year Return on Equity		Latest 12-Month Return on Equity		5-Year Return on Total Capital		5-Year Annual Sales Growth		5-Year Annual Earnings Per Share Growth	
	Rank	Percent	Rank	Percent	Rank	Percent	Rank	Percent	Rank	Percent
Distribution-specialty	(1)	16.5	(3)	14.4	(5)	11.9	(4)	14.4	(4)	11.6
Cons. goods-household products.	(2)	16.4	(1)	16.4	(1)	15.2	(11)	11.3	(12)	8.8
Transportation-airlines	(2)	16.4	(24)	6.1	(22)	8.1	(3)	15.7	(25)	-12.5
Electrical products	(4)	16.0	(4)	14.2	(3)	13.1	(5)	13.9	(6)	10.9
Information processing	(4)	16.0	(2)	14.9	(2)	13.2	(7)	12.6	(2)	12.0
Multi-cos-conglomerates	(4)	16.0	(9)	12.6	(8)	11.0	(1)	20.6	(2)	12.0
Leisure and education	(7)	15.5	(5)	13.9	(6)	11.7	(10)	11.7	(8)	10.0
Aerospace and defense	(8)	14.1	(15)	11.3	(7)	11.4	(6)	13.1	(7)	10.3
Distribution-supermarkets	(9)	13.9	(6)	13.0	(17)	10.0	(19)	8.1	(17)	5.3
Distribution-dept/var. stores . . .	(10)	13.6	(6)	13.0	(9)	10.7	(13)	10.1	(8)	10.0
Metals-nonferrous	(11)	13.5	(6)	13.0	(4)	12.5	(14)	10.0	(5)	11.5
Chemicals	(12)	12.9	(21)	10.8	(13)	10.2	(14)	10.0	(21)	1.9
Industrial equipment	(12)	12.9	(19)	10.9	(11)	10.5	(9)	11.8	(14)	7.8
Energy	(14)	12.8	(14)	11.4	(9)	10.7	(17)	9.2	(10)	9.4
Consumer goods-apparel	(15)	12.7	(11)	12.4	(14)	10.1	(20)	7.9	(15)	7.5
Automotive products	(16)	12.4	(18)	11.0	(14)	10.1	(18)	8.9	(19)	3.6
Multi-cos-agglomerates	(17)	12.3	(16)	11.2	(19)	9.5	(2)	19.1	(1)	12.4
Consumer goods-food	(18)	12.0	(10)	12.5	(12)	10.3	(23)	7.1	(16)	6.1
Utilities	(19)	11.9	(17)	11.1	(24)	6.0	(22)	7.3	(17)	5.3
Forest products and packaging. .	(20)	11.5	(12)	11.6	(21)	8.3	(12)	11.2	(11)	9.0
Finance	(21)	11.3	(12)	11.6	(14)	10.1	(7)	12.6	(13)	8.0
Building materials	(22)	11.2	(22)	9.6	(20)	8.6	(16)	9.3	(22)	1.7
Multi-cos-multi-industry	(22)	11.2	(19)	10.9	(18)	9.6	(21)	7.6	(20)	2.9
Metals-steel	(24)	8.7	(23)	7.3	(23)	7.0	(25)	3.7	(24)	-1.3
Transportation-surface	(25)	5.5	(25)	5.1	(25)	4.3	(24)	3.9	(23)	-0.7
Industry median		12.9		11.6		10.2		10.1		8.0

SOURCE: Forbes Twenty-Second Annual Report on American Industry, Jan. 1, 1970, p. 82

measures how fast the corporation or industry group is growing in terms of total sales and earnings per share.

Table 5-4A shows the ratings of performance by *Forbes* for 25 major industry groups, and Table 5-4B shows the ratings of major firms in the household and personal products industry as of end of 1969. These ratings are not only informative in terms of the past but could well indicate some clues to the immediate future of various industries. It may be well worth while to rate continuously the various industries on a quarterly basis, using the latest 12-month figures for comparison of trend. The experience in recent years has indicated that individual as well as institutional investors have become more and more shorter-term oriented. It should be rewarding to take notice and make allowance for the changes taking place in investors' behavior in both methods of analysis and final decision making.

COMPOSITE INDUSTRY DATA

For purpose of industry study, the analyst has to secure pertinent data, both historical and current, from a variety of sources: trade associations, trade journals, government publications, studies by others, advisory investment services, and the like. One source that is particularly useful is the *Industry Survey* published by the Standard & Poor's Corporation. The *Industry Survey* composite industry data is illustrated by Table 5-5, on the drug industry. These industry data are on a per-share basis and in terms of the S&P's group stock index. They are of particular interest to analysts because they cover not only the record of performance of the industry but also market valuation and some other items of interest. The analysis of these data can be usefully organized under three headings as follows:

Performance of the Industry

1. Rate of growth of sales.
2. Level and stability of profit margin.
3. Level and stability of turnover of capital which can be obtained by dividing book value into sales.
4. Stability of return on book value which is a product of capital turnover and net earnings as a percentage of sales.

Market Valuation

1. Rate of change of the price index.
2. Level and stability of price/earnings ratio.
3. Level and stability of dividend yield.

TABLE 5-5
Composite Industry Data
(Per-share data based on Standard & Poor's group stock price indexes)

The companies used for this series of composite data are: Abbott Laboratories; American Home Products; Bristol-Myers; Merck; Parke, Davis; Chas. Pfizer; Richardson-Merrell; Schering; Searle (S. D.); Squibb Beech-Nut; Sterling Drug; and Warner-Lambert. Squibb-Beech-Nut was deleted from group on April 29, 1970.

Drugs	1960	1961	1962	1963	1964	1965	1966	1967†	1968	1969P
Sales	29.21	30.44	32.87	34.87	35.33	40.41	47.47	44.27	51.04	56.30
Operating income	5.05	5.24	5.77	6.29	6.68	7.48	8.87	9.14	10.51	....
Profit margins percent	17.29	17.21	17.55	18.04	18.91	18.51	18.69	20.65	20.59	....
Depreciation	0.50	0.55	0.63	0.66	0.66	0.73	0.83	0.98	1.12	....
Taxes	2.28	2.38	2.59	2.80	2.96	3.33	3.85	3.80	4.65	....
Earnings	2.48	2.51	2.68	2.96	3.23	3.77	4.31	4.39	4.73	5.23
Dividends	1.47	1.54	1.58	1.68	1.79	2.08	2.31	2.49	2.69	2.93
Earnings as a percent of sales	8.49	8.25	8.15	8.49	9.14	9.33	9.08	9.92	9.27	9.29
Dividends as a percent of earnings	59.27	61.35	58.96	56.76	55.42	55.17	53.60	56.72	56.87	56.02
Price (1941–43 = 10) –High	69.57	80.66	79.44	75.16	82.95	106.88	108.79	136.87	139.63	165.05
–Low	53.71	62.21	50.06	61.71	72.62	82.97	88.89	102.71	111.75	127.88
Price/earnings ratios –High	28.05	32.14	29.64	25.39	25.68	28.30	25.24	31.18	29.52	31.56
–Low	21.66	24.78	18.68	20.85	22.48	22.01	20.62	22.40	23.63	24.45
Dividend yield ( ) –High	2.74	2.48	3.16	2.72	2.46	2.51	2.60	2.42	2.41	2.29
–Low	2.11	1.91	1.99	2.24	2.16	1.95	2.12	1.82	1.93	1.78
Book value	13.01	14.06	14.94	15.84	15.77	16.25	17.51	18.55	20.92	....
Return on book value, percent	19.06	17.85	17.94	18.69	20.48	23.20	24.61	23.67	22.61	....
Working capital*	8.18	8.49	8.97	9.55	9.55	10.35	11.88	14.73	14.67	....
Capital expenditures	1.13	1.10	1.09	1.06	1.12	1.45	1.95	2.37	2.32	....

SOURCE: *Basic Analysis, Drugs & Cosmetics, Industry Surveys,* Standard & Poor's Corporation, June 18, 1970.

NOTE: Per-share data are expressed in terms of the S & P Stock Price Index, i.e., stock prices, 1941–43 = 10. Each of the items shown is first computed on a true per-share basis for each company. Totals for each company are then reconstructed using the same number of shares outstanding as was used to compute our stock price index as of December 31st. This is done because the shares used on December 31st, although the latest known at the time, may differ from those reported in the annual reports which are not available for six or eight weeks after the end of the year. The sum of these reconstructed totals is then related to the base period value used to compute the stock price index. As a double check, we relate the various items to the dividends as these are the most stable series. So, for example, if total sales amount to fifteen times the total dividend payments, then, with per-share dividends at 3.50 the indicated per-share sales will be (15 × 3.50) 52.50 in terms of the S & P Stock Price Index. For comparability between the various groups, all data are on a calendar year basis, corporate data being posted in the year in which most months fall. Fiscal years ending June 30th are posted in the calendar year in which the fiscal year ends.

*Current assets less current liabilities, without allowance for long-term debt.
†McKesson & Robbins was dropped in 1967.
PPreliminary.

Other Items of Interest

1. Stability of depreciation as a percent of book value.
2. Capital expenditures as a percent of book value and sales over time.
3. Working capital as a percent of sales over time.

INDUSTRY ANALYSIS AND INVESTMENT DECISIONS

In concluding this chapter, we need to add a few words on how important industry analysis is in investment decisions. As mentioned early in this chapter, one school of thought places industry analysis and selection far ahead of company selection. In direct opposition to this approach, some analysts make their decisions by relying primarily and directly on company studies. The relative importance between industry and company studies in investment decisions, however, is not totally a matter of individual preference. The differences in circumstances of companies under study and consideration can well dictate the choice of relative emphasis between industry and company analysis. The views of the author are specified below:

1. In looking for attractive issues of securities for investment commitment, the analyst can begin with the examination of industries or directly proceed to the study of individual companies.
2. Even in the latter case, an examination of the industry outlook is still necessary, because the company in question will be affected by industry developments.
3. Where a *basic* change (new management, merger, diversification) has taken place in the corporation, so as to constitute a "special situation," primary emphasis should be logically placed on the study of the company itself.
4. Normally, equal emphasis should be given to industry and company analysis. However, in the case of conglomerates (large corporations such as Avco, Gulf & Western Industries, Ling-Temco-Vought, Litton Industries, and many others whose business are composed of many divisions covering many different industries which may or may not be closely related to one another), the logical approach is of course to concentrate on the analysis and evaluation of the company itself.
5. As a rule, the approach that begins with industry analysis and then company study is preferred to the alternative.

INDUSTRY PERFORMANCE IN THE STOCK MARKET 1965-68

The influence of industry selection can be clearly seen from referring to the varying performance of different industries in the stock market. The following four charts reproduced from *Stock Market Analysis: Facts and Principles* by

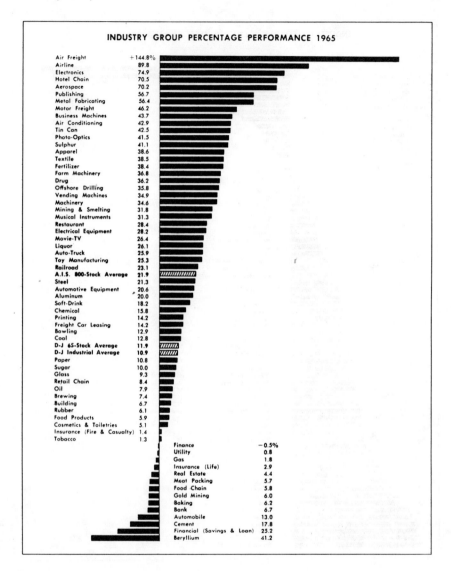

INDUSTRY GROUP PERCENTAGE PERFORMANCE 1965

Industry	%
Air Freight	+144.8%
Airline	89.8
Electronics	74.9
Hotel Chain	70.5
Aerospace	70.2
Publishing	56.7
Metal Fabricating	56.4
Motor Freight	46.2
Business Machines	43.7
Air Conditioning	42.9
Tin Can	42.5
Photo-Optics	41.5
Sulphur	41.1
Apparel	38.6
Textile	38.5
Fertilizer	38.4
Farm Machinery	36.8
Drug	36.2
Offshore Drilling	35.8
Vending Machines	34.9
Machinery	34.6
Mining & Smelting	31.8
Musical Instruments	31.3
Restaurant	28.4
Electrical Equipment	28.2
Movie-TV	26.4
Liquor	26.1
Auto-Truck	25.9
Toy Manufacturing	25.3
Railroad	23.1
A.I.S. 800-Stock Average	21.9
Steel	21.3
Automotive Equipment	20.6
Aluminum	20.0
Soft-Drink	18.2
Chemical	15.8
Printing	14.2
Freight Car Leasing	14.2
Bowling	12.9
Coal	12.8
D-J 65-Stock Average	11.9
D-J Industrial Average	10.9
Paper	10.8
Sugar	10.0
Glass	9.3
Retail Chain	8.4
Oil	7.9
Brewing	7.4
Building	6.7
Rubber	6.1
Food Products	5.9
Cosmetics & Toiletries	5.1
Insurance (Fire & Casualty)	1.4
Tobacco	1.3

Industry	%
Finance	−0.5%
Utility	0.8
Gas	1.8
Insurance (Life)	2.9
Real Estate	4.4
Meat Packing	5.7
Food Chain	5.8
Gold Mining	6.0
Baking	6.2
Bank	6.7
Automobile	13.0
Cement	17.8
Financial (Savings & Loan)	25.2
Beryllium	41.2

George A. Chestnutt, Jr., show the actual performance of different industry groups during 1965-68. The year 1965, for example, was a good year for the stock market according to the 800-stock index. However, the investors in cement stocks lost, on the average, 17.8 percent in price. The year 1966, on the other hand, was a bad year with the 800-stock average losing 9.3 percent. But if the investors had bought in beryllium, air freight, metal fabricating, or offshore drilling they would have experienced sizable capital appreciation by year end.

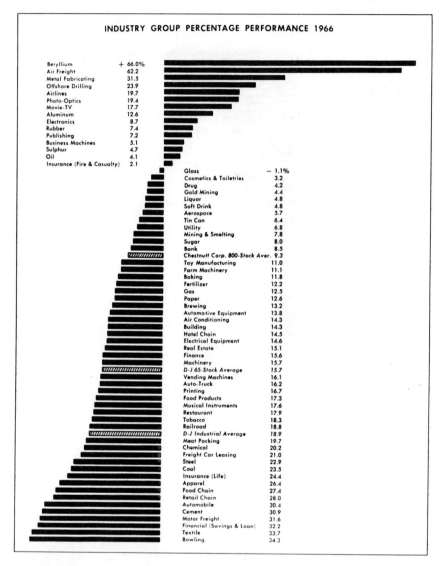

INDUSTRY GROUP PERCENTAGE PERFORMANCE 1966

Beryllium   + 66.0%
Air Freight   62.2
Metal Fabricating   31.5
Offshore Drilling   23.9
Airlines   19.7
Photo-Optics   19.4
Movie-TV   17.7
Aluminum   12.6
Electronics   8.7
Rubber   7.4
Publishing   7.2
Business Machines   5.1
Sulphur   4.7
Oil   4.1
Insurance (Fire & Casualty)   2.1

Glass	− 1.1%
Cosmetics & Toiletries	3.2
Drug	4.2
Gold Mining	4.4
Liquor	4.8
Soft Drink	4.8
Aerospace	5.7
Tin Can	6.4
Utility	6.8
Mining & Smelting	7.8
Sugar	8.0
Bank	8.5
Chestnutt Corp. 800-Stock Aver.	*9.3*
Toy Manufacturing	11.0
Farm Machinery	11.1
Baking	11.8
Fertilizer	12.2
Gas	12.5
Paper	12.6
Brewing	13.2
Automotive Equipment	13.8
Air Conditioning	14.3
Building	14.3
Hotel Chain	14.5
Electrical Equipment	14.6
Real Estate	15.1
Finance	15.6
Machinery	15.7
D-J 65-Stock Average	*15.7*
Vending Machines	16.1
Auto-Truck	16.2
Printing	16.7
Food Products	17.3
Musical Instruments	17.6
Restaurant	17.9
Tobacco	18.3
Railroad	18.8
D-J Industrial Average	*18.9*
Meat Packing	19.7
Chemical	20.2
Freight Car Leasing	21.0
Steel	22.9
Coal	23.5
Insurance (Life)	24.4
Apparel	26.4
Food Chain	27.4
Retail Chain	28.0
Automobile	30.4
Cement	30.9
Motor Freight	31.6
Financial (Savings & Loan)	32.2
Textile	33.7
Bowling	34.3

1965

Although the Dow-Jones Industrial Average outperformed the market in 1963 and 1964, making it a hard average to beat, almost everybody succeeded in beating the Dow in 1965. The average stock as represented by the A.I.S. 800 Stk. Avg. went up 21.9%, or twice the Dow's 10.9% gain.

The Airline Group, top performer in 1962 and 1963, and 4th best in 1964, took 2nd place honors in 1965 with a further gain of 89.8%. The closely related Air Freight Group stole top honors with its 144.8% gain.

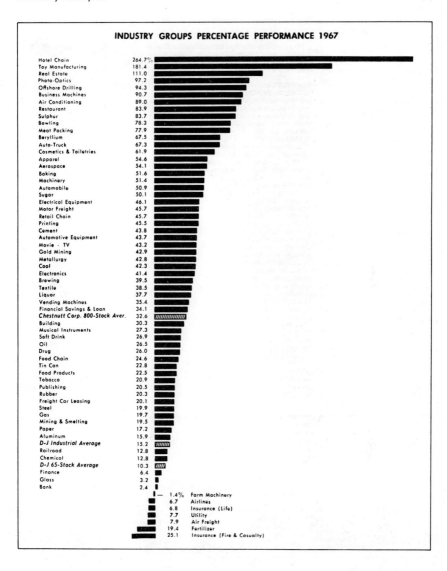

INDUSTRY GROUPS PERCENTAGE PERFORMANCE 1967

Industry	%
Hotel Chain	264.7%
Toy Manufacturing	181.4
Real Estate	111.0
Photo-Optics	97.2
Offshore Drilling	94.3
Business Machines	90.7
Air Conditioning	89.0
Restaurant	83.9
Sulphur	83.7
Bowling	78.3
Meat Packing	77.9
Beryllium	67.5
Auto-Truck	67.3
Cosmetics & Toiletries	61.9
Apparel	54.6
Aerospace	54.1
Baking	51.6
Machinery	51.4
Automobile	50.9
Sugar	50.1
Electrical Equipment	46.1
Motor Freight	45.7
Retail Chain	45.7
Printing	45.5
Cement	43.8
Automotive Equipment	43.7
Movie - TV	43.2
Gold Mining	42.9
Metallurgy	42.8
Coal	42.3
Electronics	41.4
Brewing	39.5
Textile	38.5
Liquor	37.7
Vending Machines	35.4
Financial Savings & Loan	34.1
Chestnutt Corp. 800-Stock Aver.	32.6
Building	30.3
Musical Instruments	27.3
Soft Drink	26.9
Oil	26.5
Drug	26.0
Food Chain	24.6
Tin Can	22.8
Food Products	22.5
Tobacco	20.9
Publishing	20.5
Rubber	20.3
Freight Car Leasing	20.1
Steel	19.9
Gas	19.7
Mining & Smelting	19.5
Paper	17.2
Aluminum	15.9
D-J Industrial Average	15.2
Railroad	12.8
Chemical	12.8
D-J 65-Stock Average	10.3
Finance	6.4
Glass	3.2
Bank	2.4

	%	Industry
—	1.4%	Farm Machinery
	6.7	Airlines
	6.8	Insurance (Life)
	7.7	Utility
	7.9	Air Freight
	19.4	Fertilizer
	25.1	Insurance (Fire & Casualty)

While it pays to follow new leaders when they appear and become well established, it also pays to stay with former market leaders until they have been clearly dislodged by new leaders. That is the lesson of market history.

1966

Chestnutt Corporation did not concur with the popular Dow theory characterization of the 1966 market decline as a long-term bear market. Instead, we interpreted the decline as intermediate-term and predicted new bull market highs within a year or two.

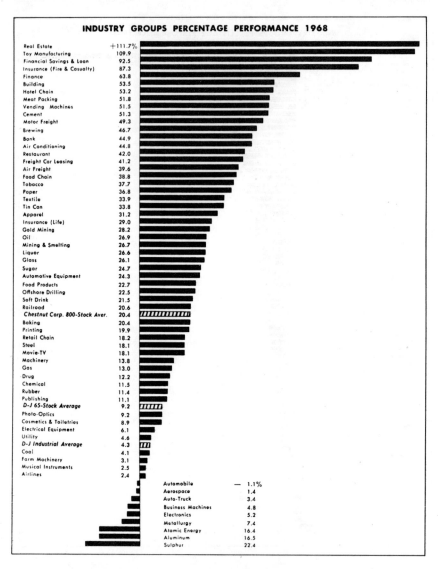

INDUSTRY GROUPS PERCENTAGE PERFORMANCE 1968

Industry	%
Real Estate	+111.7%
Toy Manufacturing	109.9
Financial Savings & Loan	92.5
Insurance (Fire & Casualty)	87.3
Finance	63.8
Building	53.5
Hotel Chain	53.2
Meat Packing	51.8
Vending Machines	51.5
Cement	51.3
Motor Freight	49.3
Brewing	46.7
Bank	44.9
Air Conditioning	44.8
Restaurant	42.0
Freight Car Leasing	41.2
Air Freight	39.6
Food Chain	38.8
Tobacco	37.7
Paper	36.8
Textile	33.9
Tin Can	33.8
Apparel	31.2
Insurance (Life)	29.0
Gold Mining	28.2
Oil	26.9
Mining & Smelting	26.7
Liquor	26.6
Glass	26.1
Sugar	24.7
Automotive Equipment	24.3
Food Products	22.7
Offshore Drilling	22.5
Soft Drink	21.5
Railroad	20.6
Chestnut Corp. 800-Stock Aver.	20.4
Baking	20.4
Printing	19.9
Retail Chain	18.2
Steel	18.1
Movie-TV	18.1
Machinery	13.8
Gas	13.0
Drug	12.2
Chemical	11.5
Rubber	11.4
Publishing	11.1
D-J 65-Stock Average	9.2
Photo-Optics	9.2
Cosmetics & Toiletries	8.9
Electrical Equipment	6.1
Utility	4.6
D-J Industrial Average	4.3
Coal	4.1
Farm Machinery	3.1
Musical Instruments	2.5
Airlines	2.4
Automobile	— 1.1%
Aerospace	1.4
Auto-Truck	3.4
Business Machines	4.8
Electronics	5.2
Metallurgy	7.4
Atomic Energy	16.4
Aluminum	16.5
Sulphur	22.4

The market continued to outperform the D-J Industrials (−9.3% vs.−18.9%), fooling many who consider the D-JI as the market.

The Airlines, in 5th place with a gain of 19.7%, made it five consecutive years of outstanding performance.

1967

This was the third year in succession that the Dow-Jones Industrial and 65-Stock Averages were outperformed by the general market. You may note also that although 36 industry groups outperformed the

800-Stock Geometric Average while only 29 groups were weaker than average, many of the strongest groups were relatively small ones, especially the top four.

During 1967 there was less follow-through in group strength than usual. Air Freight and Airlines, for example, began the year in strong positions but ended in weak positions. The strongest groups of 1967 were generally rated above average at the beginning of the year but did not attain top ranking positions until about mid-year.

1968

The Hotel Chain Group, which was 1967's top performer with a gain of 265%, came in seventh in 1968, scoring an additional 53% gain. The Toy Manufacturing Group, which was second in 1967 with a gain of 181%, came in second again in 1968 with a further gain of 110%. 1967's third best performer, Real Estate with a gain of 111%, came in first in 1968 with a further gain of 112%.

Notably absent from the chart is the industry group that went up the most, Mobile Homes. We did not begin calculating this industry group average until February 1968 and, accordingly, do not have an exact measurement for the year. Its gain was about 250%. It is obvious from an inspection of the performance of the Mobile Home stocks for the year 1967 that this Group would have been the best performer of all not only in 1968 but also in 1967.

SUGGESTED READINGS

Butler, Hartman L., "Aerospace Fundamentals and Industry Analysis," *Financial Analysts Journal*, January-February, March-April 1966.

Butler, William F., and R. A. Kavesh (eds.), *How Business Economics Forecast*, Englewood Cliffs, N.J.: Prentice-Hall, Inc., 1966, Part III.

Caves, Richard, *American Industry: Structure, Conduct, Performance*, Englewood Cliffs, N.J.: Prentice-Hall, Inc., 1964.

Cohen, J. B., and E. D. Zinbarg, *Investment Analysis and Portfolio Management*, Homewood, Ill.: Richard D. Irwin, 1967, chaps. 6-10.

Forbes Twentieth Annual Report on American Industry, Jan. 1, 1968.

Gaston, J. Frank, *Growth Patterns in Industry*, Washington, D.C.: National Industrial Conference Board, 1961.

McClow, Richard I., "Is There A Renaissance In Steel?", *Financial Analysts Journal*, July-August 1969.

Plum, Lester V. (ed.), *Investing In American Industries*, New York: Harper & Row, Publishers, 1960.

Sharpe, Eddie J., "A Review of the Food Industry," *Financial Analysts Journal*, January-February 1966.

Shubin, John A., *Managerial and Industrial Economics*, New York: The Ronald Press Company, 1961.

Standard & Poor's Corporation, *Industry Survey*.

Spigelman, Joseph H., "The Data Service Industry," *Financial Analysts Journal*, March-April, May-June, July-August 1969.

Ward, Frank F., "The Color Television Industry," *Financial Analysts Journal*, November-December 1966.

Yakowicz, Joseph V., "The Glass Container Industry," *Financial Analysts Journal*, January-February 1967.

QUESTIONS AND PROBLEMS

1. In seeking to make a long-term commitment of funds, why is it important to seek a growth industry?
2. Despite the fact that investors are ultimately concerned with earnings and dividends, why do security analysts place so much emphasis on sales of the firm and growth prospect of the industry?
3. Discuss the life-cycle theory of industry selection. What arguments are there for and against placing primary emphasis on this consideration when selecting investments?
4. Select five growth industries and defend your selection.
5. What are some of the reasons why industries show differing rates of growth?
6. Under what categories of industries—growth, cyclical, defensive, declining, do you place the following industries: steel, shipbuilding, chemical, motion pictures, automobile, air transport, drugs, and food? Why?
7. Why must an analyst always investigate the industry when looking at a particular security?
8. Select an industry and prepare a study of cost conditions and profitability in that industry.
9. What kind of information about a given industry can be usually found in the *Industry Survey* published by Standard & Poor's Corporation?
10. Prepare an industry analysis from appropriate source material, including all information which can be used as a guide to appraise the record of the leading firms in the industry.

6. Company Analysis

Even if the industry projections are right on target, the performances of individual firms within the industry are likely to vary substantially. The correct selection of an individual company remains one of the key factors in investment success. The study of an individual company can be logically arranged in four parts:

A. Analysis of record of performance in the most relevant past.
B. Comparison of record of performance with industry average and competitors.
C. Quality and background of management team and current programs.
D. Outlook of sales and profits, (1) in the year ahead, and (2) in three to five years hence.

ANALYSIS OF RECORD OF PERFORMANCE IN THE MOST RELEVANT PAST

For the purpose of historical analysis, the most relevant period for most corporations is the past five to seven years. The more distant period in the past could be affected by transient factors which are no longer important for gauging prospective performance of a company. The record of a company can be conveniently analyzed under the following six headings:

1. Growth of sales
2. Stability of profit margin
3. Turnover of capital
4. Rate of return
5. Growth of earnings
6. Degree of leverage and adequacy of working capital

As an example, the record of W. R. Grace and Company as shown in Tables 6-1 and 6-2 is analyzed below.

TABLE 6-1
Ten-Year Financial Summary*
(All dollar amounts in thousands except amount per share)

	1969	1968	1967	1966	1965	1964	1963	1962	1961	1960
Earnings Statistics										
Sales and operating revenues	$1,791,698	$1,791,759	$1,621,360	$1,349,319	$1,097,377	$876,201	$699,587	$591,532	$534,699	$552,871
Income before depreciation and taxes	124,569	167,004	150,206	137,324	116,490	104,348	84,533	72,901	61,108	54,281
Depreciation and depletion	63,172	67,538	62,910	52,033	43,901	37,542	30,404	31,500	29,218	28,201
U. S. and foreign taxes on income	26,266	38,893	35,196	25,009	24,007	24,066	20,640	18,784	13,060	9,860
Income before extraordinary items	35,131	60,573	52,100	60,282	48,582	42,740	33,489	22,617	18,830	16,220
Extraordinary items	15,900	(24,621)	3,996	10,919	10,357	3,160	–	–	–	–
Net income	51,031	35,952	56,096	71,201	58,939	45,900	33,489	22,617	18,830	16,220
Cash dividends on common stock†	30,158	27,790	27,222	21,909	19,646	16,647	13,794	9,261	7,779	7,580
Balance Sheet Statistics										
Working capital	$ 376,480	$ 327,797	$ 342,906	$ 295,125	$ 250,889	$188,841	$157,368	$146,908	$136,093	$133,052
Properties and equipment—gross	1,053,250	1,246,986	1,169,835	1,073,935	892,537	710,403	589,392	598,933	512,923	475,107
Properties and equipment—net	617,545	738,111	707,370	658,300	553,905	428,066	347,789	340,928	297,104	275,332
Capital expenditures	120,646	124,453	121,669	150,577	154,784	100,503	74,073	61,552	55,923	51,520
Long-term debt	405,928	470,700	511,724	448,653	388,911	261,978	226,228	233,944	203,485	194,501
Minority interest	22,331	62,387	53,699	49,437	20,613	19,201	15,175	36,841	30,234	28,947
Stockholders' equity—preferred stock	11,355	11,768	12,331	12,331	12,336	12,346	12,608	12,608	12,608	12,608
Stockholders' equity—common stock	624,524	603,316	579,061	546,798	463,374	391,141	338,199	288,236	254,444	240,253
Per Common Share‡										
Earnings per common and common equivalent share: Income before extraordinary items	$ 1.58	$ 2.76	$ 2.59	$ 3.31	$ 2.80	$ 2.72	$ 2.29	$ 1.93	$ 1.73	$ 1.48

Extraordinary items. . .	.73	(1.14)	.20	.61	.61	.21	—	—	—	—
Net income	2.31	1.62	2.79	3.92	3.41	2.93	2.29	1.93	1.73	1.48
Earnings per common share assuming full dilution:										
Income before extraordinary items.	1.56	2.66	2.50	3.15	2.66	2.64	2.20	1.77	1.57	1.37
Net income	2.25	1.60	2.69	3.71	3.22	2.84	2.20	1.77	1.57	1.37
Cash dividends on common stock†	1.50	1.45	1.38	1.28	1.18	1.08	.96	.84	.75	.74
Book value	30.64	29.68	29.24	29.99	27.04	25.27	23.43	24.88	24.13	23.21
Other Statistics										
Cash flow§	$97,427	$129,920	$117,855	$116,385	$94,959	$83,438	$65,813	$57,545	$49,156	$44,502
Number of common stockholders	48,607	48,450	48,051	46,478	45,053	41,790	40,142	30,919	27,814	31,306
Number of employees . . .	62,400	71,700	68,300	66,600	57,600	53,900	48,200	45,900	39,500	40,600

SOURCE: W. R. Grace & Company 1969 Annual Report.

*Includes data with respect to companies acquired in poolings of interests transactions for the year in which such transactions occurred and the preceding year. On the basis of including the operations of pooled companies prior to 1968, results for the years 1965 through 1967 would have been as follows:

	Sales and Operating Revenues	Income Before Extraordinary Items	Per Share of Common Stock		Net Income	Per Share of Common Stock	
			Including Common Equivalent Share	Assuming Full Dilution		Including Common Equivalent Share	Assuming Full Dilution
1965	$1,233,365	$53,543	$2.52	$2.42	$63,900	$3.02	$2.88
1966	1,439,709	65,832	3.06	2.93	76,751	3.57	3.41
1967	1,674,776	54,293	2.47	2.40	58,289	2.65	2.57

†The aggregate amount of cash dividends on common stock includes the dividends paid by pooled companies while the per share amount represents the rate paid by the Company only.

‡Per share figures have been adjusted to reflect two-for-one stock split in 1962 and 2% stock dividends paid on common stock each year from 1961 through 1964. Income per share is computed after deducting dividends paid on preferred stocks.

§Cash flow consists of income before extraordinary items plus provisions for depreciation and depletion and deferred income taxes.

TABLE 6-2
Grace (W. R.) & Company

[5]INCOME STATISTICS (MILLIONS) AND PER-SHARE (DOLLARS) DATA

Yr Ended Dec. 31	Sales & Oper. Rev.	Percent Op. Inc. of Sales	[1]Oper. Inc.	Depr.	Net Bef. Taxes	Net Inc.	[3]Common Share ($) Data: [2]Earns.	Divs. Paid	Price Range	Price Earns. Ratio HI LO
1970......	–	–	–	–	–	–	–	0.37½	–	–
1969......	$1,791.70	–	–	–	–	[7]35.13	[7]1.58	1.50	$49¾-25⅜	31-16
1968......	$1,738.36	10.9	189.21	$65.81	$100.35	$57.76	[6]2.86	1.45	53½-32½	19-11
1967......	1,621.36	11.2	181.46	62.91	92.93	52.10	2.59	1.37½	54¼-37¼	21-14
1966......	1,349.32	11.9	161.13	52.03	88.62	60.28	3.31	1.27½	60⅝-34⅛	18-10
1965......	1,097.38	12.1	132.65	43.90	74.17	48.58	2.80	1.17½	61⅜-47¼	22-17
1964......	876.20	13.4	117.85	37.54	66.81	42.74	2.72	[4]1.07½	59⅛-49⅜	22-18
1963......	699.59	14.2	99.47	30.40	53.64	33.49	2.30	[4]0.97½	49⅜-37⅝	21-16
1962......	591.53	14.4	85.22	31.50	41.85	22.62	1.97	0.87	42⅜-25⅜	22-13
1961......	534.70	13.2	70.80	29.22	32.96	18.83	1.81	0.77	44⅛-16⅞	24- 9
1960......	552.87	11.4	63.20	28.20	27.46	16.22	1.55	0.75	21¼-15¼	14-10

[5]PERTINENT BALANCE SHEET STATISTICS (MILLIONS)

Dec. 31	Gross Prop.	Capital Expend.	Cash Items	Inven-tories	Receiv-ables	Current Assets	Current Liabs.	Net Workg. Cap.	Cur. Ratio Assets to Liabs.	Long-Term Debt	[3]Book Val. Com. Sh.
1968......	$1,220.81	$121.38	$118.45	$335.65	$294.91	$766.71	$450.31	$316.39	1.7-1	$470.26	$27.52
1967......	1,169.84	121.67	116.68	305.89	279.43	714.52	371.62	342.91	1.9-1	511.72	27.53
1966......	1,073.94	150.58	108.44	271.92	278.19	667.70	372.57	295.13	1.8-1	448.65	28.18
1965......	892.54	154.78	108.16	206.89	196.97	520.03	269.14	250.89	1.9-1	388.91	25.93
1964......	710.40	100.50	62.59	158.39	174.38	403.37	214.52	188.84	1.9-1	261.98	24.74
1963......	589.39	54.13	58.75	128.60	130.01	322.79	165.42	157.37	2.0-1	226.23	23.90
1962......	598.93	61.60	48.26	113.15	109.41	275.96	129.05	146.91	2.1-1	233.94	25.89
1961......	512.92	55.90	57.12	90.57	90.62	242.76	106.67	136.09	2.3-1	203.48	25.11
1960......	475.11	51.50	52.52	83.92	92.52	233.12	100.07	133.05	2.3-1	194.50	24.14

SOURCE: N.Y.S.E. Stock Reports, Standard & Poor's Corporation, March 1970.

[1]Incl. net govt. subsidy. [2]Based on aver. shs. outstg.; bef. spec. chge. of $1.24 a sh. in 1968; bef. spec. crs. of $0.20 a sh. in 1967, $0.61 a sh. in 1966 & $0.61 a sh. in 1965. [3]Adj. for 2-for-1 split in 1962 & stk. divds. of 2% each in 1960-61-62. [4]Plus 2% stk. [5]Incl. all majority owned & controlled dom. & for. sub. cos.; various years restated to incl. pooling-of-interests acquisitions in subsequent year. [6]Pro-forma earns. assuming exer. of options conv. of notes debs. etc. would be $2.69 a sh. in 1968. [7]Preliminary; earns. bef. spec. cr. of $0.73 a sh.

Growth of Sales

Growth of sales is the source of expanding profits for most corporations. The study of a firm can logically begin with the examination of the stability and rates of growth of sales of a firm in the past five to ten years. If information is available, the analyst should also seek a breakdown of the total sales into groups of products and the relative growth of each group. The growth rates can be computed either on an annual or on an average basis using the compound interest table. The growth rate of sales for W. R. Grace & Company in the past five to six years is computed on both bases as in Table 6-3.

TABLE 6-3
Growth of Sales, W. R. Grace & Company

Year	Sales (millions)	Annual Percent Increase	Average Percent Increase 1963-65 to 1969
1969	$1,791.7	0	1969 sales (millions) $1,791.7
1968	1,791.8	10.5	1963-65 average sales 888.1
1967	1,621.3	20	1969/1963-65 .... 2.0
1966	1,349.3	23	Average annual growth rate 15%
1965	1,097.4	26	
1964	876.2	25	
1963	699.6		

The average annual growth rate of 15 percent can be looked up or approximated in a compound interest table by locating a close figure to 2.0 under the row of 5 years. Table 6-4 shows a condensed compound interest table.

Mergers and acquisitions often introduce discontinuities into the sales trend of a firm. Computation of growth rates of sales on a per share basis will yield much more meaningful information indicating future sales and profits prospects. As shown in Table 6-5, the average annual growth rate on per-share basis was only 9½ percent as against 15 percent on basis of total sales. This means about one third of the sales growth in the past five to seven years was simply due to adding up the sales of firms acquired in exchange for new shares.

Stability of Profit Margin

Profit margin measures what percent of a sales dollar is actual profit to the corporation. Profit margin can be measured either in terms of operating income or net income after taxes. The former is usually referred to as *operating profit margin* and the latter as *net profit margin*. As shown in Table 6-2, operating earnings are calculated before the deduction of depreciation and depletion by the Standard & Poor's Corporation. This is because of the fact that depreciation and depletion charges are mostly fixed costs, and the operating profit margin is designed to indicate profitability from current operations after deducting all variable costs. The operating profit margin and net profit margin of W. R. Grace & Company in the past ten years from 1960 to 1969 are computed in Table 6-6.

TABLE 6-4
Condensed Compound-Interest Table: 3 to 25% Rates

Years	3%	4%	5%	6%	7%	8%	9%	10%	12%	14%	16%	20%	25%
1	1.03000	1.04000	1.05000	1.06000	1.07000	1.08000	1.09000	1.10000	1.12000	1.14000	1.16000	1.20000	1.25000
2	1.06090	1.08160	1.10250	1.12360	1.14490	1.16640	1.18810	1.21000	1.25440	1.29960	1.34560	1.44000	1.56250
3	1.09273	1.12486	1.15762	1.19102	1.22504	1.25971	1.29503	1.33100	1.40493	1.48154	1.56090	1.72800	1.95313
4	1.12551	1.16986	1.21551	1.26248	1.31080	1.36049	1.41158	1.46410	1.57352	1.68896	1.81064	2.07360	2.44141
5	1.15927	1.21665	1.27628	1.33823	1.40255	1.46933	1.53862	1.61051	1.76234	1.92541	2.10034	2.48832	3.05176
6	1.19405	1.26532	1.34010	1.41852	1.50073	1.58687	1.67710	1.77156	1.97382	2.19497	2.43640	2.98598	3.81470
7	1.22987	1.31593	1.40710	1.50363	1.60578	1.71382	1.82804	1.94872	2.21068	2.50227	2.82622	3.58318	4.76837
8	1.26677	1.36857	1.47746	1.59385	1.71819	1.85093	1.99256	2.14359	2.47596	2.85259	3.27841	4.29982	5.96046
9	1.30477	1.42331	1.55133	1.68948	1.83846	1.99900	2.17189	2.35795	2.77308	3.25195	3.80296	5.15978	7.45058
10	1.34392	1.48024	1.62889	1.79085	1.96715	2.15892	2.36736	2.59374	3.10585	3.70722	4.41144	6.19174	9.31323
11	1.38423	1.53945	1.71034	1.89830	2.10485	2.33164	2.58043	2.85312	3.47855	4.22623	5.11726	7.43008	11.64153
12	1.42576	1.60103	1.79586	2.01220	2.25219	2.51817	2.81266	3.13843	3.89598	4.81790	5.93603	8.91610	14.55192
13	1.46853	1.66507	1.88565	2.13293	2.40984	2.71962	3.06580	3.45227	4.36349	5.49241	6.88579	10.69932	18.18989
14	1.51259	1.73168	1.97993	2.26090	2.57853	2.93719	3.34173	3.79750	4.88711	6.26135	7.98752	12.83918	22.73737
15	1.55797	1.80094	2.07893	2.39656	2.75903	3.17217	3.64248	4.17725	5.47357	7.13794	9.26552	15.40702	28.42171
16	1.60471	1.87298	2.18287	2.54035	2.95216	3.42594	3.97031	4.59497	6.13039	8.13725	10.74800	18.48843	35.52714
17	1.65285	1.94790	2.29202	2.69277	3.15882	3.70002	4.32763	5.05447	6.86604	9.27646	12.46768	22.18611	44.40892
18	1.70243	2.02582	2.40662	2.85434	3.37993	3.99602	4.71712	5.55992	7.68997	10.57517	14.46251	26.62333	55.51115
19	1.75351	2.10685	2.52695	3.02560	3.61653	4.31570	5.14166	6.11591	8.61276	12.05569	16.77652	31.94800	69.38894
20	1.80611	2.19112	2.65330	3.20714	3.86968	4.66096	5.60441	6.72750	9.64629	13.74349	19.46076	38.33760	86.73617

SOURCE: Douglas A. Hayes, *Investments: Analysis and Management*, 2d ed. New York: The Macmillan Company, 1966.

TABLE 6-5
Growth of Sales Per Share, W. R. Grace & Company

Year	Sales* Per Share	Annual Percent Increase	Average Percent Increase 1963-65 to 1969
1969	87.92	0	1969 sales per share 87.92
1968	87.50	1.5	1963-1965 average sales
			per share 55.96
1967	86.37	20	1969/1963-65 . . . . .1.57
1966	72.13	15	Average annual growth
			rate of sales per share 9½%
1965	62.97	14	
1964	55.29	12	
1963	49.61		

*Data from *The Value Line Investment Survey*, May 8, 1970.

The operating profit margin reached a high of 14 percent in 1961. Then it began its uninterrupted long decline. For 1969, partly a recession year, the operating profit margin reached a low of 7 percent, which was only half of what it was eight years ago in 1961. The net profit margin on the other hand showed improvement from 1960 to 1965, and then began its deterioration. The improvement of net profit margin during 1961-65, however, was partly attributable to favorable changes in income tax rates and regulations pertaining to depreciation and depletion charges. Another factor was the fact that the net income in 1964 and 1965 included sizable amount of income from extraordinary items.

Turnover of Capital

Turnover of capital measures how fast sales are being generated by each dollar of capital invested. Turnover of capital is usually calculated as a ratio between sales and common equity. The greater the turnover of capital the larger

TABLE 6-6
Operating and Net Profit Margins, W. R. Grace & Company

Year	Sales (millions)	Operating Income before Depreciation and Taxes	Net Income	Operating Income as Percent of Sales	Net Income as Percent of Sales
1969	$1,791.7	$124.6	$51.0	7.0	2.8
1968	1,791.8	167.0	36.0	9.3	2.0
1967	1,621.4	150.2	56.1	9.3	3.5
1966	1,349.3	137.3	71.2	10.2	5.3
1965	1,097.4	116.5	58.9	10.6	5.4
1964	876.2	104.3	45.9	11.2	5.2
1963	699.6	84.5	33.5	12.1	4.8
1962	591.5	72.9	22.6	12.3	3.8
1961	534.7	61.1	18.8	14.0	3.5
1960R	552.9	54.3	16.2	9.8	2.9

R Recession.

is the profit to the corporation, assuming profit margin unchanged. The turnover of capital of W. R. Grace & Company in the ten years from 1960 to 1969 is computed in Table 6-7. The turnover of capital varied from a low of 2.06 in 1962 to a high of 2.98 in 1968. The range of variation was about 45 percent. There was substantial improvement in turnover of capital since 1964.

TABLE 6-7
Turnover of Equity Capital, W. R. Grace & Company

Year	Sales (millions)	Common Equity (millions)	Sales over Common Equity
1969	$1,791.7	$624.5	2.87
1968	1,791.8	603.3	2.98
1967	1,621.4	579.1	2.78
1966	1,349.3	546.8	2.46
1965	1,097.4	463.4	2.37
1964	876.2	391.1	2.24
1963	699.6	338.2	2.07
1962	591.5	288.2	2.06
1961	534.7	254.4	2.10
1960[R]	552.9	240.3	2.30

[R]Recession.

Rate of Return on Common Equity

Rate of return on common equity measures the profitability of the business, i.e., the percent being earned on each dollar of capital contributed by the shareholders or retained from earnings in the business. Rate of return on common equity is a product of two factors: (1) net profit margin, and (2) turnover of equity capital. Algebraically, the relationships among them can be expressed as

$$\underset{\text{(net profit margin)}}{\frac{\text{Net Income after Tax}}{\text{Sales}}} \times \underset{\substack{\text{(turnover} \\ \text{of equity)}}}{\frac{\text{Sales}}{\text{Common Equity}}} = \underset{\substack{\text{(rate of return on} \\ \text{common equity)}}}{\frac{\text{Net Income after Tax}}{\text{Common Equity}}}$$

Table 6-8 shows the net profit margin, turnover of equity, and rate of return on common equity of the W. R. Grace & Company for the years 1960 through 1969. The rate of return on common equity had been improving from 1960 to 1966, but it was declining during 1967-69. While the turnover of common equity continued to show its improvement in the last few years, the sharp decrease in net profit margin since 1966 was more than offsetting the slight improvement in turnover of common equity. This accounted for the deterioration in rate of return on common equity since 1966.

Growth of Earnings

Rate of growth of earnings can be computed using a compound interest table as in the case of growth of sales discussed earlier. Average earnings per

TABLE 6-8
Rate of Return on Common Equity,
W. R. Grace & Company

Year	Net Profit Margin	Turnover of Common Equity	Rate of Return on Common Equity
1969	2.8	2.87	8.1
1968	2.0	2.98	6.0
1967	3.5	2.78	9.7
1966	5.3	2.46	13.0
1965	5.4	2.37	12.8
1964	5.2	2.24	11.6
1963	4.8	2.07	9.9
1962	3.8	2.06	7.8
1961	3.5	2.10	7.3
1960[R]	2.9	2.30	6.7

[R] Recession.

share of W. R. Grace & Company as shown in Table 6-10 was $1.71 during 1960-62 and $2.31 during 1967-69. Dividing the former into the latter figure, we get a ratio of 1.35; by locating a close figure to 1.35 under the row of seven years (treating the 1960-62 average as 1961, and the 1967-69 average as 1968) in a compound interest table, the average annual growth rate is obtained at 4.4 percent.

Least-Squares Method

The rate of growth of earnings, obtained through using a compound interest table as above or through averaging annual growth rates for individual years, provides results which are approximate but sufficient for most practical purposes. However, if the analyst wants the real growth rate of the period, he should employ a method known as the *least-squares method*. The least-squares technique can yield a trend line best fit to the historical data and with known mathematical relationships. For instance, the sum of the squares of deviations about this trend line is known to be less than the sum of the squares of the deviations about any other line of the same mathematical type. That is why this method is known as least-squares method. Since the time series is viewed here as a geometric rather than an arithmetic progression, the function to be used to describe the data is the exponential equation in the form of $Y = ab^x$, where Y represents trend value, x the time scale, a for a constant, and b a ratio at which the series is changing.

The least-squares method involves several steps. First, the exponential equation has to be converted into linear logarithmic form: $\log Y = \log a + x \log b$. The second step is to solve two normal equations for the values of $\log a$ and $\log b$. The two normal equations are

(1) $\Sigma \log Y = n (\log a) + \log b (\Sigma x)$
(2) $\Sigma x (\log Y) = \log a (\Sigma x) + \log b (\Sigma x^2)$

Since the x origin may be taken at the middle of the period, $\Sigma x = 0$; these two normal equations may be written in short form as below:

(1) $\Sigma \log Y = N \log a$

(2) $\Sigma x (\log Y) = \log b (\Sigma x^2)$

The final step is to look up the antilog of the $\log b$ to get the value of b. If, for example, $\log b$ is found to be 0.0607, then b is 1.15, and the growth rate for the period is 15 percent. For purpose of illustration, the calculation of annual growth rate of domestic demand for gasoline during 1940-58 is shown in Table 6-9.

TABLE 6-9
Computation of Geometric Straight-Line Trend, Average Monthly Domestic Demand for Gasoline, 1940–58
(Millions of barrels)

Year	x	x^2	Demand, y	$\log y$	$x \log y$
1940	−9	81	49.1	1.69108	−15.21972
1941	−8	64	55.6	1.74507	−13.96056
1942	−7	49	49.1	1.69108	−11.83756
1943	−6	36	47.4	1.67578	−10.05468
1944	−5	25	52.7	1.72181	−8.60905
1945	−4	16	58.0	1.76343	−7.05372
1946	−3	9	61.3	1.78746	−5.36238
1947	−2	4	66.3	1.82151	−3.64302
1948	−1	1	72.6	1.86094	−1.86094
1949	0	0	76.1	1.88138	0
1950	+1	1	82.9	1.91855	+1.91855
1951	+2	4	90.8	1.95809	+3.91618
1952	+3	9	96.4	1.98408	+5.95224
1953	+4	16	100.5	2.00217	+8.00868
1954	+5	25	102.6	2.01115	+10.05575
1955	+6	36	111.2	2.04610	+12.27660
1956	+7	49	114.4	2.05843	+14.40909
1957	+8	64	116.1	2.06483	+16.51864
1958	+9	81	118.2	2.07262	+18.65358
		570	1521.3	35.75556	+14.10760

SOURCE: *Business Statistics*, 1959; or Ya-Lun Chou, *Statistical Analysis* (New York: Holt, Rinehart & Winston, Inc., 1969), p. 566.

Substituting the values in the normal equations, we have

(1)

$$35.75556 = 19 \log a$$
$$\log a = 1.88187$$

(2)

$$14.10760 = 570 \log b$$
$$\log b = .02475$$

The trend equation in logarithmic form is

$$\log Y_c = 1.88187 + .02475x$$

(origin 1949, x unit, 1 year; Y unit, average monthly
domestic demand for gasoline in millions of barrels)

To look up the antilog of $\log a$ and $\log b$, we can write the trend equation in natural form:

$$Y_c = (76.18)(1.059)^x$$

origin, 1949 x unit, 1 year

The annual growth rate of domestic demand for gasoline during 1940-58 was therefore 5.9 percent.

Causes of Growth of Earnings

The calculation of the growth rate of earnings per share during a past period indicates the degree of success or failure the corporation had achieved in a past period, but the growth rate tells us nothing about the causes underlying the growth. Therefore, we now turn to the discussion of these causes.

Growth of earnings per share can be discussed in terms of two causal factors: (1) capital base—book value per share, and (2) profitability—or average rate of return on equity. Growth of earnings will result if either or both factors are increased. For the majority of corporations, the reason earnings per share grew steadily over the years is the enlargement of capital base. The increase in book value per share is caused mainly by plowing back part of the corporate earnings, and in some cases the sale of new shares at a premium over book value. The relationship between book value, rate of return, percent of earnings retained and plowed back, and earnings growth rate can be illustrated in the following hypothetical example.

Corporate data of ABC Corporation in 1970:

Book value per share	$20.00
Earnings per share	3.00
Rate of return on equity	15%

Earnings growth rate in 1971 under two assumptions below:
(a) The 15 percent rate of return is maintained.
(b) All earnings are retained and plowed back.
Then:

Book value per share, beginning of year	$23.00
Rate of return	15%
Earnings per share 15% × $23.00	$ 3.45
Earnings growth rate 3.45/3.00	15%

Earnings growth rate in 1971 under another set of conditions:
(a) The 15 percent rate of return is maintained.
(b) 40 percent of earnings are retained and plowed back.
Then:

Book value per share, beginning of year $21.20
Rate of return. 15%
Earnings per share $21.20 × 15% . . . $ 3.18
Earnings growth rate   3.18/3.00 . . . .   6%

If the rate of return is assumed constant over a period of time, a general formula is available for computing earnings growth rate. The formula is

Earnings growth rate = rate of return on equity × (1 - dividend payout ratio)

Using the formula, we can get the same growth rates in the two hypothetical cases above:

$$15\% \times (1 - 0\%) = 15\%$$
$$15\% \times (1 - 60\%) = 6\%$$

In cases where the rate of return on common equity has been either declining or increasing over a period of years, the earnings growth rate computed on the basis of average rate of return portrays neither the actual historical performance nor the potentials of the corporation. An alternative computation of earnings growth rate on the basis of rate of return on new investments is often necessary and revealing. The rate of return on new investments is a ratio between the increase in earnings and the increase in book value per share over a period of time. It suggests the degree of profitability on investments to capital from retained earnings or otherwise.

In Table 6-10, growth of earnings per share of W. R. Grace & Company from 1960 to 1969 are shown in relation to changes in book value per share, dividend payout ratio, and rates of return on common equity. Rates of growth of earnings are computed on three bases: (1) average rate of return over the period 1960-69, (2) rate of return on new investments from 1960-62 to 1967-69, and (3) compound interest rate from 1960-62 to 1967-69. The growth rates were 5.1 percent on basis of average rate of return, 4.4 percent on basis of compound interest rate method, and 5.6 percent on basis of rate of return on new investments. The three different calculations provide growth rates within a narrow range, varying from a low of 4.4 percent to a high of 5.6 percent. Based on this information, it seems, the future earnings growth rate will be most likely around 5 percent. If we assume on the other hand that the corporation will earn on the average a rate of return of about 9 percent and that the dividend payout ratio will be higher than before, say, around 50 percent, then the future earnings growth rate will be 9% × (1 - 50%) = 4.5 percent.

Degree of Leverage and Adequacy of Working Capital

By leverage we mean the utilization of long-term debt in the capital structure. Since bond interest is tax-deductible, the real cost to the corporation at the present level of income tax rates is only half as much as the fixed interest charges on the bond. If the corporation earns a rate of return higher than the

TABLE 6-10
Analysis of Growth of Earnings Per Share, W. R. Grace & Company

Year	Earnings Per Share	Book Value Per Share	Dividend Per Share	Dividend Payout Ratio, Percent	Rate of Return on Common Equity
1969	1.58	30.64	1.50	95	8.1
1968	2.76	29.68	1.45	52.5	6.0
1967	2.59	29.24	1.38	53.3	9.7
1966	3.31	29.99	1.28	38.8	13.0
1965	2.80	27.04	1.18	42.0	12.8
1964	2.72	25.27	1.08	39.8	11.6
1963	2.29	23.43	.96	42.0	9.9
1962	1.93	24.88	.84	43.5	7.8
1961	1.73	24.13	.75	43.3	7.3
1960	1.48	23.21	.74	50.0	6.7
1960–69 average	2.32	26.75			9.3
1960–68 average				45.0	
1967–69/ 1960–62 average	1.35				
Increase: Earnings 1960-62 to 1967–69	.59				
Book value 1960-62 to 1967–69		5.80			
Increase of earnings to Increase of book value					10.2

Growth rate computations:
Based on average rate of return . . . . 9.3 X (1 − 45%) = 5.1%
Based on rate of return on new investments 10.2 X (1 − 45%) = 5.6%
Compound interest rate method . . . . . . 1.35 for 7 years = 4.4%

real cost of the bond to the corporation, profits will increase, and vice versa. Therefore the utilization of a "reasonable" amount of long-term debt in the capital structure may enhance the rate of growth of earnings and should not be frowned upon. However, bond-interest costs are fixed charges. They have to be met under all business conditions if the issuing corporation wants to stay in business. Excessive use of debt in the capital structure should therefore be regarded as a sign of possible trouble ahead.

The adequacy of working capital is usually measured by the so-called *current ratio* which measures current assets to current liabilities. A 2-to-1 ratio is usually considered adequate for most corporations. For large corporations, working capital is usually found adequate and therefore does not require much analysis.

The capital structure and current ratio of the W. R. Grace & Company for the period 1960 to 1969 is shown in Table 6-11. As can be seen from the table, the Grace Company used long-term debt quite liberally in the capital structure. It is doubtful that the company can raise much further from the current level the percentage of long-term debt in total capitalization. The ratio between current assets and current liabilities decreased from 2.3 in 1960 to 1.7 in 1968. The reduction in the ratio may represent more efficient use of current assets, but could also mean a little tightness on working capital.

TABLE 6-11

Capital Structure and Current Ratio, W. R. Grace & Company

Year	Long-Term Debt	Preferred Stock	Common Stock	Total Capital, Millions	Long-Term Debt as Percent of Total Capital	Current Assets to Current Liabilities
1969	405.9	11.4	624.5	1,041.8	39	—
1968	470.7	11.8	603.3	1,085.8	43.5	1.7
1967	511.7	12.3	579.1	1,103.1	46.5	1.9
1966	448.7	12.3	546.8	1,007.8	44.5	1.8
1965	388.9	12.3	463.4	864.6	45	1.9
1964	262.0	12.3	391.1	665.4	39.5	1.9
1963	226.2	12.6	338.2	577.0	39	2.0
1962	233.9	12.6	288.2	534.7	44	2.1
1961	203.5	12.6	254.4	470.5	43.5	2.3
1960[R]	194.5	12.6	240.3	447.4	43.5	2.3

[R]Recession.

COMPARISON OF RECORD OF PERFORMANCE WITH INDUSTRY AVERAGE AND COMPETITORS

After a careful analysis of the record of performance of a corporation in the most relevant past, the next step is to compare the record with industry average and competitors to see whether the corporation is winning or losing in the competitive race of the industry.

Comparability of Corporate Data

Unfortunately, earnings per share as reported by corporations are often not strictly comparable because of differences in treatment of the following items:
Inventory valuation
Method of depreciation
Consolidation practice
Convertible senior security
Accounting for merger
Research and development expenditures

Inventory Valuation

There are three commonly used methods of valuing inventory: (1) first-in-first-out method (FIFO), (2) last-in-first-out method (LIFO), and (3) average-cost method. The FIFO method assumes what is left on hand at the end of a fiscal period is recently purchased, and therefore should be valued at recent purchase prices. The LIFO method assumes just the opposite, and the inventory is valued under this method at older purchase prices, sometimes prices which existed many years previous. Under the average-cost method, cost of each unit of inventory is recomputed each time when a new purchase is made. The inventory on hand is therefore costed at weighted average purchase price.

If the purchase price remains constant over time, the three methods provide the identical results: (a) the same value of inventory on hand, and (b) the same amount for cost of goods sold.[1] However, under conditions of rising price level, the FIFO method will value inventory at higher recent purchase price, and allocate less to cost of goods sold. As a result, total earnings will be higher. Under the LIFO method, inventory will be costed at lower older prices, and the recent purchases at higher prices will be allocated to cost of goods sold. Therefore earnings will be lower. The average-cost method will yield a earnings figure somewhere between the results from the FIFO and LIFO methods.

Methods of Depreciation

The most commonly used methods of depreciation are three: (1) straight-line method, (2) sum-of-the-years-digits method, and (3) double-declining-balance method. For purpose of writing off faster the cost of equipment (accelerated depreciation), the corporation can use either method 2 or method 3. Since depreciation is an expense, the greater the amount of depreciation the smaller the amount of earnings. The earnings of a corporation will therefore be less if faster depreciation methods are used.

Consolidation Practice

Practices vary widely in respect to reporting earnings of partly owned subsidiaries and affiliates. One method is to include only the dividends or remittances actually received by the parent company from subsidiaries. Another method is to combine the financial statements of the parent company and all subsidiaries as one unit. Allowance is made for minority interest in earnings and assets of partly owned subsidiaries. The difference in treatment of subsidiary earnings can often affect the reported earnings of the parent company substantially.

Convertible Senior Security

Some corporations, especially those that have numerous acquisitions, often make extensive use of convertible bonds and preferred stocks in their capital structure. When and if these securities are converted there will be substantial

---

[1] The formula for computing cost of goods sold is

(Beginning inventory + purchases) - Ending inventory = Cost of goods sold

increase in the number of common shares outstanding, thereby reducing appreciably the per-share earnings of the corporation.

Accounting for Merger

There are two methods currently in use to record the financial results of a merger. One method is known as *purchase* and the other as *pooling of interests*. The two methods create different impacts on the future earnings of the acquiring corporation. For purpose of illustration, a hypothetical example is set up as follows:

Company	A (Acquiring firm)	B
Market price of common stock per share . .	$20	$10
Book value of common stock per share. . . .	15	5

Merger term based on market
  prices: ½ share of Common A for 1 share of Common B
Accounting problem: ½ share of Common A has a book value of $7½, whereas 1 share of Common B has a book value of $5. The accounting problem is, how do we account for the difference of $2½ for each ½ share common issued for acquiring company B in the books of company A?

If the merger is treated as a "purchase," the excess of value offered over the book value purchased ($7½ - $5 = $2½) is set up as goodwill which will be written off against earnings over a future period. The main disadvantage of this method is that future earnings will be lowered by the amortization of goodwill. If the merger, on the other hand, is looked upon as a "pooling of interests," the accounting treatment is simply to combine the balance sheets of the two companies. No goodwill will arise and any premium paid over book value acquired ($2½ for each half share common issued in this case) is charged against capital surplus account of the acquiring corporation. The advantage of this method is that future earnings will be free from any charges from amortization of goodwill. However, the differences in accounting treatment to merger among firms provide another reason why earnings figures of different corporations are not strictly comparable.

Research and Development Expenditures

Research and development expenditures have assumed increasing importance in recent years of fast-changing technology. The accounting treatment of this item varies widely among corporations. Some large corporations may conservatively charge off R&D expenditures against current income. Other corporations may capitalize all or part of the R&D expenditures, and write them off against future income. The effect on per-share earnings is quite obvious. Expensing R&D expenditures will lower the per-share earnings, whereas capitalization of R&D expenditures will raise per-share earnings in the short run.

The discussions above serve to indicate why per-share earnings of corporations are not strictly comparable. The ideal solution is, of course, to make proper adjustments of reported earnings of corporations so that their adjusted earnings can be compared with one another. However, there are two practical difficulties. One is the lack of sufficient published information to make all the adjustments necessary. The other is the amount of time required of the analyst to make these adjustments. As a practical matter, stockholders (except the industry specialist) often forgo most of the adjustments of corporate earnings. The alternative is to refer to some of the corporate data as adjusted by professional investment services.

Cash-Flow Analysis

One of the key aspect of investment analysis is to ascertain and analyze the past *trend* of profitability of a corporation on its total capital and on its equity and in relation to its competitors. Unfortunately, corporate earnings data as mentioned above are not strictly comparable among corporations, and in many cases not even for the same corporation over a span of years. The main problem arises from the fact that there is no uniform accounting treatment among corporations to items like inventory valuation, allocation of cost for depreciation and depletion, or consolidation practice. Among these factors the difference in accounting practice toward depreciation and depletion charges is probably the most important single factor responsible for noncomparability of corporate earnings data.

To cope with the problem, financial analysts in recent years began to favor a new concept, *cash flow*, for the purpose of measuring *trend* of profitability of corporations. Cash flow is defined as corporate earnings after taxes plus noncash charges such as depreciation and depletion. Though the cash-flow concept does not eliminate all the factors causing noncomparability of corporate earnings data among corporations, it nonetheless provides better approximations for measuring trends in corporate profitability. Should the cash-flow concept be defined on a pretax basis (cash flow = net corporate earnings plus depreciation and depletion and corporate taxes), it would form an even better basis for measuring trends in profitability, because the size of corporate taxes is also indirectly affected by the amount of depreciation and depletion charges taken for the current year.[2]

Growth of Sales

Growth of sales usually forms the base of growth of earnings. Growth of sales can be aided by a variety of factors, such as rising level of domestic business activity, development of new products, expansion of productive facilities, and active acquisition programs. Table 6-12 shows relative growth of sales of some

[2] J. B. Cohen and E. D. Zinbarg, *Investment Analysis and Portfolio Management*, Homewood, Ill.: Richard D. Irwin, 1967, p. 199.

TABLE 6-12
Sales Record
(1957-59=100)

	[4]Air Prod.	Air Red.	[6]Allied Chem.	Amer. Cyan.	Amer. Enka	[1]Atlas Chem.	Big Three Ind.	[1]Cabot	Celanese	Cheme-tron	[8]Com'l. Solv.	Dexter	Dia-mond	Dow Chem.	[1]du-Pont	[9]FMC Corp.	[8]Free-port Sul.	[6]GAF Corp.	[1]Grace (W.R.)
1969	539	258	194	199	311	209	370	239	551	242	154	263	433	251	182	431	326	455	392
1968	492	232	186	187	289	194	332	214	553	197	162	221	420	230	173	421	353	358	392
1967	446	219	183	171	225	173	252	191	489	191	141	186	329	193	155	402	302	355	345
1966	391	228	183	174	244	166	249	185	449	198	142	178	318	183	159	284	251	330	295
1965	295	200	165	158	234	143	220	165	385	173	136	151	167	164	151	284	186	165	240
1964	271	180	153	142	211	131	175	147	308	130	139	119	143	150	139	254	137	131	178
1963	260	162	142	130	181	130	136	134	247	117	129	113	128	135	129	189	115	121	153
1962	253	152	128	119	167	123	124	129	140	114	120	100	126	129	121	155	99	122	129
1961	212	137	[5]124	110	138	118	115	117	125	109	95	⋯	119	117	111	127	92	111	117
1960	148	121	113	106	116	114	100	121	116	110	93	⋯	117	114	108	111	92	109	121
1959	117	106	106	107	132	102	⋯	114	117	100	105	⋯	110	113	107	105	96	108	104

Average net sales in 1957-59 base period, in millions of dollars; months indicate year end:

	[4]Air Prod.	Air Red.	[6]Allied Chem.	Amer. Cyan.	Amer. Enka	[1]Atlas Chem.	Big Three Ind.	[1]Cabot	Celanese	Cheme-tron	[8]Com'l. Solv.	Dexter	Dia-mond	Dow Chem.	[1]du-Pont	[9]FMC Corp.	[8]Free-port Sul.	[6]GAF Corp.	[1]Grace (W.R.)
	41.1 Sept.	188.6 Dec.	679.4 Dec.	547.0 Dec.	82.5 Dec.	69.3 Dec.	[14]17.0 Dec.	78.4 Sept.	227.0 Dec.	120.7 Dec.	67.0 Dec.	[12]18.9 Dec.	124.9 Dec.	717.4 [11]Dec.	2,009 Dec.	326.7 Dec.	57.3 Dec.	146.7 Dec.	456.9 Dec.

	Her-cules	Int'l. Min.	Int'l. Salt	Mon-santo	Nalco	Nat'l. Chem-search	[10]Nat'l. Distl.	[16]Oak-ite	Olin Corp.	Penn-walt	Products Research & Chem.	Reich-hold	Richard-son	Rohm & Haas	Stauffer	[3]Texas Gulf	Union Carb.	VWR United	Witco Chem.
1969	295	466	188	292	392	667	282	162	183	500	689	226	454	236	251	483	208	182	408
1968	284	467	177	281	333	583	231	155	170	496	691	216	373	224	241	496	191	174	393
1967	254	306	156	247	282	499	216	144	143	455	574	183	348	199	213	405	181	160	345
1966	250	278	131	243	262	468	221	138	139	272	239	176	342	196	193	212	184	156	338
1965	210	245	131	222	216	355	201	124	148	252	221	153	251	184	164	158	147	135	303
1964	210	210	117	204	187	280	202	116	129	176	192	146	152	169	140	113	133	127	234
1963	201	171	114	180	148	220	190	111	123	166	198	138	151	150	130	99	119	123	212
1962	193	153	107	160	136	178	191	110	117	153	213	136	139	138	119	94	116	112	185
1961	149	123	99	140	127	139	181	106	111	117	155	128	117	126	113	94	111	100	176
1960	132	117	103	134	119	100	169	105	106	111	109	124	100	115	110	94	110	⋯	165
1959	111	105	104	131	117	⋯	109	103	111	107	105	126	⋯	114	115	102	109	⋯	163

Average net sales in 1957-59 base period, in millions of dollars; months indicate year end:

	Her-cules	Int'l. Min.	Int'l. Salt	Mon-santo	Nalco	Nat'l. Chem-search	[10]Nat'l. Distl.	[16]Oak-ite	Olin Corp.	Penn-walt	Products Research & Chem.	Reich-hold	Richard-son	Rohm & Haas	Stauffer	[3]Texas Gulf	Union Carb.	VWR United	Witco Chem.
	253.1 Dec.	107.5 Dec.	30.0 June	663.3 Dec.	40.5 Dec.	147.03 [2]Apr.	247.9 Dec.	[15]17.0 Dec.	632.1 Dec.	81.9 Dec.	154.04 Sept.	80.1 Dec.	[14]28.0 Dec.	188.9 Dec.	198.9 Dec.	62.5 Dec.	1,407.6 Dec.	[13]112.2 [2]Feb.	58.0 Dec.

SOURCE: Chemicals: Basic Analysis, *Industry Survey*, Standard & Poor's Corporation, July 2, 1970.
[1]Based on sales and operating revenues. [2]Of foll. cal. yr. [3]Based on gross revenues. [4]Based on total revenues. [5]Incl. Union Texas Natural Gas. [6]Based on gross sales. [7]Year ended Dec. 31 in 1960 and prior yrs. [8]After deduct. Fed. withdrawal tax paid on products sold. [9]Incl. revenues from leased mach. and processes. [10]Based on net sales, after deducting excise taxes. [11]Yrs. end. May 31 of foll. cal. yr. in 1960 & pr. yrs. [12]1961 = 100. [13]1961-62 = 100. [14]1960 = 100. [15]1958-60 = 100. [16]Incl. oth. income pr. to 1964.

37 general and specialty chemical corporations during the period 1959-69. Sales during 1957-59 were taken as 100. The sales of W. R. Grace & Company in 1969 was nearly four times the sales figure in 1959. The fast growth of sales was to a large extent attributable to its active acquisition programs.

Research Expenditures

Research expenditures are instrumental for new-product development. The amount of money spent on research programs and in relation to sales provide good indications whether or not the corporation concerned can keep up with its competitors. Unfortunately, corporations are not required as of now to report these expenditures either to their stockholders or to the Securities and Exchange Commission in their 10-K statements. In a recent survey conducted by Forbes for their Second Annual Directory Issue, only about 40 percent of 870 companies surveyed were willing to reveal their research and development expenditures for 1969. Even among those reporting, the R&D figures may not be on a compatible basis. Nonetheless, these figures constitute an important piece of information, and wherever possible, the analyst should look for them. Table 6-13 shows the research and development expenditures of 18 chemical firms in absolute amounts and in relation to sales for 1969.

TABLE 6-13
Research and Development Expenditures of
18 Major Chemical Firms in 1969

Company	Research and Development Expenditures in 1969 (millions)	Sales in 1969 (millions)	Percent of Sales
Air Reduction	10.5	487.3	2.2
Allied Chemical	30.0	1,316.1	2.3
Am. Cyanamid	44.9	1,087.1	4.1
Celanese Corp.	48.6	1,249.9	3.9
Chemetron	2.9	292.2	1.0
Diamond Shamrock	10.1	541.3	1.9
Dow Chemical	87.3	1,797.1	4.9
Ethyl	16.0	509.3	3.1
Freeport Sulphur	8.4	175.2	4.8
FMC Corp.	30.7	1,409.3	2.2
GAF	13.3	606.3	2.2
Hercules, Inc.	23.2	746.0	3.1
Int'l. & Mineral Chem.	6.2	500.8	1.2
Koppers	7.8	533.3	1.5
Monsanto	101.5	1,938.8	5.2
Rohm & Haas	28.6	446.2	6.4
Stauffer Chemical	12.2	498.7	2.4
Union Carbide	71.2	2,933.0	2.4

SOURCE: *Forbes* (Dimensions of American Business, 2nd Annual Directory Issue), May 15, 1970, p. 202.

TABLE 6-14
Comparative Company Analysis
Capital Expenditures
(Millions of dollars)

	Air Prod.	Air Red.	Allied Chem.	Amer. Cyan.	Amer. Enka	Atlas Chem.	[4]Big Three Ind.	Cabot	Celanese	Cheme-tron	Com'l. Solv.	Dexter	Dia-mond	[2]Dow Chem.	du-Pont	FMC Corp.	[3]Free-port Sul.	GAF Corp.	[3]Grace (W.R.)
1969	42.54	55.30	185.17	15.80	23.35	6.63	14.05	17.47	176.40	27.55	6.24	4.10	41.76	370.6	391.4	79.44	10.63	22.09	120.65
1968	36.41	34.90	91.40	56.81	15.75	5.45	16.38	30.30	127.40	19.59	6.71	5.40	55.04	306.3	332.4	69.64	40.91	43.58	124.45
1967	37.94	42.60	128.10	56.07	27.33	8.78	6.71	32.34	163.10	19.97	22.90	6.00	79.87	192.3	453.7	71.80	57.58	39.93	121.67
1966	44.01	32.90	224.20	108.43	37.53	12.62	13.35	27.47	281.30	21.58	9.68	1.50	53.20	241.5	531.1	75.20	46.94	31.57	150.58
1965	43.65	45.10	180.20	129.53	19.11	9.59	11.66	20.03	287.00	20.62	5.95	...	28.72	248.3	326.9	51.64	21.82	24.99	154.78
1964	23.77	53.20	143.70	49.11	21.10	4.02	14.82	18.64	151.00	17.65	7.12	...	14.50	166.1	290.1	50.01	7.23	11.10	100.50
1963	25.73	22.30	99.10	45.05	20.97	4.26	...	9.84	88.35	13.45	6.30	...	15.72	82.0	370.0	22.25	15.75	8.45	54.13
1962	21.12	33.80	107.30	35.15	9.74	10.15	...	16.45	31.30	11.85	5.16	...	11.67	69.0	245.0	32.68	6.02	12.68	61.60
1961	[5]17.51	22.20	141.10	46.49	11.12	12.15	...	13.31	24.57	9.47	2.61	...	16.80	115.0	204.9	18.40	5.83	6.17	55.90
1960	18.70	16.90	58.20	48.29	8.33	3.03	...	16.93	26.75	6.49	2.33	...	15.15	148.0	213.7	23.42	8.42	7.44	51.50
1959	7.47	31.10	40.80	35.50	11.54	4.22	...	10.80	12.47	5.87	1.35	...	9.52	102.0	174.0	16.12	10.87	5.89	32.26
Yr. Ends	Sept.	Dec.	Dec.	Dec.	Dec.	Dec.	Dec.	Sept.	Dec.	Dec.	Dec.	Dec.	Dec.	[8]Dec.	Dec.	Dec.	Dec.	Dec.	Dec.

	Her-cules	Int'l. Min.	Int'l. Salt	Mon-santo	Nalco	[7]Nat'l. Chem-search	Nat'l. Distl.	Oak-ite	Olin Corp.	Penn-walt	[7]Products Research & Chem.	Reich-hold	[9]Richard son	Rohm & Hass	Stauffer	[3]Texas Gulf	Union Carb.	VWR United	Witco Chem.
1969	63.59	19.18	6.52	219.87	12.61	...	43.10	0.63	76.70	22.20	1.01	10.76	4.60	54.24	59.59	47.00	322.23	...	17.99
1968	109.25	23.27	4.84	134.99	6.94	0.45	30.70	0.34	79.28	19.93	2.13	6.68	3.90	38.78	24.47	30.00	347.15	1.99	15.09
1967	129.68	56.94	10.45	160.39	5.34	1.09	54.00	1.93	74.50	27.32	1.36	5.33	4.58	40.51	45.09	34.00	478.20	1.02	10.01
1966	69.22	69.43	6.03	210.97	6.90	1.26	32.40	...	42.76	24.84	...	3.86	3.83	50.52	38.80	138.79	393.64	...	16.37
1965	65.30	52.76	2.85	295.16	5.20	1.69	12.30	...	107.06	16.05	...	3.63	2.80	43.99	50.37	58.74	242.18	...	8.09
1964	25.49	25.10	4.54	218.11	2.24	0.67	30.56	...	65.13	9.97	...	5.65	1.45	28.80	39.75	18.66	271.24	...	5.77
1963	31.49	23.20	4.80	114.50	3.09	...	28.55	...	57.88	13.59	...	5.52	2.93	23.37	17.13	14.51	169.50	...	4.74
1962	35.64	28.86	5.11	168.83	10.33	...	28.36	...	53.73	12.82	...	3.14	4.20	19.94	20.46	17.67	145.08	...	5.63
1961	41.57	13.23	2.23	153.82	3.94	...	29.90	...	36.86	9.73	...	4.03	2.44	21.69	29.61	18.83	167.50	...	8.38
1960	58.80	12.14	4.83	121.25	2.28	...	75.84	...	48.88	10.59	...	9.66	2.53	30.85	29.16	5.23	219.77	...	4.33
1959	70.80	13.93	7.29	76.25	1.56	...	25.51	...	30.19	8.00	...	11.79	...	19.20	14.42	5.30	136.56	...	2.41
Yr. Ends:	Dec.	[6]June	June	Dec.	Dec.	[1]Apr.	Dec.	Dec.	Dec.	Dec.	Sept.	Dec.	[10]Dec.	Dec.	Dec.	Dec.	Dec.	[1]Feb.	Dec.

NOTE—Data was obtained from annual reports and SEC statements.

[1]Of the following calendar year. [2]Approximate. [3]As reported to SEC. [4]Net expend. aft. 1965. [5]Reflects merger of Houndry Process Corp. [6]Yr. end Dec. 31 in 1960 & pr. yrs. [7]Net expend. [8]Yrs. end May 31 of foll. cal. yr. in 1960 and pr. yrs. [9]Net additions pr. to 1965. [10]Yrs. end Apr. 30 in 1960 & pr. yrs.

Capital Expenditures
(as Percentage of Gross Plant)

	Air Prod.	Air Red.	Allied Chem.	Amer. Cyan.	Amer. Enka	Atlas Chem.	Big Three Ind.[1]	Cabot	Celanese	Cheme-tron	Com'l. Solv.	Dexter	Dia-mond	Dow Chem.	du-Pont	FMC Corp.	Free-port Sul.	GAF Corp.	Grace (W.R.)
1969	12.7	10.2	9.0	9.4	7.4	5.8	22.2	6.0	11.8	11.8	4.1	11.7	5.5	16.11	8.6	10.2	3.8	5.1	11.5
1968	12.2	6.7	4.9	5.9	5.4	5.0	29.4	10.7	7.6	9.4	4.6	17.4	7.6	14.9	7.7	9.7	15.2	10.4	10.0
1967	12.2	8.8	6.6	6.0	9.8	8.3	16.0	12.6	8.8	10.6	16.2	23.0	11.4	11.0	11.1	10.9	25.2	10.5	10.3
1966	14.1	7.2	11.4	11.7	14.9	12.7	33.2	12.7	16.4	12.6	8.1	7.3	9.6	14.4	14.3	12.8	25.3	9.5	14.0
1965	22.6	10.3	10.1	15.0	8.9	10.9	36.0	10.2	19.5	13.6	4.9	...	10.9	16.3	10.0	11.9	15.5	13.6	17.3
1964	15.7	12.8	8.8	6.4	10.5	5.0	36.5	10.3	12.4	13.1	6.1	...	6.0	12.3	9.6	12.9	6.0	7.2	13.3
1963	19.8	6.2	6.6	6.2	11.6	5.5	...	5.9	12.1	10.7	5.8	...	6.8	6.6	13.2	6.5	13.8	5.6	9.2
1962	20.0	9.6	7.5	4.9	6.0	13.6	...	10.3	7.5	10.5	5.0	...	5.3	5.5	9.8	12.1	6.0	8.9	10.7
1961	22.6	6.9	10.4	6.7	7.3	18.3	...	9.1	6.3	8.9	3.1	...	8.0	8.8	8.9	7.6	5.8	4.7	10.9
1960	30.8	5.8	5.5	7.4	5.8	5.4	...	12.5	7.2	6.6	2.9	...	8.2	11.8	9.9	10.2	8.7	5.8	10.8
1959	24.2	12.2	4.0	5.8	8.6	7.9	...	8.9	3.6	6.1	1.7	...	5.5	8.9	8.7	6.1	26.2	4.7	9.0

	Her-cules	Int'l. Min.	Int'l. Salt	Mon-santo	Nalco	Nat'l. Chem-search[3]	Nat'l. Distl.	Oak-ite	Olin Corp.	Penn-walt	Products Research & Chem.[3]	Reich-hold	Richard-son[2]	Rohm & Haas	Stauffer	Texas Gulf	Union Carb.	VWR United	Witco Chem.
1969	7.9	4.9	7.4	8.9	16.6	...	7.7	7.6	7.3	8.1	14.9	10.0	9.6	11.1	14.8	11.4	7.4	...	13.6
1968	14.6	5.3	5.9	5.8	10.9	8.6	6.1	4.4	8.2	7.9	33.3	8.3	10.1	8.8	6.6	7.4	8.2	8.2	12.2
1967	13.1	13.6	13.4	7.1	9.4	22.7	11.3	26.2	8.1	9.6	28.0	7.1	12.9	9.8	11.6	8.9	12.1	4.4	8.8
1966	14.2	20.6	8.7	9.9	13.2	31.0	7.8	...	5.1	14.1	...	5.7	11.3	13.4	11.2	39.0	11.1	...	15.5
1965	6.4	19.4	4.4	15.0	11.4	55.8	3.6	...	11.3	10.2	...	5.6	10.0	13.2	16.4	26.7	8.3	...	9.0
1964	8.3	11.6	7.2	12.8	5.5	43.2	9.2	...	8.1	7.6	...	8.6	13.5	9.8	14.1	11.9	10.0	...	10.5
1963	10.3	11.9	8.1	7.5	8.0	...	6.9	...	7.7	10.2	...	4.9	26.4	8.7	6.9	10.3	6.8	...	9.3
1962	12.9	15.5	8.8	12.0	28.8	...	7.6	...	7.5	10.4	...	5.3	44.8	8.1	8.5	15.3	6.1	...	12.6
1961	20.6	8.3	4.2	12.6	15.2	...	7.2	...	5.4	9.4	...	7.0	28.5	9.4	13.0	18.4	7.3	...	25.6
1960	9.2	7.6	9.5	11.1	10.1	...	19.7	...	7.2	9.2	...	17.7	30.3	15.4	14.0	5.6	10.0	...	17.1
1959		9.6	16.9	8.8	7.5	...	11.9	...	4.7	7.6	...	14.4	...	11.1	7.8	5.3	6.9	...	11.3

DEFINITION—Capital expenditures during fiscal year divided by gross plant at the end of the fiscal year.

SOURCE: Chemicals: Basic Analysis, Industry Surveys, Standard & Poor's Corporation, July 2, 1970.

[1] Net expend. divided by net property aft. 1965. [2] Net additions pr. to 1965. [3] Net additions divided by net property.

Capital Expenditures

A comparison of capital expenditures by corporations in the same industry yields important information as to how new the plant and equipment are and how fast they are being expanded. Other things being equal, a higher rate of new capital expenditures signals better prospects for the firm. Table 6-14 shows capital expenditures in millions and as a percentage of gross plant for most firms in the chemical industry during the period 1959-69.

Control of Costs and Profitability

Profitability of operations as expressed in the form of operating or net profit margin is affected by three elements: selling prices, output, and control of costs. Since changes in selling prices and level of output are usually industry-wide, a comparison of the trend in the operating and net profit margins of firms will yield important clues as to how each firm is controlling its costs of production and distribution. Table 6-15 shows the comparison of operating profit margin (operating income before depreciation as percent of sales) between major chemical firms during 1959-69. Table 6-16 shows the comparison of net profit margin (net income after tax as percent of sales) for the same firms.

Growth of Earnings

Table 6-17 shows the relative growth of net income among major chemical firms during the period 1959 to 1969.

A still better comparison is in terms of growth of earnings per share, because the growth of net income may be due to an increase in the number of shares outstanding from enlargement of capitalization. The comparison of growth of earnings per share can be either in terms of annual growth rates or as relatives of a basic period as shown in Table 6-18.

MANAGEMENT AND CURRENT PROGRAMS

The quality and efficiency of management are the most important factors that will determine the future prospects of a corporation. It is true that if the management has not changed in many years its quality is already reflected in the record of performance of the corporation. The question is why should we examine management and its current programs in addition to our quantitative analysis of the record of the company as discussed above. The reasons are several.

1. The present management may be dominated by key individuals. They may soon leave the corporation because of retirement, death, or other reasons. The important question is whether second-line or senior executives of comparable quality are available and will take command with equal efficiency.

TABLE 6-15
Profit Margins
(Percent)

	COMPOSITE DATA																				
	425 Indus-trials	Chemical Cos.	Chemical Cos. Excl. duPont	Sulphur Cos.	[6]Air Prod.	Air. Red.	[1]Allied Chem.	Amer. Cyan.	Amer. Enka	Atlas Chem.	Big Three Ind.	Cabot	Celanese	Cheme-tron	Com'l. Solv.	Dexter	Dia-mond	Dow Chem.	du-Pont	FMC Corp.	[7]Free-port Sul.
1969	...	...	...	...	22.3	13.6	16.3	18.6	22.8	11.8	28.3	20.1	22.0	11.1	11.55	18.3	14.5	23.2	27.6	12.0	24.5
1968	15.8	21.3	18.8	46.0	21.9	13.8	15.4	19.6	23.8	11.6	25.9	18.3	21.3	11.8	9.9	17.4	15.8	23.3	29.7	13.6	33.2
1967	15.5	21.0	19.3	37.6	22.0	16.2	18.1	16.8	18.2	11.4	28.4	20.3	19.9	14.5	10.7	15.9	18.7	25.3	26.7	12.0	31.3
1966	16.4	23.5	21.4	32.8	22.0	17.1	20.5	20.3	24.6	21.1	30.5	22.5	21.4	15.5	17.0	16.8	21.2	24.9	30.0	13.6	29.6
1965	16.3	24.9	22.2	27.2	22.6	17.4	20.2	22.1	21.7	12.0	30.8	17.6	23.3	15.2	18.3	20.4	20.4	24.8	32.4	15.7	26.9
1964	15.9	25.1	21.9	25.8	20.9	15.4	21.1	21.7	22.1	11.7	24.6	15.8	23.7	12.8	18.9	18.9	21.2	23.6	32.1	14.4	23.8
1963	15.2	25.1	22.2	24.7	18.7	16.5	22.0	22.0	20.0	9.9	24.1	17.2	25.8	11.6	18.6	16.1	20.1	24.2	32.4	14.8	24.6
1962	15.2	25.1	22.2	28.4	18.1	17.6	21.5	21.5	20.4	10.7	19.7	18.4	24.3	9.1	18.9	16.1	21.9	24.2	32.9	13.8	26.2
1961	14.7	24.0	21.6	29.6	18.9	17.6	20.9	20.9	19.4	13.4	19.2	21.2	22.0	9.5	21.0	...	22.0	23.1	30.2	14.7	28.6
1960	14.7	24.1	22.1	28.4	14.3	21.0	19.5	19.5	10.4	14.1	14.9	22.9	21.1	10.1	20.4	...	24.1	23.3	29.3	14.5	28.5
1959	15.3	26.7	24.0	29.8	10.1	21.6	21.0	21.0	19.0	15.3	...	25.8	25.0	8.9	15.9	...	23.9	28.5	33.0	13.8	30.9

	GAF Corp.	Grace (W.R.)	Her-cules	Int'l. Min.	Int'l. Salt	Mon-santo	Nalco	Natl. Chem.	[5]Nat'l. Distl.	Oak-ite	Olin Corp.	Penn-walt	Products Research & Chem.	Reich-hold	Richard-son	Rohm & Hass	Stauffer	[3] [4]Texas Gulf	Union Carb.	VWR United	Witco Chem.
1969	9.6	8.7	19.4	7.5	25.8	18.3	21.7	...	16.2	20.5	12.2	12.5	16.0	10.5	10.3	21.0	18.2	32.6	20.6	4.1	10.0
1968	10.9	10.9	21.0	11.0	23.7	20.8	22.3	21.0	17.0	19.3	14.1	14.8	19.0	11.1	11.9	22.6	18.7	39.4	19.7	4.2	11.9
1967	10.4	11.2	19.4	12.8	19.9	20.7	20.5	20.5	19.1	18.3	15.2	15.7	17.7	8.7	12.4	21.0	18.9	39.9	20.6	4.0	11.6
1966	[2]29.5	11.9	20.9	17.6	18.9	21.8	20.0	21.6	17.4	18.5	15.0	14.2	20.3	9.8	13.4	23.6	21.8	32.6	24.4	3.8	12.5
1965	14.4	12.1	18.9	15.9	22.1	23.3	19.9	18.6	15.9	15.9	15.4	14.2	16.5	7.4	12.6	25.0	21.6	26.0	26.7	4.2	11.2
1964	13.6	13.4	18.8	14.9	18.4	24.9	20.6	18.8	14.0	13.2	14.4	16.9	13.3	7.8	12.9	27.1	21.4	23.0	25.6	3.6	11.0
1963	12.9	14.2	18.8	12.5	18.8	23.6	21.0	18.8	13.9	11.2	14.1	16.7	14.9	7.1	13.9	26.2	20.5	20.2	26.0	3.9	10.1
1962	14.0	14.4	21.0	12.5	23.0	23.2	20.0	18.3	15.0	...	14.6	17.5	13.7	8.2	13.1	26.5	21.7	28.7	26.9	4.1	9.6
1961	10.2	13.2	21.9	14.2	26.3	23.1	20.3	15.6	16.9	...	14.9	19.1	14.4	4.2	13.5	22.6	21.5	31.1	25.6	...	8.1
1960	12.9	11.4	21.6	14.4	27.6	23.3	18.8	12.2	18.0	...	14.9	19.4	14.1	7.3	8.3	26.9	22.8	30.5	26.2	...	7.4
1959	13.8	12.1	23.3	13.3	28.3	25.4	19.7	...	...	...	16.1	18.5	...	7.4	...	29.5	24.1	30.6	29.3	...	7.7

SOURCE: Chemicals: Basic Analysis, *Industry Surveys*, Standard & Poor's Corporation, July 2, 1970.

[1]Based on sales and operating revenues. [2]After depreciation. [3]Based on gross revenues. [4]Before depreciation and capital stock in all years. [5]Based on net sales after excise taxes. [6]Based on total revenues. [7]Based on gross sales.

*Profit margins are derived by dividing operating income by sales. Operating income is usually the balance left from sales after deducting operating costs, selling, general and administrative expenses, local and state taxes; provision for bad debts and pensions; but before other income and before deducting depreciation charges, debt service charges if any, Federal taxes, and any special revenues.

TABLE 6-16
Net Income
(As a percentage of sales)

COMPOSITE DATA

	425 Indus-trials	Chemical Cos.	Chemical Cos. Excl. duPont	Sulphur Cos.	Mon-santo	3Air Prod.	Air Red.	Nat'l. Chem.	Allied Chem.	Amer. Cyan.	Amer. Enka	1Atlas Chem.	Big Three Ind.	Cabot	Celanese	Cheme-tron	Coml. Solv.	Dexter	Dia-mond	Dow Chem.	du-Pont	FMC Corp.	6Free-port Sul.
1969	...	P6.7	P5.9	P18.8	5.7	6.1	4.2	9.5	5.2	8.3	8.6	4.6	8.3	7.5	6.1	3.8	2.1	6.5	5.7	8.3	9.7	4.8	16.3
1968	6.1	7.2	6.2	22.9	6.2	5.8	4.4	10.1	3.2	8.4	8.2	4.1	8.6	7.6	4.6	4.3	1.4	6.1	6.6	8.2	10.7	5.5	21.3
1967	6.1	7.4	6.6	23.7	6.0	5.9	6.0	10.3	5.6	7.5	5.8	3.9	9.2	6.8	5.3	6.1	4.6	6.2	8.4	9.5	10.1	5.6	18.7
1966	6.6	9.2	8.3	21.6	7.0	6.1	6.8	11.3	7.2	9.9	9.5	5.1	10.2	8.4	6.5	6.9	6.6	6.7	8.4	9.3	12.2	6.2	22.4
1965	6.8	9.9	8.8	18.6	8.4	6.1	6.8	9.7	7.5	10.8	8.1	5.6	9.8	6.1	7.5	6.4	7.4	7.1	7.8	9.2	13.5	6.2	20.3
1964	6.6	10.5	8.4	17.4	8.4	5.6	5.5	9.5	7.8	10.5	7.9	5.1	7.2	4.8	7.8	5.2	7.4	6.0	7.4	8.7	16.9	5.4	19.5
1963	6.2	10.3	7.6	16.4	7.0	5.7	5.5	9.5	7.5	9.3	6.3	3.2	6.3	6.7	8.0	4.4	6.9	7.2	6.7	8.3	18.3	5.3	19.3
1962	5.9	10.3	7.5	19.3	7.4	5.5	5.7	9.1	6.7	9.1	6.2	3.2	5.5	6.7	8.7	3.2	6.1	7.2	6.9	7.8	18.5	5.2	22.4
1961	5.7	10.1	7.2	20.3	7.4	5.4	5.8	8.0	7.3	8.2	5.1	4.5	5.4	8.0	7.2	3.4	7.8	...	7.2	7.2	18.8	5.8	24.4
1960	5.7	10.4	7.9	21.2	7.6	3.9	7.3	6.4	6.7	8.1	0.7	4.2	3.9	9.3	7.5	3.3	8.6	...	8.5	7.9	17.6	5.7	24.9
1959	6.0	11.5	8.7	20.8	8.5	2.9	7.4	...	7.0	9.0	5.2	5.5	...	11.2	8.5	3.1	4.0	...	8.2	10.4	20.0	6.3	27.2

	GAF Corp.	Grace (W.R.)	Her-cules	Int'l. Min.	Int'l. Salt	Nalco	5Nat'l. Distl.	Oak-ite	Olin Corp.	Penn-walt	Products Research & Chem.	Reich-hold	Richard-son	Rohm & Haas	Stauffer	4Texas Gulf	Union Carb.	VWR United	Witco Chem.
1969	2.5	2.0	5.9	0.6	11.9	9.4	5.2	9.2	4.4	4.2	6.3	4.0	3.6	7.5	6.3	20.3	6.4	1.4	4.1
1968	3.7	3.4	7.4	2.6	7.6	9.8	5.8	8.7	5.3	5.6	8.1	4.3	4.4	8.2	6.5	23.1	5.8	1.6	4.7
1967	3.6	3.0	7.3	4.3	8.8	9.1	4.7	8.8	6.0	5.6	8.2	3.3	4.9	7.8	7.2	24.5	6.7	1.7	4.8
1966	5.5	4.5	8.5	8.2	8.1	9.4	4.5	9.1	5.4	5.7	9.0	4.3	4.9	9.6	8.8	21.2	9.3	1.6	4.7
1965	6.3	4.4	7.5	7.7	9.0	9.3	3.8	7.4	5.3	5.9	6.6	2.9	4.5	10.4	9.1	18.3	11.0	1.8	4.7
1964	5.6	4.9	7.1	7.0	9.0	8.6	5.4	6.0	5.1	6.4	5.8	3.1	3.9	10.5	8.6	16.4	10.1	1.5	4.4
1963	4.6	4.8	6.6	5.6	7.1	7.9	4.8	5.2	4.7	5.9	5.0	2.0	3.8	9.6	7.8	15.0	9.6	1.5	3.8
1962	5.1	3.8	6.9	5.4	9.0	9.0	3.1	4.8	4.7	5.8	4.9	2.3	3.9	9.3	8.1	20.6	9.8	1.6	3.2
1961	4.5	3.5	7.4	6.0	13.0	9.3	7.4	4.5	4.6	5.8	6.6	3.4	3.8	8.8	7.7	21.4	9.1	1.6	3.1
1960	3.2	2.9	8.3	6.2	12.2	8.7	5.6	5.5	5.0	5.4	6.6	0.2	2.7	9.8	9.0	23.3	10.2	...	3.2
1959	4.4	2.9	8.3	5.5	13.6	8.8	8.0	4.9	5.3	5.2	6.8	3.8	...	10.7	9.7	21.0	11.2	...	3.2

SOURCE: Chemicals: Basic Analysis, *Industry Surveys*, Standard & Poor's Corporation, July 2, 1970.
1Based on sales and operating revenues. 2Adjusted. 3Based on total revenues. 4Based on gross revenues; net is after depletion after 1959. 5Based on net sales, less excise taxes. 6Based on gross sales. P—Preliminary.

TABLE 6-17
Net Income
(1957-59 = 100)

	Air Prod.	Air Red.	Allied Chem.	Amer. Cyan.	Amer. Enka	Atlas Chem.	Big Three Ind.	Cabot	Celanese	Cheme-tron	Com'l. Solv.	Dexter	Dia-mond	Dow Chem.	du-Pont	FMC Corp.	Free port Sul.	GAF Corp.	Grace (W.R.)
1969	851	136	160	181	739	180	795	171	413	208	114	237	370	231	92	381	211	251	251
1968	758	131	96	174	657	151	741	155	313	189	79	185	418	211	96	426	299	350	433
1967	679	166	164	143	359	127	600	124	321	264	231	158	420	203	81	344	240	313	339
1966	616	194	210	192	642	159	662	149	361	300	329	165	425	189	101	396	238	367	431
1965	462	172	198	189	522	152	559	97	351	261	353	148	198	168	106	327	160	250	347
1964	391	126	190	166	459	126	327	68	297	163	361	98	159	146	122	252	114	177	286
1963	381	112	170	135	313	80	221	86	243	125	313	112	129	125	123	185	95	133	239
1962	359	110	136	121	283	75	177	83	149	89	259	100	132	113	93	148	94	151	162
1961	239	95	145	100	195	100	159	89	116	92	288	...	129	93	108	133	95	86	135
1960	148	110	121	95	23	102	100	108	108	98	253	...	160	100	99	119	98	118	116
1959	88	100	118	106	191	107	...	123	123	80	149	...	137	131	109	116	107	116	118
Yr.	1.60	14.89	42.55	49.15	2.99	3.67	0.66	8.20	18.47	5.37	1.91	[6] 1.37	8.28	64.43	385.5	17.66	13.51	6.06	13.99
ends:	Sept.	Dec.	Dec.	Dec.	Dec.	Dec.	Dec.	Sept.	Dec.	Dec.	Dec.	Dec.	Dec.	Dec.	Dec.	Dec.	Dec.	Dec.	Dec.

Average net income in 1957-59 base period, in millions of dollars; months indicate yr. ends:

	Her-cules	Int'l. Min.	Int'l. Salt	Mon-santo	Nelco	Nat'l. Chem.	Nat'l. Distl.	Oak-ite	Olin Corp.	Penn-walt	Products Research & Chem.	Reich-hold	Richard-son	Rohm & Hass	Stauffer	Texas Gulf	Union Carb.	VWR United	Witco Chem.
1969	223	49	159	224	424	1,240	157	355	182	455	700	215	601	189	178	416	130	160	478
1968	271	205	150	236	374	1,067	144	324	207	602	908	220	692	196	175	484	109	180	520
1967	237	309	97	202	296	962	183	304	195	347	760	125	636	166	173	421	119	171	467
1966	271	386	75	230	281	822	176	300	172	335	348	170	617	200	190	190	167	159	455
1965	202	319	84	251	230	540	135	218	179	321	236	105	421	203	168	123	158	152	401
1964	193	247	58	235	185	416	117	168	149	244	180	106	219	189	134	78	132	119	295
1963	169	161	57	170	134	324	98	138	133	213	160	65	218	154	113	63	112	114	228
1962	159	140	69	160	140	253	105	127	123	193	168	74	200	137	108	82	111	111	170
1961	142	128	86	140	136	173	100	114	116	146	167	7	167	108	98	85	99	100	154
1960	138	120	96	139	120	100	105	139	138	131	116	99	100	120	111	93	110	...	148
1959	119	97	100	153	117	...	114	121	135	121	116	114	...	130	125	90	120	...	146
Yr.	19.68	6.38	4.23	48.91	3.53	30.45	23.16	0.71	27.73	3.78	70.25	3.37	80.75	17.77	17.78	14.76	14.34	[9] 1.77	2.04
ends:	Dec.	June	[2] June	Dec.	Dec.	[1] Apr.	Dec.	Dec.	Dec.	Dec.	Sept.	Dec.	Dec.	Dec.	Dec.	Dec.	Dec.	[1] Feb.	Dec.

Average net income in 1957-59 base period, in millions of dollars; months indicate yr. ends:

DEFINITION: Net income is simply the net profit after all charges as reported by the company.
SOURCE: Chemicals: Basic Analysis, *Industry Surveys*, Standard & Poor's Corporation July 2, 1970.

[1] Of the following calendar year. [2] Yr. end. Dec. 30 in 1960 & pr. yrs. [3] 1960 = 100. [4] Yrs. end. Apr. 30 in 1965 & Pr. yrs. [5] Yrs. end. May 31 of foll. cal. yr. in 1960 & pr. years. [6] 1962 = 100. [7] 1958-60 = 100. [8] 1960 = 100. [9] 1961 = 100.

TABLE 6-18

Comparison of Earnings Growth Between Three Chemical Firms

Year	Earnings Per Share			Earnings Per Share 1958-60 = 100			Percent Growth of Earning over Previous Year		
	Allied Chem.	American Cyanamid	W. R. Grace	Allied Chem.	American Cyanamid	W. R. Grace	Allied Chem.	American Cyanamid	W.R. Grace
1969	2.44	2.02	1.58	108	181	116	67	5	-42
1968	1.46	1.93	2.76	64	173	203	-41	21	9
1967	2.50	1.59	2.54	110	142	187	-23	-25	-23
1966	3.26	2.13	3.32	144	190	244	4	1	19
1965	3.14	2.11	2.80	138	188	205	2	13	3
1964	3.08	1.86	2.72	136	166	200	11	23	18
1963	2.77	1.51	2.30	122	135	169	26	8	16
1962	2.19	1.39	1.97	97	124	145	- 6	21	9
1961	2.33	1.15	1.81	103	103	133	- 9	5	17
1960	2.57	1.10	1.55	114	98	114	2	-10	- 2
1959	2.51	1.23	1.58	110	110	116	46	19	65
1958	1.72	1.03	.96	76	92	71			

2. The present management may remain in place for some time. However, there may be a new change in business philosophy toward such important questions as diversification, acquisition, foreign market, or production outside of the country.

3. Some corporations may have a brilliant record, and therefore their stocks are selling at high price-earnings ratios. An independent examination of the quality of management through interviews and plant visits could confirm or contradict the market implication that the good record achieved will be likely repeated in the future.

4. If the mangement is relatively new, the statistical record of the corporation is a poor indication of the future prospects of the firm. This constitutes an added reason why the background and record of the new management should be carefully evaluated. The evaluation of the quality and efficiency of the management of a firm should cover several aspects:
   (a) Background of the management team
   (b) Objectives, organization, and planning of the firm
   (c) Management and the past record of the firm
   (d) Current and prospective programs of the firm

Background of the Management Team

The first question is to identify the people who make the key decisions of the firm. In some corporations this may be a one-man show. The person may be the president or the board chairman. In other corporations the management team may include the president, the board chairman, and a few senior vice-presidents. After identifying the key people who represent the top management, the analyst should proceed to investigate their background, which should include age, education, training, experience, and years of service, and jobs held in this corporation.

Objectives, Organization, and Planning of the Firm

A better managed corporation should reflect itself in its objectives, organization, and the planning process. The analyst should inquire whether the corporation has clearly stated corporate objectives that may be expressed in the form of market share, annual rate of growth of earnings, or rate of return on common equity. In respect to organization, the analyst should ask what philosophy of organization (centralized or decentralized) does the firm adopt? Are line and staff functions well organized? How often does the board of directors meet? Who are on the board? How many people are reporting to the chief executive? Is the chief executive overburdened by administrative details of routine operations? Who heads the planning unit? What is the planning process?

Management and the Past Record of the Firm

The analyst should first find out what have been the rates of growth of sales, per-share earnings, and the rates of return on common equity earned by the corporation in the past five to ten years. Then he should find out whether the record was better, worse, or just comparable with the industry average. Next, he should inquire whether the better or poorer record of the firm compared to industry average can be largely attributable to the present management.

Current and Prospective Programs of the Firm

The analyst should be particularly interested in inquiring about the programs which are currently in progress and the programs the management is contemplating to put into effect in the near future. A good management should be always forward-looking and well prepared for any changes on the horizon. Interesting and well-thought-out current and prospective programs are the earmarks of a good and efficient management.

OUTLOOK OF SALES AND PROFITS

The analysis of the past record of a corporation, its comparison to industry average and competitors, and the evaluation of the quality of management are all preliminary steps to the most important part of a company analysis—namely, the evaluation and forecast of prospective profitability. Except possibly in the case of public utilities, a forecast of earnings beyond five years is subject to so many uncertainties that even corporate management itself rarely attempts it. As a general rule the analyst is usually called upon to make estimates of sales and earnings (1) in the current year or next twelve months, and (2) for three to five years.

Estimates of Sales and Profits in the Year Ahead

Stock prices are often found to be importantly affected by the level of earnings in the year ahead. Therefore, to the extent that earnings forecast for the next year is accurate, the analyst has important advantage over others.

One method to estimate the earnings for next year is through the projection of next year's income statement. First, on basis of product mix, industry outlook, and general business outlook, a sales forecast is made. Then a projection on basis of past relationships to sales is made for operating and nonoperating expenses. Finally, deduction is made for fixed charges and income taxes. The resultant figure is the amount of net earnings for next year. When divided by number of shares outstanding, the per-share earnings are obtained.

Alternatively, after the sales forecast for next year is made, the analyst then decides on appropriate rates for operating profit and net profit margins to be applied to sales to get earnings for next year.

Whichever method is used by the analyst, he can usually enlist the help of the corporation to supply him with information on the operations of next year. Often the analyst is supplied with management's own estimates of sales and profits for next year. Statistical advisory services such as Standard & Poor's, Value Line, and Moody's forecast year-ahead earnings for most issues listed on the New York Stock Exchange. A reference to these estimates should also be helpful.

Estimates of Sales and Profits in Three to Five Years

The estimate of sales and profits in three to five years is subject to more error than the estimate for the current year or the next twelve months ahead. Few managements formally forecast sales and profits in three to five years. The statistical investment advisory agencies do not try it either. However, the earning power of a corporation in three to five years will have an important bearing on investment decisions of long-term investors.

As in the case of the estimate of earnings for the year ahead, one way to estimate earnings in three to five years is through projection of income statement. Alternatively, he can first forecast sales in three to five years and then select appropriate operating and net profit margins to be applied to sales to get gross and net earnings.

Another method is through the utilization of the rate of return on total capital and on common equity. The analyst first determines the historical norm for rates of return on total capital and on common equity. Then he forecasts the level of total capital and common equity in three to five years. Last, he chooses "appropriate" rates of return on total capital and on common equity to be applied to the respective levels of total capital and common equity. Since the rate of return on common equity is the product of net profit margin (net profit/sales) and turnover of capital (sales/common equity), the analyst should first examine the levels of these two elements in the past before he decides on the rate of return on common equity in the future period.

Irrespective of the method of forecast the analyst uses, the task of estimating earnings in three to five years is a difficult one. In order to obtain good results the analyst must make a thorough analysis, both financial and technological, of the operation of the company and have a good grasp of the problems and opportunities of the industry of which the company is a part.

Success in investment depends in no small degree on the correct estimate of the profitability of a firm both in the near term and in a longer term of three to five years hence.

APPENDIX A

Graphic Presentation of Data

Statistical data are usually presented in tables and graphs or charts. A chart often enables the reader to generally visualize the results at a glance. However, data in tabular form are necessary for exact statistical analysis.

The type of chart to be employed in any case depends primarily on the purpose of the chart. If the purpose is to emphasize changes in absolute units between different points of time, a conventional chart with arithmetic scales for both the Y and X axes should be used. In investment analysis, however, we are more often interested in relative change or the rates of change, rather than absolute change in magnitude. For this purpose, a special chart is employed in which the vertical scale Y is ruled so that *equal space represents equal percentage changes* rather than equal amounts of change. The horizontal scale X on the other hand is ruled arithmetically as in a conventional chart of arithmetic scale.

Figure 6-1 is a ratio chart drawn on a semilogarithmic paper. As shown in the vertical Y scale, the distance from 1 to 10 is the same as the distance between 100 to 1,000. The same distance represents that in both cases the larger number is ten times greater than the smaller number.

In order to aid in the interpretation of the meaning of different types of curves on a ratio chart, several pairs of hypothetical curves are drawn in Figure 6-1, with brief notations on the meaning of each curve. In short, a straight line in a ratio chart represents change at a constant rate. The steeper the slope of the line the greater the rate of change. If two lines are parallel to each other, the rate of change for each is the same. For a curve, the curvature indicates whether the rate of change is accelerating or decelerating.

In a ratio chart drawn on semilogarithmic paper, the growth rates of a time series can be approximated by measuring roughly the slope of the curve of the

Figure 6-1

Meaning of Curve Shapes on Ratio Chart

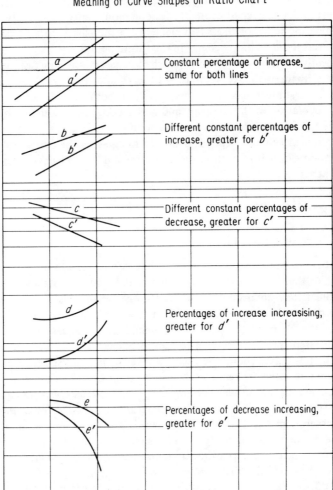

plotted time series. In Figure 6-2 the data of our previous example on domestic monthly demand for gasoline during 1940-58 are plotted on a semilogarithmic paper. In addition we draw several lines of constant growth rates from the same origin, the starting point of the plotted curve. By reference to these lines, the user of the chart can readily determine the approximate rate of growth of the plotted time series between any two years. For example, between 1943 and 1951 the demand for gasoline grew relatively fast at about 9 percent. For the whole period from 1940 to 1958, the annual growth rate was somewhere between 5 and 6 percent.

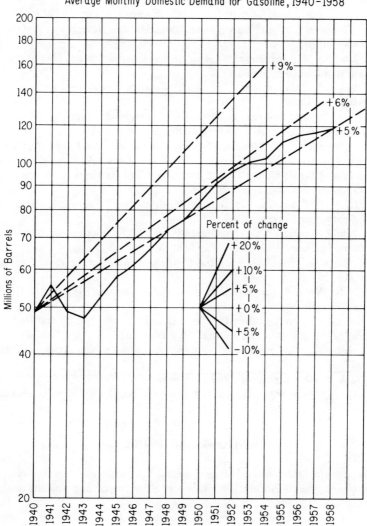

Figure 6-2

Average Monthly Domestic Demand for Gasoline, 1940–1958

SUGGESTED READINGS

Babcock, Guilford C., "The Concept of Sustainable Growth," *Financial Analysts Journal*, May-June 1970.

Bennett, William M., "Capital Turnover vs. Profit Margins," *Financial Analysts Journal*, March-April 1966.

Briloff, Abraham J., "The Accounting Profession at the Hump of the Decades," *Financial Analysts Journal*, May-June 1970.

Cohen, J. B., and E. E. Zinbarg, *Investment Analysis and Portfolio Management*, Homewood, Ill.: Richard D. Irwin, Inc., 1967.

Forbes Twentieth Annual Report on American Industry, Jan. 1, 1968.

Graham, Benjamin, et al., *Security Analysis*, 4th ed. New York: McGraw-Hill Book Company, 1962.

Hayes, Douglas A., *Investments: Analysis and Management*, New York: The Macmillan Company, 1966.

Hill, William P., "Management Appraisal," *Financial Analysts Journal*, September-October 1966.

Kendrick, J. W., and D. Creamer, *Measuring Company Productivity*, Washington, D.C.: National Industrial Conference Board, Inc., 1965.

Murphy, Joseph E., Jr., "Relative Growth of Earnings Per Share—Past and Future," *Financial Analysts Journal*, November-December 1966; "Return on Equity Capital, Dividend Payout and Growth of Earnings Per Share," *Financial Analysts Journal*, May-June 1967.

Myers, John H., "More on Depreciation Manipulation," *Financial Analysts Journal*, September-October 1969.

Parker, James E., "New Rules for Determining EPS," *Financial Analysts Journal*, January-February 1970.

Penrose, Edith T., *The Theory of the Growth of the Firm*, Oxford: Basil Blackwell, 1959.

Plum, Lester V., (ed.), *Investing in American Industries*, New York: Harper & Row, Publishers, 1960.

Powers, James T., "Accounting Principles Board Opinion No. 15 and Its Implications," *Financial Analysts Journal*, May-June 1970.

Shubin, John A., *Managerial and Industrial Economies*, New York: The Ronald Press Company, 1961.

Standard & Poor's Corporation, *Industry Survey*.

Stone, David, "Input-Output and the Multi-Product Firm," *Financial Analysts Journal*, July-August 1969.

QUESTIONS AND PROBLEMS

1. How important do you consider the factor of management in the evaluation of an enterprise for investment purposes? How do you appraise the quality of management?
2. How do we go about determining the competitive position of a company within an industry?
3. Compute earnings growth rates of Magnavox common in the past ten years based on (a) average rate of return on equity, (b) rate of return on new investments, and (c) compound-interest-rate method. What growth rate of earnings do you think it will likely achieve in the next few years?
4. Select a company and make an analysis of its record in the past ten years including growth of sales and earnings, stability of profit margin, turnover of capital, rate of return, and degree of leverage.
5. Compare General Motors, Ford, and Chrysler, and indicate which common stock of these three companies is a better buy at current market price.

6. Why are earnings per share of different corporations often not strictly comparable?
7. What procedure will you use in estimating earnings per share of a corporation in the next year or two?
8. As a prospective investor in the stocks of a corporation, which ratios do you consider important?

7. Valuation of the "General Market"

THE "GENERAL MARKET"

The general level of stock prices is most frequently measured by two well-known indexes. They are (1) The Dow Jones Industrial Average, and (2) the Standard & Poor's index of "425" Industrial Common Stocks.

DJIA

The Dow Jones Industrial Average consists of 30 common stocks of the most impressive names of corporations in the United States.[1] The present average is worked back to 1914. The average is probably more used than the S&P's 425 among both professionals and laymen alike. The DJIA is an arithmetic index. The earnings, dividends, prices, and P/E ratios reported of the index represent what a share of the average company in the index has achieved or has been appraised in the stock market.

S&P's "425"

The Standard & Poor's 425 is an index of 425 industrial common stocks. Its coverage is much broader than the DJIA, and is therefore more representative of the general market. However, the index is weighed by the value of shares outstanding of each corporation in the index. It thus represents more of the bigger companies than the average company in the index.

---

[1] The 30 companies are Allied Chemical, Alcoa, American Can, American Telephone, American Tobacco, Anaconda, Bethlehem Steel, Chrysler, Du Pont, Eastman Kodak, General Electric, General Foods, General Motors, Goodyear, International Harvester, International Nickel, International Paper, Johns-Manville, Owens-Illinois, Procter & Gamble, Sears Roebuck, Standard Oil of California, Standard Oil of New Jersey, Swift & Co., Texaco, Union Carbide, United Aircraft, U.S. Steel, Westinghouse Electric, and Woolworth.

IMPORTANCE OF THE VALUATION OF THE "GENERAL MARKET"

The purposes of the valuation of the general market are basically twofold:

1. To determine if the general level of security prices is relatively high or low in terms of past and prospective earnings, so that the investor can decide whether he or the institution should pursue a relatively aggressive, neutral, or defensive investment policy.
2. To take the valuation of the general market as a bench mark against which to measure the relative attractiveness of individual stocks and industry groups. For example, a certain stock or industry group has been selling in the past at about 90 percent of P/E of DJIA; now it is selling at only, say, 75 percent of the P/E of DJIA. Other things being equal, this may mean the stock or stock group is underpriced relative to the general market, and therefore deserves further investigation.

THEORIES OF VALUATION OF COMMON STOCK

Though there have been numerous theories advanced in the past for the explanation of valuation of common stocks, analytically they come under two basic approaches:[2] (1) the theory of present-worth approach, and (2) the capitalization approach.

The Theory of Present Worth

The theory of present worth expresses a truism. That is, the present worth of a security, aside from market price, is equal to the future stream of cash income discounted at appropriate rates. Mathematically, it can be expressed by the formula

$$V = \frac{C_1}{1+i} + \frac{C_2}{(1+i)^2} + \frac{C_3}{(1+i)^3} \cdots \frac{C_n}{(1+i)^n}$$

where V is the present worth, C_1 the cash income in period 1, i the discount rate or rates deemed appropriate by investor, and n the life of the investment. C_n includes not only dividend but also the liquidating proceeds from a stock.

The application of this theory to the valuation of a specific stock or stock index entails, however, quantification of several factors: (a) earnings growth rates, (b) growth durations, (c) dividend payout ratios, (d) discount rates, and (e) P/E ratio at time of sale of stock. The theory, though conceptually sound, requires considerable estimation in its practical application.

[2] Stanley, S.C. Huang, *Corporate Earning Power & Valuation of Common Stocks* Larchmont, N.Y.: Investors Intelligence, Inc., 1968.

The Capitalization Approach

The traditional standard approach to the valuation of common stock is some form of the capitalization approach. Judging from current practice and literature, the approach seems to continue to hold its preeminent position today.

The bases of capitalization are either one or a combination of several value-determining factors of common stocks—book value, dividend, earnings, or cash flow.[3] Since all the value-determining factors are subject to wide fluctuation in the short run because of the play of some chance factors, a norm or some kind of average over a time span is usually sought.

The rate of capitalization or its reciprocal—the multiplier—should theoretically bear some relationship to interest rates on savings deposits and yields on government and corporate securities.[4] However, the relationship has not been a consistent and steady one, especially since 1930.[5] The rate of capitalization varies widely among stocks and stock groups at a given time because of (1) differences in quality of the stock and earnings expectation, and (2) shift of investors' favoritism. The rate of capitalization also varies substantially for the same stock over a period of time for any combination of several causes: (1) change in overall attitudes of investors toward common stocks, their profitability and safety, (2) change in corporate performance, and (3) change of expectation of the stock, the general market, and the economy. It can be readily seen that the seeking of a norm in capitalization rate rests on even less tangible ground than in the case of capitalization base.

Though the capitalization approach is seemingly proceeding on inexact and opinionated bases, it is nevertheless grounded on the realization that few of us can foresee very far, and thus a historical perspective should be emphasized.

Capitalize Earnings

Among the several methods of capitalization approach, the most widely used is the capitalization of earnings. The reason for the popularity of this method is due not so much to theoretical considerations as to its practical ease and convenience, and the avoidance of the need to forecast the dividend payout ratio.

Under this method, it is argued that earnings, whether distributed as dividends or retained in the business for further investment, belong to the owner and represent his annual gross total return. As long as management is presumed to be acting in the best interests of the stockholders and selecting an appropriate

[3] Cash flow is equivalent to earnings after taxes plus noncash charges such as depreciation and depletion allowances.

[4] If a stock earns $1 per share, and the rate of capitalization is 10 percent, then the stock is worth $10. Alternatively, we can say the multiplier is 10.

[5] Nicholas Molodovsky, "The Many Aspects of Yields," *Financial Analysts Journal*, March-April 1962. Reprinted in E. Bruce Fredrikson (ed.), *Frontier of Investment Analysis*, rev. ed. (Scranton, Pa.: Intext Educational Publishers, 1971).

dividend policy, the question of how a given return is split between cash dividend and retained earnings (potential capital gains) is relatively insignificant. Hence the investor needs only to concentrate on the total amount of after-tax earnings.[6]

In the estimate of earnings base, as noted before, a norm or some kind of average is usually sought. Some look back on demonstrable or recorded earning power. Others lean heavily on the current and immediately prospective earning power. Still others look far into the future. In terms of historical development, the pendulum seems to swing from emphasis on record in the past to current thinking—emphasis on prospective earnings.

The assignment of a capitalization rate or multiplier has a pattern somewhat similar to the estimate of earnings base. Some would simply take the historical norm of the multiplier of the stock. Others would emphasize the current multiplier, or multipliers in the recent past. Still others are looking for upgrading in the multiplier.

What has been said above about the estimate of earnings base and capitalization rate are of course rough generalizations. The same can probably be said in terms of different categories of stocks, different growth prospects, rather than in terms of people—investors or analysts—of different inclinations. In other words, the same investor or analyst is conceivably following different patterns, emphasizing relatively more the past, current, or future, when he deals with different categories of stocks.

EARNINGS, QUARTERLY PRICE INDEXES, PRICE-EARNINGS RATIOS OF DJIA, 1936-70

The price index of DJIA at the end of each quarter since 1936, its earnings of preceding twelve months, and price-earnings ratios at end of each quarter during 1936-70 are shown in Table 7-1. Figure 7-1 shows year-end price of DJIA with annual earnings since 1936. Figure 7-2 shows annual range of P/E (quarterly price index to preceding 12 months' earnings) of DJIA during 1936-70. Examination of the record shows distinguishing patterns for several subperiods during the span 1936-70. The subperiods are: (1) 1936-44, (2) 1945-49, (3) 1950-61, and (4) 1962-70.

1936-44

1. Earnings during the period, except the recession year 1938, fluctuated sidewise.

---

[6] Franco-Modigliani and Merton H. Miller, "The Cost of Capital, Corporation Finance and the Theory of Investment," *American Economic Review*, June 1958; "The Cost of Capital and the Theory of Investment: Comments and Replies," *American Economic Review*, September 1959.

TABLE 7-1
Price, Earnings, and Price-Earnings Ratios, DJIA, 1936–70

Year	End of Quarter	DJIA Index	Preceding 12-Months Earnings	Price/ Earnings Ratio	Year	End of Quarter	DJIA Index	Preceding 12-Months Earnings	Price Earnings Ratio
1936	1	156.3	7.06	22.1	1949	1	177.1	23.79	7.4
	2	157.7	8.08	19.5		2	167.4	23.95	7.0
	3	167.8	9.26	18.1		3	182.5	24.66	7.4
	4	179.9	10.07	17.9		4	200.1	23.54	8.5
1937	1	186.4	11.12	16.8	1950	1	206.1	23.20	8.9
	2	169.3	11.97	14.1		2	209.1	24.99	8.4
	3	154.6	12.26	12.6		3	226.4	27.15	8.3
	4	120.9	11.49	10.5		4	235.4	30.70	7.7
1938	1	99.0	9.81	10.1	1951	1	247.9	32.40	7.7
	2	133.9	7.74	17.3		2	242.6	31.83	7.6
	3	141.5	6.13	23.1		3	271.2	29.02	9.3
	4	154.8	6.01	25.8		4	269.2	26.59	10.1
1939	1	131.8	6.49	20.3	1952	1	269.5	25.11	10.7
	2	130.6	7.17	18.2		2	274.4	24.06	11.4
	3	152.5	7.94	19.2		3	270.6	24.37	11.1
	4	150.2	9.11	16.5		4	291.9	24.78	11.8
1940	1	148.0	10.13	14.6	1953	1	279.9	25.78	10.9
	2	121.9	10.87	11.2		2	268.3	26.93	10.0
	3	132.6	11.15	11.9		3	264.0	27.63	9.6
	4	131.1	10.92	12.0		4	280.9	27.23	10.3
1941	1	122.7	11.05	11.1	1954	1	303.5	27.20	11.2
	2	123.1	11.16	11.0		2	333.5	27.52	12.1
	3	126.8	11.66	10.9		3	360.5	27.00	13.4
	4	111.0	11.64	9.5		4	404.4	28.18	14.4
1942	1	99.5	10.87	9.2	1955	1	409.7	29.65	13.8
	2	103.3	9.96	10.4		2	451.4	32.11	14.1
	3	109.1	9.21	11.8		3	466.6	34.41	13.6
	4	119.4	9.22	13.0		4	488.4	35.78	13.7
1943	1	136.5	9.36	14.6	1956	1	511.8	36.02	14.2
	2	143.4	9.76	14.7		2	492.8	35.51	13.9
	3	140.1	9.77	14.3		3	475.3	33.65	14.1
	4	135.9	9.74	14.0		4	499.5	33.34	15.0
1944	1	138.8	9.86	14.1	1957	1	474.8	34.30	13.8
	2	148.4	9.93	14.9		2	503.3	34.82	14.4
	3	146.7	10.08	14.6		3	456.3	36.70	12.4
	4	1152.3	10.07	15.1		4	435.7	36.08	12.1
1945	1	154.4	10.37	14.9	1958	1	446.8	32.56	13.7
	2	165.3	10.70	15.4		2	478.2	29.41	16.3
	3	181.7	10.67	17.0		3	532.1	27.97	19.0
	4	192.9	10.56	18.3		4	583.7	27.94	20.9
1946	1	199.8	9.76	20.5	1959	1	601.7	31.04	19.4
	2	205.6	10.24	20.1		2	643.6	35.71	18.0
	3	172.4	11.56	14.9		3	631.7	35.70	17.7
	4	177.2	13.63	13.0		4	679.4	34.31	19.8
1947	1	177.2	16.62	10.7	1960	1	610.6	33.82	18.2
	2	177.3	18.10	9.8		2	640.6	31.26	20.5
	3	177.5	18.66	9.5		3	580.1	31.64	18.3
	4	181.2	18.80	9.6		4	615.9	32.21	19.1
1948	1	177.2	19.01	9.3	1961	1	676.6	29.53	22.9
	2	189.5	19.60	9.7		2	684.0	29.29	23.4
	3	178.3	20.94	8.5		3	701.2	29.03	24.2
	4	177.3	23.07	7.7		4	731.1	31.91	22.9

TABLE 7-1 (*Continued*)

Year	End of Quarter	DJIA Index	Preceding 12-Months Earnings	Price Earnings Ratio	Year	End of Quarter	DJIA Index	Preceding 12-Months Earnings	Price Earnings Ratio
1962	1	707.0	34.11	20.7	1967	1	866.0	56.67	15.3
	2	561.3	34.74	16.2		2	860.3	54.27	15.8
	3	579.0	35.52	16.3		3	926.7	52.73	17.6
	4	652.1	36.43	17.9		4	905.1	53.87	16.8
1963	1	682.5	37.35	18.3	1968	1	840.7	53.98	15.6
	2	706.7	38.71	18.3		2	897.8	55.71	16.1
	3	732.8	40.18	18.2		3	935.8	57.05	16.4
	4	763.0	41.21	18.5		4	943.8	57.89	16.3
1964	1	813.3	42.60	19.1	1969	1	935.5	59.34	15.8
	2	831.5	44.46	18.7		2	873.2	59.47	14.7
	3	875.4	45.88	19.1		3	813.1	59.60	13.6
	4	874.1	46.43	18.8		4	800.4	57.02	14.0
1965	1	889.1	48.55	18.3	1970	1	785.6	54.07	14.5
	2	868.0	50.84	17.1		2	683.5	53.18	12.8
	3	930.6	52.74	17.6		3	760.7	51.83	14.7
	4	969.3	53.67	18.1		4	838.9	50.99 E	16.4E
1966	1	924.8	55.05	16.8					
	2	870.1	56.23	15.5					
	3	774.2	57.36	13.5					
	4	785.7	57.68	13.6					

EEstimated.

2. The price index of DJIA showed a downward trend until 1941, and then moved up steadily during 1943-44.

3. Except the recession year 1938, the annual range of P/E, like the price index, declined gradually until 1941 and then moved up steadily during 1942-44. The average P/E during the period was about 14.

4. War and economic condition were the two governing factors during the period. Before 1942, the recession of 1937-38 and uncertainty of the outcome of war dominated the scene, pushing price and P/E downward. From 1942 onward confidence in victory of war and booming war economy raised both price and P/E.

1945-49

1. Earnings during this early postwar period increased sharply, with the price level of the average practically unaffected.

2. As a consequence the P/E ratio moved down continuously, reaching a low of 7 in 1949.

3. The opposite movement of earnings and P/E was the most important feature of this period. Fear of postwar recession, surprise of cold war, and the general view that corporate profits were inflated due to low depreciation charges were considered by many the main factors contributing to the diverging trends of earnings and P/E ratios.

Figure 7-1

Annual Earnings and Price Index at Year End, DJIA, 1936-70

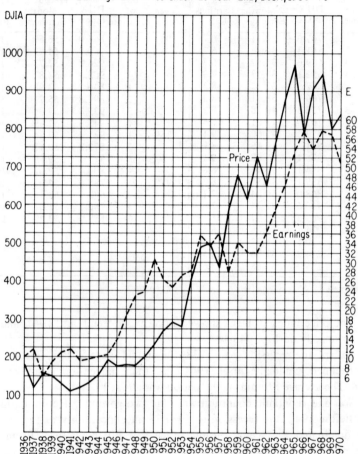

1950-61

1. Earnings during the period were only slightly increased.

2. Both price and P/E showed a distinct upward trend, parallel to each other. The mean P/E in 1950 was 8, and in 1961 it reached a high of 24, tripled in eleven years.

1962-70

1. Earnings resumed its upward trend, but began to level off after 1966, dropping sharply in 1970.

2. Price index had a similar pattern as earnings, rising at first during 1962-65 and then moving downward and sidewise.

3. P/E ratio had a downward adjustment during the period.

Figure 7-2

Annual Range of P/E (Price to preceding 12 months' earnings), DJIA, 1936-70

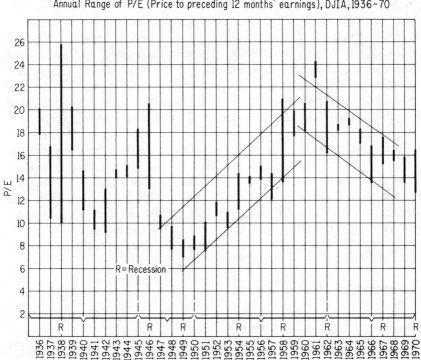

VALUATION OF DJIA ON BASIS OF EARNINGS RECORD

The Concept of Price-Earnings Ratio

The most widely used concept in the stock market, now and in the past— and very likely also in the future—is the price-earnings ratio. The P/E ratio relates conventionally the price of a stock to the earnings per share earned during the past year, or earnings anticipated for the current year.

There are good reasons why this ratio is so widely and persistently used by practically all concerned with investment in stocks. First, the ratio indicates an elementary point that the price of a stock should be expressed in terms of earnings, whether past, current, or prospective, because it is the earning power upon which the price of a stock is predicated. Second, while the ratio is simple and readily understandable, it is very useful to compare (1) one stock against another, and (2) one stock or stock average against itself over a period of time in terms of the same standard—that is, the number of current dollars paid by investors for a dollar of earnings. Third, a comparison of the level, variation, and trend of P/E of a stock over a period of time can provide some ideas as to the level of multiplier (or its reciprocal, the capitalization rate) that one should as- to a stock for its valuation.

However, the concept is not without deficiencies, and investors should be aware of them. The P/E ratio is a quotient of two factors, the price of a stock and its earnings per share. Earnings for a given year can vary substantially from the past because of the influence of factors like cyclical variation of general business, nonrecurrent items, changes in government regulation on depreciation and tax rates, and changes in accounting practice of the firm, while the basic earning power of the corporation is by no means really changed. The numerator —price—fluctuates even more widely and quickly because of influence from changes in investors' enthusiasm as well as changes in reported or current earnings. Consequently the P/E ratio can be quite erratic over a period of time.

In normal times when earnings are growing, the P/E ratio measures investors' enthusiasm about a stock or growth potential expected of it. However, in times of recession the P/E ratio could also go up for a different reason. The earnings of a cyclical stock in time of recession could drop much faster than its price, thereby raising its P/E ratio, which is of course different in meaning from an increase in P/E under conditions of earning improvements. It is important that the investor distinguish and interpret correctly the two types of increase in price-earnings ratio.

Range of P/E of DJIA, 1936-70

The annual range of P/E (price to preceding 12 months' earnings at end of each quarter) of Dow Jones Industrial Average during 1936-67 was shown in Figure 7-2. Analysis of the pattern of the chart reveals several interesting characteristics as follows:

1. As mentioned above, in time of recession the P/E ratio can rise sharply such as in years of 1938, 1946, 1958, and 1962.
2. Ignoring the recession year 1938, the P/E ratio varied between 10 and 20 from 1936 to 1946. The mean P/E was about 14.
3. There was a distinct upward trend of P/E during the period 1947 to 1961. The low was down to 7 in 1949, and the high of 24 was established in 1961.
4. There was a downward adjustment in P/E during the period 1962-70. The mean P/E during this period was 16.6.

VALUATION OF DJIA ON BASIS OF PRICE-ACTUAL EARNINGS RATIOS

Valuation of DJIA on basis of price-actual earnings ratios consists of these steps:

1. To find out the actual earnings of the DJIA in the previous 12 months.
2. To select a range of P/E multiplier deemed "reasonable" for the index under the present circumstances.

3. Multiplication of actual 12 months' earnings by the selected range of multiplier will yield a range of valuation for the DJIA.

Suppose at the beginning of 1970 an investor desired a valuation of DJIA. He found that the actual earnings of DJIA in the previous 12 months were $57.02. He then selected a range of 13 to 15 as the "appropriate" P/E for DJIA. The resultant range of valuation will be 855.3 (57.02 × 15) at the upper limit and 741.3 (57.02 × 13) at the lower limit.

The critical question under this method is therefore the selection of an "appropriate" range of P/E multiplier to be applied to the actual earnings of DJIA. There is no mechanical rule that can be suggested to help the investor in his choice of "appropriate" range of P/E for DJIA. However, a historical perspective is definitely helpful. As mentioned before, the mean P/E was about 14 from 1936 to 1946. After a prolonged uplifting in the postwar period, the mean P/E in the eight years from 1962 to 1970 was 16.6. Besides historical perspective, some indications can be derived also from a careful weighing of the following factors:

(a) Profit outlook of the economy.
(b) Outlook of inflationary tendencies.
(c) Historical comparison between the levels of bond interest and dividend yield on stocks.
(d) Potential demand for stocks from institutional investors.
(e) Size of supply of new stocks of investment grade.

VALUATION OF STANDARD & POOR'S 425 ON BASIS OF EARNINGS RECORD

Price, Earnings, and P/E

The price index of S&P's 425 at end of each quarter, earnings in preceding 12 months, and price-earnings ratios at end of each quarter during 1936-1970 are shown in Table 7-2.

Annual Range of P/E

Figure 7-3 shows the annual range of P/E (price to preceding 12 months' earnings) of S&P's 425 Industrial Index. The chart pattern is very similar to that for DJIA as shown in Figure 7-2. The only difference between the two charts is that since the DJIA represents 30 blue-chip companies, the average has usually sold at slightly higher P/E than the broader index of the 425. For example, between 1936 and 1946, the lowest P/E was 8 for "425," and 9 for DJIA. In the postwar period the highest P/E reached 22.4 for the 425 in 1961 as compared to 24.2 for DJIA. The mean P/E during 1962-70, however, was 17.3 for the 425 as compared to 16.6 for DJIA.

TABLE 7-2
Price, Earnings, and Price-Earnings Ratios,
S&P's "425" Industrials Index, 1936-1970

Year	End of Quarter	Price* Index	Preceding 12-Months Earnings	Price Earnings Ratio	Year	End of Quarter	Price* Index	Preceding 12-Months Earnings	Price Earnings Ratio
1936	1	14.24	.70	20.4	1949	1	14.86	2.45	6.1
	2	14.09	.80	17.6		2	13.92	2.47	5.6
	3	15.16	.85	17.8		3	15.28	2.48	6.2
	4	16.50	.92	17.9		4	16.49	2.42	6.8
1937	1	17.39	1.02	17.1	1950	1	16.98	2.47	6.9
	2	15.07	1.09	13.8		2	17.66	2.66	6.7
	3	13.51	1.16	11.7		3	19.56	2.85	6.9
	4	10.26	1.08	9.5		4	20.58	2.93	7.0
1938	1	8.39	.90	9.3	1951	1	21.65	2.93	7.4
	2	11.43	.68	16.8		2	21.27	2.81	7.6
	3	12.30	.52	23.8		3	23.71	2.60	9.1
	4	13.07	.56	23.4		4	24.23	2.55	9.5
1939	1	10.74	.64	16.8	1952	1	24.63	2.49	9.9
	2	10.55	.69	15.3		2	25.35	2.43	10.5
	3	12.71	.73	17.4		3	24.77	2.43	10.2
	4	12.17	.81	15.1		4	26.89	2.46	10.9
1940	1	11.92	.92	13.0	1953	1	25.44	2.48	10.2
	2	9.52	.98	9.7		2	24.30	2.55	9.6
	3	10.32	1.04	9.9		3	23.33	2.60	9.0
	4	10.37	1.01	10.3		4	24.87	2.59	9.6
1941	1	9.74	1.02	9.6	1954	1	27.14	2.66	10.2
	2	9.77	1.05	9.3		2	29.68	2.75	10.8
	3	10.19	1.14	9.0		3	33.29	2.76	12.1
	4	8.78	1.11	7.9		4	37.24	2.89	12.8
1942	1	8.11	.98	8.3	1955	1	37.76	3.08	12.3
	2	8.45	.88	9.6		2	42.98	3.35	12.8
	3	8.99	.81	11.1		3	46.29	3.58	12.9
	4	9.94	.83	12.0		4	48.44	3.78	12.8
1943	1	11.64	.84	13.9	1956	1	51.76	3.86	13.4
	2	12.36	.86	14.4		2	50.21	3.75	13.3
	3	12.00	.85	14.1		3	48.50	3.59	13.5
	4	11.60	.75	15.5		4	50.08	3.53	14.2
1944	1	11.88	.76	15.7	1957	1	46.98	3.52	13.3
	2	12.89	.76	17.0		2	51.21	3.55	14.4
	3	12.66	.75	17.0		3	45.78	3.60	12.7
	4	13.05	.78	16.7		4	42.86	3.50	12.2
1945	1	13.35	.80	16.7	1958	1	44.93	3.25	13.8
	2	14.38	.84	17.1		2	48.16	3.02	15.9
	3	15.69	.83	19.0		3	53.60	2.95	18.2
	4	16.78	.82	20.5		4	58.97	2.95	20.0
1946	1	17.39	.72	24.0	1959	1	59.01	3.18	18.5
	2	17.70	.67	26.5		2	62.82	3.50	17.9
	3	14.58	.74	19.8		3	60.99	3.55	17.2
	4	14.75	.92	16.1		4	64.50	3.53	18.2
1947	1	14.79	1.18	12.5	1960	1	59.02	3.52	16.8
	2	14.95	1.37	11.0		2	60.52	3.37	18.0
	3	14.82	1.51	9.8		3	56.70	3.39	16.7
	4	15.18	1.59	9.6		4	61.49	3.39	18.1
1948	1	14.87	1.70	8.8	1961	1	68.78	3.22	21.4
	2	16.53	1.88	8.8		2	68.40	3.18	21.5
	3	15.26	2.09	7.3		3	70.25	3.21	21.8
	4	15.12	2.33	6.5		4	75.72	3.37	22.4

TABLE 7-2 (*Continued*)

Year	End of Quarter	Price* Index	Preceding 12-Months Earnings	Price Earnings Ratio	Year	End of Quarter	Price* Index	Preceding 12-Months Earnings	Price Earnings Ratio
1962	1	73.36	3.55	20.6	1967	1	96.71	5.76	16.8
	2	57.34	3.67	15.6		2	97.71	5.63	17.3
	3	58.80	3.73	15.7		3	105.05	5.62	18.7
	4	66.00	3.87	17.0		4	105.11	5.65	18.6
1963	1	69.71	3.91	17.8	1968	1	98.2	5.90	16.6
	2	72.76	4.03	18.0		2	108.8	5.90	18.4
	3	75.47	4.16	18.1		3	112.2	6.20	18.0
	4	79.25	4.24	18.7		4	113.0	6.20	18.2
1964	1	83.87	4.42	19.0	1969	1	110.1	6.45	17.1
	2	86.66	4.59	18.9		2	107.5	6.25	17.2
	3	89.12	4.75	18.7		3	102.8	6.40	16.1
	4	89.62	4.83	18.5		4	101.5	6.40	15.8
1965	1	90.98	4.97	18.3	1970	1	98.6	5.80	16.9
	2	89.12	5.15	17.3		2	79.9	5.45	14.7
	3	95.61	5.29	18.0		3	92.6	5.80	15.9
	4	98.47	5.51	17.8		4	100.9	5.15	17.8
1966	1	95.51	5.67	16.8					
	2	90.72	5.79	15.7					
	3	81.65	5.84	14.0					
	4	85.24	5.89	14.4					

*1941–43 = 10.

Figure 7-3

Annual Range of P/E (Price to preceding 12 months' earnings), S & P's "425" Industrials, 1936–1970

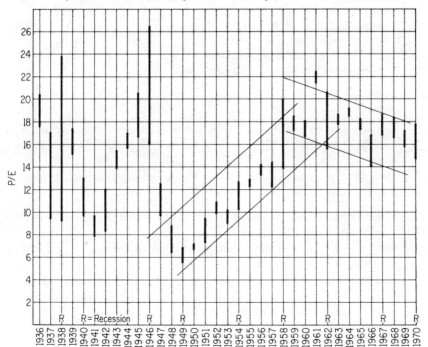

Valuation of S&P's 425

The procedure for the valuation of S&P's 425 is the same as for DJIA. The only difference lies in the magnitude of P/E to be assigned to each index for their valuation. Since the 425 index represents a cross section of the 425 larger industrial companies, its valuation tends to be more representative of the general market than that for DJIA, though the latter is better known and more widely used than the former.

VALUATION OF DJIA IN TERMS OF PRESENT-WORTH APPROACH

As mentioned before, there are basically two approaches to valuation. One is the capitalization approach, the other the present-worth approach. Table 7-3,

TABLE 7-3
Present Worth of DJIA Under Assumed Conditions

1. Per share normal earnings, DJIA (defined arbitrarily as 3-year moving average centered)	$ 1	$ 1
2. Growth rate of earnings assumed for next 50 years	4%	3½%
3. Earnings 50 years later	7.11	5.58
4. P/E ratio assumed 50 years later	16	16
5. Price index, DJIA, 50 years later	$113.8	$89.3
6. Discount rate assumed (rate of return desired by investors	8%	8%
7. Present worth of $1.00 to be received 50 years later . . .	.021	.021
8. Present worth of future selling price (line 5 × line 7) . . .	2.39	1.87
9. Dividend payout ratio assumed at a constant rate	65%	65%
10. Present worth of 50 years' growing dividends*	$ 14.3	$13.1
11. Present worth of dividends and selling price (line 8 + line 10)	$ 16.7	$15.0
12. Ratio: present worth of dividends + selling price to current normal earnings	16.7	15.0

*Calculations are on basis of tables in Robert M. Soldofsky and James T. Murphy's *Growth Yields on Common Stocks*, published by Bureau of Business and Economic Research, State University of Iowa, 1961.

illustrates the application of the present-worth approach to the valuation of DJIA. Here we assume several conditions:

(a) Dividend payout ratio is assumed at a constant rate of 65 percent of net earnings.

(b) The growth rate of net earnings for DJIA in the next 50 years is assumed at an annual rate of 3½ to 4 percent.

(c) The P/E ratio for DJIA 50 years later is assumed to be around 16.

(d) The discount rate or the rate of return desired by investors on stocks in the DJIA is assumed at 8 percent.

On the basis of these assumptions, the price-normal earnings (defined arbitrarily as an average of last year's earnings, current year, and next year's estimated earnings) ratio for DJIA is found in Table 7-3 at about 15 on basis of 3½ percent dividend growth, and at 16.7 on basis of 4 percent dividend growth. Multiplying these price-normal earnings ratios by the estimated normal earnings of DJIA at the time results in valuation for DJIA.

VALUATION OF DJIA ON BASIS OF ANTICIPATED AVERAGE EARNING POWER

The valuation of stocks or stock indexes should be theoretically based on estimated future average earning power of the respective stocks or stock indexes, because the value of a stock as an asset item derives not from past earnings but from incomes it *will provide* to the owner in the years ahead. However, past earnings are important because of two reasons: (1) they represent actual achievements of the corporation, and (2) they provide the basis for the estimate of future earning power.

The length of the period for which future earnings are possible to be estimated depends chiefly on the nature and the size of the company and of the industry of which it is a part.

Statements by various corporate managements indicate that they generally attempt tentatively to forecast earnings not more than three to five years into the future. It follows, therefore, that corporate outsiders should not aim their forecast for a period longer than the managements themselves feel competent to estimate.

Observations of the experience in the stock market and the general pattern of investors' behavior, on the other hand, indicate that, aside from earnings in the last few years, the estimates of earning in the current year and in the near future play a very important role in influencing stock prices.

The considerations and thoughts mentioned above suggest that a reasonable estimate of corporate earning power at any time should be based partly on what was *realized* and partly on what can be *reasonably projected* into the future. For most corporations, we propose that average earning power be measured by a moving average of seven years' earnings centered; this means that the earning power of a corporation at a given time is calculated at an arithmetic average of actual earnings of three years past plus estimated earnings for the current year and three more future years.

Our method, of course, is arbitrary, but requires some thoughts. For example, if the period be lengthened to nine or eleven years, the analyst has to project earnings five to seven years into the future. This will raise questions of feasibility and usefulness of estimates so far ahead. If average earning power be measured purely on basis of projected future earnings, too much reliance is placed on the competence of the analyst. Besides, we know that investors do not ignore actual level of earnings as one of the factors determining the price they are willing to pay. On the other hand, measuring average earning power on historical basis tends to ignore different growth propsects. We also know that investors are keenly concerned with prospective earnings in the current year and the immediate years following. Therefore we are of the view that a seven-year-moving-average-centered estimate of earnings is probably one of the best compromises. In the case of stock averages such as DJIA or S&P's "425," a five-year-moving-average-centered earnings figure may be substituted. This will reduce the period of forecast from 3-4 years to 2-3 years.

In Tables 7-4 and 7-5 we illustrate how a semi-mechanical valuation of DJIA based on estimated average earning power (measured by five-year and seven-year moving-average-centered) and adjusted price-earnings ratios can be arrived at.

The steps for semimechanical valuation of DJIA are as follows:

1. Estimate earnings for the current year and two to three years following.

TABLE 7-4
Semimechanical Valuation of DJIA on Basis of Estimated Average Earning Power
(Five-year-moving-average-centered)

	(1)	(2)	(3)	(4)	(5)	(6)
Year	Earnings Per Share	Average Earning Power, 5-Year Moving Average Centered	Mean Price of High and Low	Adjusted P/E (3/2)	Basic Multiplier, Average Adjusted P/E, Last 3 Years	Valuation for DJIA (2 × 5)
1950	30.70	25.7	215.9	8.4	8.5	218
1951	26.59	26.6	257.7	9.7	8.0	213
1952	24.78	27.5	274.0	10.0	8.5	234
1953	27.23	28.5	275.0	9.7	9.4	268
1954	28.18	29.7	353.5	11.9	9.8	290
1955	35.78	32.1	438.0	13.6	10.5	337
1956	33.74	32.3	492.0	15.2	11.7	378
1957	36.08	33.5	470.5	14.0	13.6	455
1958	27.95	32.8	510.5	15.6	14.3	468
1959	34.31	32.5	627.0	19.3	14.9	485
1960	32.21	32.6	625.8	19.2	16.3	532
1961	31.91	35.2	672.6	19.0	18.0	635
1962	36.43	37.6	630.9	16.8	19.2	720
1963	41.21	41.9	707.0	16.8	18.3	767
1964	46.51	47.1	828.9	17.6	17.5	825
1965	53.67	50.6	904.9	17.9	17.1	865
1966	57.68	53.3	869.7	16.3	17.4	925
1967	53.87	55.4	864.7	15.6	17.1	950
1968	57.89	54.9	897.0	16.3	16.6	910
1969	57.02	54.6	876.2	16.0	16.1	880
1970[E]	48.00	56.2	720.0*	12.8	16.0	900
1971[E]	56.00					
1972[E]	62.00					

[E]Estimated.
*Mean price of high and low during the period January–August 1970.

TABLE 7-5
Semimechanical Valuation of DJIA on Basis of Estimated Average
Earning Power
(Seven-year-moving-average-centered)

	(1)	(2)	(3)	(4)	(5)	(6)
Year	Earnings Per Share	Estimated Average Earning Power, 7-Year Moving Average Centered	Mean Price of High and Low	Adjusted P/E (3/2)	Basic Multiplier, Average Adjusted P/E, Last 3 Years	Valuation for DJIA (2 X 5)
1950	30.70	25.0	215.9	8.7	8.6	215
1951	26.59	26.4	257.7	9.8	8.4	222
1952	24.78	28.0	274.0	9.8	8.8	246
1953	27.23	29.8	275.0	9.2	9.4	280
1954	28.18	30.0	353.5	11.8	9.6	288
1955	35.78	30.4	438.0	14.4	10.3	313
1956	33.74	32.0	492.0	15.4	11.8	378
1957	36.08	32.5	470.5	14.5	13.9	452
1958	27.95	33.0	510.5	15.6	14.8	488
1959	34.31	33.2	627.0	18.8	15.2	505
1960	32.21	34.4	625.8	18.4	16.3	560
1961	31.91	35.8	672.6	18.9	17.6	630
1962	36.43	39.5	630.9	16.0	18.7	740
1963	41.21	43.0	707.0	16.4	17.8	770
1964	46.51	46.0	828.9	18.0	17.1	785
1965	53.67	49.0	904.9	18.5	16.8	825
1966	57.68	52.0	869.7	16.7	17.6	915
1967	53.87	55.0	864.7	15.7	17.7	975
1968	57.89	53.5	897.0	16.8	17.0	910
1969	57.02	56.0	876.2	15.7	16.4	920
1970[E]	48.00	57.0	720.0*	12.6	16.1	920
1971[E]	56.00					
1972[E]	62.00					
1973[E]	64.00					

[E]Estimated.
*Mean price of high and low during the period January–August 1970.

2. Compute average earning power on the basis of either a five-year or seven-year moving average of earnings centered.
3. Divide mean price of yearly high and low by average earning power to get adjusted P/E ratio. This ratio measures how the average earning power of the index is appraised in the market.
4. Take an average of adjusted P/E in the last three years to get a basic multiplier.
5. Multiply the basic multiplier for the year by average earning power to get valuation of DJIA for the year.

As can be seen from the table, the valuation of DJIA did not deviate too much from the mean price of yearly high and low, except the current year 1970. Better results can be expected if one more step is added—that is, *the analyst will make some adjustments of the historically derived basic multiplier based on his appraisal of current conditions.* However, even without this added step, we believe the resultant valuation of DJIA can usefully serve as a bench mark to evaluate whether the general market is relatively high or low or about right at the moment. For example, the Dow Jones Industrial Average as of the middle of August 1970 was around 720, whereas our semimechanical valuation pointed to a level around 920 which is derived on basis of a basic multiplier of 16.1 and an estimated average earning power of DJIA at $57.0. In view of the experience in the past ten years, a basic multiplier of 16.1 for DJIA cannot be considered as too high. Therefore, at the current level of 720 for DJIA in August 1970, the market is estimating the earning power of DJIA at $44.7 (using the 16.1 multiplier) which is even lower than the estimated $48 for a recession year. As has happened before in recession years, stock buyers as a whole at this point become unduly conservative not only in earnings estimates but also in the size of multiplier they apply. The result is a sizable gap between market price and valuation level. As of mid-August 1970, the market price index is lower than our valuation level by more than 20 percent, this should indicate to investors that now is most likely a good time to acquire stocks of good grade for investment purposes.[7]

SUGGESTED READINGS

Bernhard, Arnold, *The Evaluation of Common Stocks*, New York: Simon and Schuster, 1959.

Bing, Ralph A., "Appraising Our Methods of Stock Appraisal," *Financial Analysts Journal*, May-June 1964.

Bonham, Howard B., Jr., "Equity Investment Return in 1970," *Financial Analysts Journal*, May-June 1968.

Graham, Benjamin, "The Future of Financial Analysis," *Financial Analysts Journal*, May-June 1963; "Some Investment Aspects of Accumulation Through Equities," *Journal of Finance*, May 1962.

Graham, Benjamin, et al., *Security Analysis*, 4th ed. New York: McGraw-Hill Book Company, 1962.

Hammel, J. E., and D. A. Hodes, "Factors Influencing Price-Earnings Multiples," *Financial Analysts Journal*, January-February 1967.

Hayes, Douglas A., "The Dimensions of Analysis," *Financial Analysts Journal*, September-October 1966.

[7]The level of stock prices rose in the remainder of the year since our valuation in mid-August 1970. The Dow-Jones Industrial Average finished the year at 838.9 which was about 120 points higher than the level in mid-August. Our valuation models indicated a "normal" level of 900 to 920 for the year. The actual figure of 838.9 for DJIA at year end was still lower than our valuation level, but within 10 percent, whereas in mid-August the market price index was lower than our valuation level by more than 20 percent. As said before, the main advantage of carefully establishing a valuation level on basis of sound procedures as illustrated by various methods in this chapter is to enable the investor to maintain a reasonable perspective so that he can profit from the extremes of pessimism or optimism prevailing in the marketplace.

Hoddleson, D., and A. Lipper III, "Buy Low, Sell High," *Barron's*, June 1967.

Huang, Stanley S. C., *Corporate Earning Power and Valuation of Common Stock*, Larchmont, N.Y.: Investors Intelligence, Inc., 1968.

McWilliams, James D., "Prices, Earnings and P/E Ratios," *Financial Analysts Journal*, May-June 1966.

Molodovsky, Nicholas, Catherine May and Sherman Chottiner, "Common Stock Valuation," *Financial Analysts Journal*, March-April 1965.

Murphy, Joseph E., "Earnings Growth and Price Change in the Same Time Period," *Financial Analysts Journal*, January-February 1968.

Murphy, J. E., and H. W. Stevenson, "Price/Earnings Ratios and Future Growth of Earnings & Dividends," *Financial Analysts Journal*, November-December 1967.

Wendt, Paul F., "Current Growth Stock Valuation Methods," *Financial Analysts Journal*, March-April 1965.

QUESTIONS AND PROBLEMS

1. What is the difference between the Dow Jones Industrial Average and Standard & Poor's 425 Industrial Index of stock prices? Which one is more representative of the market?

2. What are some of the practical difficulties in applying the present-worth approach to the valuation of common stocks?

3. Explain the capitalization approach to the valuation of common stocks.

4. What has been the pattern of price-earnings ratios in the past ten years?

5. What do you think of the present level of price-earnings ratios? Will it increase, decrease, or stay constant in the year ahead? Why?

6. Discuss the usefulness and limitations of the concept of price-earnings ratio in the valuation of common stock.

7. Review the changes of stock prices in the last six months as measured by Dow Jones Industrial Average. What factors in your opinion were chiefly responsible for the increase or decrease in stock prices during these months?

8. Prepare a valuation for Dow Jones Industrial Average for the past three years, current year, and the next year on basis of any one of the methods discussed in this chapter.

8. Valuation of Common Stocks

As mentioned in the previous chapter, theories of valuation of common stocks are basically of two types:

1. The present-worth approach.
2. The capitalization approach.

The present-worth approach arrives at valuation of a common stock through discounting its future income to the owner, mainly dividends but also including liquidating proceeds at time of sale.

The capitalization approach capitalizes most commonly the actual average earning power or anticipated future average earning power of the stock. The base of capitalization can be also dividends, cash flow, or a combination of earnings and dividends.

PRESENT-WORTH APPROACH AND DISCOUNT TABLES

The present-worth theory expresses a basic truth—that the value of a stock, aside from its market price, is but the sum of future stream of cash income to the owner discounted at appropriate rates. However, its practical application must await the construction of tables composed of numerous combinations of underlying factors, such as earnings growth rate, dividend payout ratio, growth duration, discount rate, and P/E ratio at time of sale.

Discount Tables by Guild

The first step in the construction of discount tables was taken by S. E. Guild in his book *Stock Growth and Discount Tables*[1] published in 1931. As

[1] S. E. Guild, *Stock Growth & Discount Tables* Boston: Financial Publishing Co., 1931, p. 163.

TABLE 8-1
For Equivalent Total Return of 7 Percent

When it is Estimated That

The Trend of Growth in Earnings during the period will be at an annual rate of. . . . 10%

and

The Proportion of Earnings to be Paid out in Dividends during the period will be. . . 40%

and

The Stock will Sell at the end of the period at a ratio of—

(a) Dividend to Market Price (Dividend Yield) . . .	2.0%	2.4%	2.8%	3.2%	3.6%	4.0%	4.8%	5.6%
or								
(b) Earnings to Market Price	5%	6%	7%	8%	9%	10%	12%	14%
or								
(c) Market Price to Earnings	20.00	16.67	14.29	12.50	11.11	10.00	8.33	7.14

Years Required:

1	20.97	17.55	15.09	13.26	11.83	10.70	8.97	7.75
2	21.97	18.45	15.93	14.04	12.58	11.40	9.64	8.38
3	22.99	19.38	16.79	14.85	13.34	12.13	10.32	9.03
4	24.05	20.33	17.67	15.68	14.13	12.88	11.03	9.69
5	25.14	21.31	18.58	16.53	14.94	13.66	11.74	10.38
6	26.26	22.32	19.51	17.41	15.76	14.45	12.48	11.08
7	27.40	23.35	20.47	18.30	16.61	15.27	13.25	11.80
8	28.59	24.42	21.46	19.23	17.49	16.10	14.03	12.54
9	29.80	25.52	22.47	20.18	18.39	16.97	14.84	13.30
10	31.05	26.64	23.51	21.15	19.32	17.86	15.66	14.09
15	37.82	32.77	29.17	26.47	24.36	22.68	20.15	18.35
20	45.61	39.81	35.66	32.56	30.14	28.22	25.32	23.25

SOURCE: S. E. Guild, *Stock Growth & Discount Tables* (Boston: 1931), Financial Publishing Co., p. 163.

The figures in the body of this table are the number of times its earnings per share at which a stock is selling at present.

shown from one of his tables reproduced here, the underlying factors are six in all:

1. Equivalent total return (the return the investor desires or the discount rate deemed appropriate by the investor for the stock)—top of the table, assumed at 7%
2. Trend of growth of earnings estimated—top of the table 10%
3. Dividend payout ratio assumed—top of the table 40%
4. P/E ratio assumed at time of sale . . . . any number
on row C

5. Years required (growth duration assumed)—left-hand side
   of table . . . . 1 to 20 years
6. P/E ratio at which the stock is selling now—body of the table

If an investor has some idea or estimates about five of the six factors, he can find out the numerical value of the remaining factor simply by referring to the table.

For purpose of illustration, let us suppose that an investor intends to buy a certain stock and he has the following estimates:

1. Growth of earning estimated at 10%
2. Dividend payout ratio estimated at 40%
3. Growth period estimated for . . . . 10 years
4. P/E ratio of the stock 10 years from now 20
5. He desires a total return of 7 percent or he considers a rate
   of discount appropriate for the stock at 7%

The question is at what price does the stock correspond to its real value—or, in other words, what is the present worth of the stock (the dividend stream plus final selling price 10 years from now) under these conditions? By reference to the table, we find that the stock is worth about 31.05 times its current earnings. If the actual P/E at the time is substantially below 31.05, the stock should be rated a good buy. On the other hand, if the current actual P/E is above 31.05, then the stock is considered overvalued in terms of present worth of future income.

Price-Dividend Ratios by Soldofsky and Murphy

In 1961 Soldofsky and Murphy jointly published their book, "Growth Yields on Common Stock—Theory & Tables." It includes so called one-step and two-step growth yields tables. The one-step table is based on the assumption of one growth period of a constant dividend growth rate, whereas the two-step tables are based on two growth periods of constant but different dividend growth rates. Their tables, not like Guild's tables, are constructed directly on basis of dividend growth rates, and, therefore, *the figures in the body of the tables are price-dividend ratios instead of price-earnings ratios as in the case of Guild's tables.* The main improvement over Guild's tables is that their scope and coverage is much broader as to enhance the usefulness of the tables in practical application.

A simple example will serve to illustrate the use of their two-step tables. Suppose that to a given investor IBM is having these attributes: namely, its dividend will likely grow at 15 percent per year for the next 10 years, and then continue to grow at 10 percent for 10 more years, and subsequently stay at the level reached; and the appropriate rate of discount is assumed to be 6½ percent. The question is, what is a reasonable price for the stock? The answer can be easily found in Table 8-2. The present worth of IBM under these conditions

TABLE 8-2
Growth Yields on Common Stock—Selected Values
Two Growth Rates
Dividend Growth Yields (Columns)*

Growth Periods—Years			6½%	6¾%	7%	8%	9%	10%
First Period	Second Period	Total						
			Growth Rates 15%, 6%†					
5	5	10	$ 35.55	$ 34.08	$ 32.71	$ 28.10	$ 24.53	$ 21.70
5	10	15	42.08	40.20	38.45	32.60	28.12	24.59
10	5	15	58.49	55.70	53.13	44.52	37.96	32.82
5	15	20	48.45	46.10	43.93	36.70	31.24	26.99
10	10	20	68.06	64.57	61.35	50.68	42.64	36.43
15	5	20	92.11	87.04	82.38	66.99	55.50	46.71
5	20	25	54.66	51.78	49.14	40.43	33.94	28.99
10	15	25	77.39	73.12	69.19	56.28	46.71	39.44
15	10	25	106.14	99.88	94.15	75.41	61.62	51.22
5	30	35	66.60	62.53	58.82	46.90	38.35	32.03
10	25	35	95.32	89.26	83.74	66.01	53.33	44.00
15	20	35	133.09	124.15	116.04	90.03	71.56	58.08
20	15	35	181.90	168.92	157.16	119.70	93.37	74.36
5	45	50	83.22	77.09	71.60	54.55	43.00	34.91
10	40	50	120.31	111.15	102.94	77.50	60.33	48.33
15	35	50	170.64	157.05	144.89	107.30	82.08	64.59
25	25	50	328.42	299.39	273.52	194.49	142.58	107.43
			Growth Rates 15%, 10%†					
5	5	10	40.89	39.13	37.51	32.03	27.80	24.46
5	10	15	55.01	52.36	49.92	41.75	35.54	30.70
10	5	15	66.31	63.03	60.00	49.90	42.23	36.26
5	15	20	71.58	67.71	64.15	52.40	43.64	36.94
10	10	20	87.00	82.20	77.77	63.20	52.34	44.06
15	5	20	103.57	97.66	92.22	74.34	61.09	51.01
5	20	25	91.02	85.51	80.46	64.06	52.11	43.18
10	15	25	111.29	104.43	98.15	77.76	62.93	51.85
15	10	25	133.90	125.42	117.67	92.53	74.30	60.74
5	30	35	140.50	130.03	120.58	90.80	70.24	55.66
10	25	35	173.08	160.02	148.24	111.15	85.57	67.43
15	20	35	211.07	194.86	180.23	134.23	102.58	80.20
20	15	35	254.56	234.54	216.49	159.86	121.04	93.72
5	45	50	250.51	226.25	204.84	140.93	100.59	74.31
10	40	50	310.47	280.19	253.48	173.76	123.47	90.73
15	35	50	382.66	344.93	311.65	212.43	149.91	109.29
25	25	50	570.70	512.64	461.48	309.45	214.28	152.96

SOURCE: R. M. Soldofsky and J. T. Murphy, *Growth Yields on Common Stock—Theory and Tables* (Ames, Iowa: State University of Iowa, 1961), p. 118.

*Growth yields for rates up to and including 4 percent are based upon discounting the expected income stream for 200 years. A 100-year income stream was used in determining growth yields beginning with 4¼ percent through 10 percent, and a 50-year stream was used for 12 percent and above. In all cases, however, at least 99 percent of the value of a perpetuity is included at each growth yield. In most cases much of the final 1 percent of the value of a perpetuity is included despite the foreshortening of the discount period.

†The first of these two growth rates applies to the first growth period; the second growth rate applies to the second growth period.

should be 87.00 times current dividend. At the current divident of $4.80 in 1970, it should be worth about $417.

Price-Dividend Ratios by Bauman

In 1963 W. Scott Bauman published his present-worth tables in his book *Estimating the Present Value of Common Stocks by the Variable Rate Method.* His tables, like those of Soldofsky and Murphy are in terms of price-dividend ratios. However, he differs from them and Guild in two important respects:

1. Bauman argues that high rate of growth is usually temporary. What is normally observed in corporate life is the phenomenon of decreasing rate of

TABLE 8-3
25-Year Transition Period
Price-Dividend Ratios

Initial Growth Rates (Percent)	Initial Discount Rates							
	5%	6%	6½%	7%	8%	9%	10%	12%
Depressed								
0	24.3	18.8	17.0	15.4	31.1	11.4	10.1	8.3
1	26.8	20.6	18.5	16.8	14.2	12.3	10.9	8.8
2	29.5	22.6	20.2	18.3	15.4	13.3	11.7	9.4
3	32.6	24.8	22.1	19.9	16.7	14.3	12.5	10.1
Constant								
4	36.0	27.2	24.2	21.7	18.1	15.5	13.5	10.8
High								
5	39.8	29.8	26.5	23.7	19.6	16.7	14.5	11.5
6	44.0	32.8	29.0	25.9	21.4	18.1	15.7	12.3
8	53.8	39.7	34.9	31.1	25.3	21.3	18.3	14.2
10	65.9	48.1	42.1	37.3	30.1	25.1	22.4	16.3
12	80.7	58.3	50.8	44.8	35.9	29.7	25.1	18.9
14	99.0	70.9	61.5	54.0	42.9	35.2	29.5	21.9
16	121.5	86.3	74.5	65.2	51.4	41.8	34.8	25.5
18	149.1	105.0	90.3	78.7	61.6	49.7	41.2	29.8
20	182.8	127.9	109.6	95.2	73.9	59.3	48.7	34.9
25	303.8	209.1	177.8	153.2	117.1	92.5	74.9	52.0
30	502.1	341.1	288.1	246.5	186.0	144.9	115.8	78.4
35	823.9	553.7	465.1	395.7	205.2	227.3	179.6	118.7
40	1,341.2	893.1	746.7	632.2	467.1	356.2	278.6	180.5
50	3,463.0	2,273.0	1,886.4	1,585.1	1,153.0	865.5	665.9	417.4
60	8,630.9	5,603.9	4,625.0	3,864.1	2,778.1	2,060.4	1,565.7	956.4
70	20,775.4	13,376.7	10,992.2	9,143.2	6,513.8	4,785.5	3,601.4	2,155.9

SOURCE: W. Scott Bauman, *Estimating the Present Value of Common Stocks by Variable Rate Method* (Ann Arbor: Bureau of Business Research, University of Michigan 1963), p. 75.

growth after an initial period of rapid growth. Therefore in his construction of tables, Bauman includes a transitional period during which a high rate of growth is assumed to decline evenly and gradually to the rate at which an average company will grow proportionally to the economy which is assumed at 4 percent.

2. Bauman contends that since the dividend estimate is subject to greater uncertainty for each succeeding future year, the discount rate in his view should be gradually increased to offset this growing uncertainty of dividend estimates. In constructing his tables, he assumed that the discount rate will increase yearly by .0075 times the initial discount rate.

Using again IBM for illustration, if the stock has an initial high growth rate of 16 percent, the transitional period is assumed for 25 years, and the initial discount rate is considered appropriate at 6½ percent, then the present worth of the stock in terms of price-dividend ratio is found in Table 8-3 at 74.5. At the current dividend of $4.80 in 1970, the stock is worth $358.

Price-Normal Earnings Ratios by Molodovsky, May and Chottiner

Molodovsky, May, and Chottiner published an article entitled "Common Stock Valuation: Theory and Tables" in the *Financial Analysts Journal* for March 1965. Their approach represents another variant in the application of the present-worth theory. The distinquishing features of their approach are as follows:

1. The calculations of Molodovsky, May, and Chottiner are in terms of price-earnings ratios, as in the case of Guild's tables. However, they eliminate Guild's explicit assumptions of dividend payout ratio by way of inserting a built-in relationship between growth rate and dividend payout ratio which they found through correlation analysis. The following statement indicates their reasoning and methodology:

> Corporate earnings can either be paid out as dividends or reinvested in the company. The relative mix is primarily a function of the investment opportunities of the firm.
> Low dividend payouts are a result of high investment return which in turn causes high earnings growth. High dividend payouts are a result of low investment return which in turn causes low earnings growth. Our tables are computed by using the hypothesis that the payout ratio is a function of earnings growth. An equation was applied to the Cowless commission data and the Standard and Poor's 500 for the period 1871 to 1962. Using the least square criterion, a multiple regression was obtained expressing the relation between pay-out ratios and current and lagged earnings growth rates.[2]

---

[2] Nicholas Molodovsky, Catherine May and Sherman Chottiner, "Common Stock Valuation: Theory and Tables," *Financial Analysts Journal*, April–March 1965.

TABLE 8-4

Investment Values of Normal Earnings of $1 at 7 Percent Return

Projected Earnings Growth Rate 9.0%

Years Constant Growth	YEARS DIMINISHING GROWTH									
	2	4	6	8	10	12	14	16	18	20
2	12.1	12.9	13.8	14.6	15.5	16.3	17.2	18.0	18.9	19.7
4	14.1	15.0	15.9	16.7	17.6	18.5	19.4	20.3	21.1	22.0
6	16.2	17.1	18.0	18.9	19.9	20.8	21.7	22.6	23.5	24.4
8	18.3	19.3	20.3	21.2	22.2	23.1	24.1	25.0	25.9	26.9
10	20.6	21.6	22.6	23.6	24.6	25.5	26.5	27.5	28.5	29.5
12	22.9	24.0	25.0	26.0	27.0	28.1	29.1	30.1	31.1	32.1
14	25.3	26.4	27.5	28.6	29.6	30.7	31.7	32.8	33.8	34.9
16	27.9	29.0	30.1	31.2	32.3	33.4	34.5	35.6	36.7	37.8
18	30.5	31.6	32.8	33.9	35.1	36.2	37.3	38.5	39.6	40.7
20	33.2	34.4	35.6	36.8	37.9	39.1	40.3	41.5	42.7	43.8
22	36.0	37.2	38.5	39.7	40.9	42.2	43.4	44.6	45.8	47.1
24	38.9	40.2	41.5	42.8	44.0	45.3	46.6	47.9	49.1	50.4
26	41.9	43.3	44.6	45.9	47.3	48.6	49.9	51.2	52.5	53.8
28	45.1	46.5	47.8	49.2	50.6	52.0	53.3	54.7	56.1	57.4
30	48.3	49.8	51.2	52.6	54.1	55.5	56.9	58.3	59.7	61.2

Projected Earnings Growth Rate 13.0%

Years Constant Growth	YEARS DIMINISHING GROWTH									
	2	4	6	8	10	12	14	16	18	20
2	13.1	14.4	15.8	17.3	18.8	20.4	22.0	23.6	25.3	27.1
4	16.3	17.8	19.4	21.0	22.7	24.4	26.2	28.1	30.0	32.0
6	19.9	21.6	23.3	25.1	27.0	29.0	31.0	33.0	35.2	37.4
8	23.9	25.8	27.7	29.8	31.9	34.0	36.2	38.5	40.9	43.4
10	28.4	30.5	32.7	34.9	37.2	39.6	42.1	44.7	47.4	50.1
12	33.4	35.7	38.1	40.7	43.3	45.9	48.7	51.6	54.5	57.6
14	38.9	41.5	44.3	47.1	50.0	52.9	56.0	59.2	62.5	66.0
16	45.1	48.1	51.1	54.2	57.4	60.8	64.2	67.8	71.5	75.3
18	52.0	55.3	58.7	62.2	65.8	69.5	73.3	77.3	81.4	85.7
20	59.8	63.4	67.2	71.1	75.1	79.2	83.5	87.9	92.5	97.3
22	68.4	72.4	76.6	81.0	85.4	90.1	94.9	99.8	104.9	110.2
24	78.0	82.5	87.2	92.0	97.0	102.2	107.5	113.0	118.7	124.6
26	88.7	93.7	98.9	104.3	109.9	115.7	121.6	127.8	134.1	140.7
28	100.6	106.3	112.1	118.1	124.3	130.7	137.4	144.2	151.3	158.6
30	113.9	120.2	126.7	133.4	140.3	147.5	154.9	162.6	170.5	178.7

Projected Earnings Growth Rate 10.0%

Years Constant Growth	YEARS DIMINISHING GROWTH									
	2	4	6	8	10	12	14	16	18	20
2	12.3	13.3	14.3	15.3	16.3	17.3	18.3	19.3	20.3	21.3
4	14.6	15.6	16.7	17.7	18.8	19.8	20.9	22.0	23.1	24.1
6	17.0	18.1	19.2	20.3	21.4	22.6	23.7	24.8	26.0	27.1
8	19.6	20.8	21.9	23.1	24.3	25.4	26.6	27.8	29.0	30.2
10	22.3	23.5	24.8	26.0	27.2	28.5	29.7	31.0	32.3	33.6
12	25.2	26.5	27.8	29.1	30.4	31.7	33.0	34.4	35.7	37.1
14	28.2	29.6	30.9	32.3	33.7	35.1	36.5	37.9	39.3	40.8
16	31.4	32.8	34.3	35.7	37.2	38.7	40.2	41.7	43.2	44.7
18	34.8	36.3	37.8	39.4	40.9	42.5	44.0	45.6	47.2	48.8
20	38.4	40.0	41.6	43.2	44.8	46.5	48.1	49.8	51.5	53.2
22	42.1	43.8	45.5	47.3	49.0	50.7	52.5	54.2	56.0	57.8
24	46.1	47.9	49.7	51.5	53.4	55.2	57.1	58.9	60.8	62.7
26	50.3	52.2	54.1	56.1	58.0	59.9	61.9	63.9	65.9	67.9
28	54.8	56.8	58.8	60.9	62.9	64.9	67.0	69.1	71.2	73.3
30	59.5	61.6	63.8	65.9	68.1	70.2	72.4	74.6	76.8	79.1

Projected Earnings Growth Rate 14.0%

Years Constant Growth	YEARS DIMINISHING GROWTH									
	2	4	6	8	10	12	14	16	18	20
2	13.3	14.8	16.4	18.0	19.7	21.5	23.4	25.3	27.3	29.4
4	16.9	18.6	20.4	22.2	24.2	26.2	28.3	30.5	32.8	35.1
6	20.9	22.9	24.9	27.0	29.2	31.5	33.9	36.3	38.9	41.6
8	25.5	27.7	30.0	32.4	34.9	37.5	40.2	43.0	46.0	49.0
10	30.7	33.2	35.8	38.5	41.4	44.3	47.4	50.6	53.9	57.4
12	36.6	39.5	42.4	45.5	48.7	52.1	55.5	59.2	63.0	66.9
14	43.3	46.6	49.9	53.4	57.1	60.8	64.8	68.9	73.2	77.7
16	51.0	54.6	58.4	62.4	66.5	70.8	75.3	80.0	84.9	90.0
18	59.6	63.8	68.1	72.6	77.3	82.2	87.3	92.6	98.1	103.9
20	69.4	74.1	79.0	84.1	89.5	95.0	100.8	106.9	113.1	119.7
22	80.6	85.9	91.5	97.3	103.3	109.6	116.2	123.1	130.2	137.6
24	93.2	99.3	105.6	112.2	119.0	126.2	133.7	141.4	149.5	158.0
26	107.6	114.4	121.6	129.1	136.9	145.0	153.5	162.3	171.5	181.1
28	123.9	131.7	139.8	148.3	157.1	166.4	176.0	186.0	196.4	207.3
30	142.4	151.2	160.5	170.1	180.1	190.6	201.5	212.9	224.8	237.1

11.0%

Years Constant Growth	YEARS DIMINISHING GROWTH									
	2	4	6	8	10	12	14	16	18	20
2	12.6	13.7	14.8	15.9	17.1	18.2	19.4	20.6	21.9	23.1
4	15.2	16.3	17.5	18.8	20.0	21.3	22.5	23.8	25.2	26.5
6	17.9	19.2	20.5	21.8	23.2	24.5	25.9	27.3	28.7	30.1
8	20.9	22.3	23.7	25.1	26.6	28.0	29.5	31.0	32.5	34.1
10	24.2	25.7	27.2	28.7	30.2	31.8	33.4	35.0	36.6	38.3
12	27.7	29.2	30.9	32.5	34.2	35.8	37.6	39.3	41.1	42.9
14	31.4	33.1	34.8	36.6	38.4	40.2	42.0	43.9	45.8	47.8
16	35.4	37.3	39.1	41.0	42.9	44.9	46.9	48.9	51.0	53.0
18	39.8	41.7	43.7	45.8	47.9	50.0	52.1	54.3	56.5	58.7
20	44.4	46.5	48.7	50.9	53.1	55.4	57.7	60.0	62.4	64.8
22	49.4	51.7	54.1	56.4	58.8	61.2	63.7	66.2	68.8	71.4
24	54.8	57.3	59.8	62.3	64.9	67.5	70.2	72.9	75.7	78.5
26	60.6	63.3	66.0	68.7	71.5	74.3	77.2	80.1	83.1	86.1
28	66.9	69.8	72.7	75.6	78.6	81.6	84.7	87.8	91.0	94.3
30	73.6	76.7	79.8	83.0	86.2	89.5	92.8	96.2	99.6	103.1

15.0%

Years Constant Growth	YEARS DIMINISHING GROWTH									
	2	4	6	8	10	12	14	16	18	20
2	13.6	15.2	17.0	18.8	20.7	22.7	24.8	27.1	29.4	31.9
4	17.5	19.4	21.4	23.5	25.7	28.1	30.5	33.1	35.8	38.6
6	22.0	24.2	26.5	29.0	31.5	34.2	37.0	40.0	43.1	46.4
8	27.2	29.8	32.4	35.3	38.2	41.3	44.6	48.0	51.6	55.4
10	33.3	36.2	39.3	42.4	45.9	49.5	53.3	57.3	61.5	65.8
12	40.2	43.6	47.2	50.9	54.9	59.0	63.4	68.0	72.8	77.9
14	48.3	52.2	56.3	60.6	65.2	70.0	75.0	80.3	85.9	91.7
16	57.6	62.1	66.8	71.8	77.1	82.6	88.5	94.6	101.0	107.8
18	68.3	73.5	79.0	84.8	90.9	97.3	104.0	111.1	118.5	126.3
20	80.7	86.7	93.1	99.8	106.8	114.2	121.9	130.1	138.7	147.7
22	95.0	102.2	109.3	117.0	125.1	133.7	142.6	152.1	162.0	172.4
24	111.6	119.6	128.1	137.0	146.4	156.2	166.6	177.5	188.9	200.9
26	130.7	140.0	149.8	160.0	170.9	182.2	194.2	206.8	220.0	233.9
28	152.8	163.5	174.8	186.7	199.2	212.3	226.1	240.7	256.0	272.0
30	178.3	190.7	203.7	217.4	231.9	247.1	263.0	279.8	297.5	316.0

12.0%

Years Constant Growth	YEARS DIMINISHING GROWTH									
	2	4	6	8	10	12	14	16	18	20
2	12.8	14.0	15.3	16.6	17.9	19.3	20.7	22.1	23.5	25.0
4	15.7	17.1	18.4	19.9	21.3	22.8	24.3	25.9	27.5	29.1
6	18.9	20.4	21.9	23.4	25.0	26.6	28.3	30.0	31.8	33.5
8	22.4	24.0	25.7	27.3	29.1	30.9	32.7	34.6	36.5	38.4
10	26.2	28.0	29.8	31.6	33.5	35.5	37.5	39.5	41.6	43.8
12	30.4	32.3	34.3	36.3	38.4	40.6	42.8	45.0	47.3	49.6
14	35.0	37.1	39.3	41.5	43.8	46.1	48.5	51.0	53.5	56.1
16	40.0	42.3	44.7	47.1	49.6	52.2	54.8	57.5	60.3	63.1
18	45.5	48.0	50.6	53.3	56.1	58.9	61.7	64.7	67.7	70.8
20	51.5	54.3	57.2	60.1	63.1	66.2	69.3	72.6	75.9	79.3
22	58.1	61.2	64.3	67.5	70.8	74.2	77.6	81.2	84.8	88.5
24	65.3	68.7	72.1	75.6	79.3	82.9	86.7	90.6	94.6	98.7
26	73.2	76.9	80.7	84.6	88.5	92.6	96.7	101.0	105.3	109.8
28	81.9	86.0	90.1	94.3	98.6	103.1	107.6	112.3	117.1	121.9
30	91.4	95.9	100.4	105.0	109.8	114.6	119.6	124.7	129.9	135.3

16.0%

Years Constant Growth	YEARS DIMINISHING GROWTH									
	2	4	6	8	10	12	14	16	18	20
2	13.9	15.7	17.6	19.6	21.7	24.0	26.4	29.0	31.7	34.6
4	18.1	20.2	22.5	24.9	27.4	30.1	32.9	35.9	39.1	42.5
6	23.2	25.6	28.3	31.1	34.0	37.2	40.5	44.1	47.8	51.8
8	29.1	32.0	35.1	38.4	41.9	45.6	49.5	53.6	58.1	62.7
10	36.0	39.4	43.1	46.9	51.0	55.4	60.0	64.9	70.1	75.6
12	44.2	48.2	52.5	57.0	61.8	66.9	72.4	78.1	84.2	90.7
14	53.8	58.5	63.5	68.9	74.5	80.5	86.9	93.7	100.8	108.4
16	65.0	70.6	76.5	82.8	89.4	96.5	104.0	111.9	120.4	129.3
18	78.3	84.8	91.8	99.2	107.0	115.3	124.1	133.4	143.3	153.8
20	93.9	101.6	109.7	118.4	127.6	137.3	147.7	158.6	170.3	182.6
22	112.2	121.2	130.8	141.0	151.8	163.2	175.4	188.3	202.0	216.5
24	133.7	144.3	155.6	167.5	180.2	193.7	208.0	223.2	239.2	256.2
26	159.0	171.5	184.7	198.8	213.7	229.5	246.3	264.1	283.0	303.0
28	188.7	203.4	218.9	235.5	253.0	271.6	291.3	312.3	334.5	358.0
30	223.6	240.9	259.2	278.6	299.2	321.1	344.3	368.9	394.9	422.6

SOURCE: Nicholas Molodovsky, Catherine May, and Sherman Chottiner, "Common Stock Valuation: Theory & Tables," *Financial Analysts Journal*, March—April 1965, p. 117.

2. The pattern of growth assumed resembles to some extent Bauman's hypothesis. Specifically, they construct their tables on basis of the following growth pattern:

(a) A high but constant growth rate for the first period.

(b) A transitional period during which the growth rate will decline to zero rate.

(c) Zero growth rate is extended indefinitely.

3. The price-earnings ratios in the body of tables are not price-current earnings ratios but rather price-normal earnings ratios. "Normal earnings are not a precise figure. They may be found by trend-line analysis using the least-squares criterion. Even so, judgment must enter in the selection of trend periods. A less satisfactory but still acceptable approach is to determine normal earnings by averaging last year's earnings, the current level of earnings, and next year's expected earnings."[3]

Using again IBM for illustration, if the investor wants a 7 percent return and believes that

(a) The earnings of the stock will grow at 12 percent annually for the next 10 years, (b) The transitional period is 20 years during which the earnings growth rate will decline from 12 percent to zero growth rate at the end of the period, then the present worth in terms of price-normal earnings ratio is found in Table 8-4 at 43.8. At the current level of earnings around $8.85 in 1970, the stock is worth about $388.

Limitation of the Present-Worth Approach

The present-worth tables constructed by various theorists noted above are helpful in putting the present-worth theory into operational form. However, the main difficulty in the application of the approach still remains—that is, it carries an implied assumption that one can at least roughly forecast the rates, duration, and pattern of growth of earnings or dividends of the stock for a long period ahead. Such implication creates some doubts in the minds of many investors as to the usefulness of this approach as a main method of valuation.

THE CAPITALIZATION APPROACH

As mentioned in the previous chapter, the traditional standard approach to the valuation of common stock is some form of the capitalization approach. Judging from current practice, the approach still holds the preeminent position today.

The bases of capitalization are either one or a combination of several value-determining factors of common stocks—book value, dividends, earnings, or cash

---

[3] Molodovsky, May, and Chottiner, *op. cit.*, p. 105.

flow. However, the most commonly used base is earnings per share. Since in the short run the value-determining factors are all subject to wide fluctuation due to the influence of chance factors, a norm or some kind of average over a longer time span is usually taken as the base of capitalization.

The rate of capitalization or its reciprocal, the multiplier, varies widely among stocks and stock groups depending on the quality of the stock, earnings expectation, industry difference, and shifts in investors' favor. The rate of capitalization also varies substantially for the same stock over a period of time for any combination of several factors: (1) change in overall attitude of investors toward common stocks, their profitability, and safety, (2) change in actual corporate performance, (3) change of expectation of the stock, the general market, and the economy. It can readily be seen that the seeking of a norm in capitalization rate is even more difficult than in the case of capitalization base.

Though the capitalization approach is seemingly proceeding on some inexact and opinionated basis, it is nevertheless grounded on the realization already stated that few of us can foresee very far, and therefore a historical perspective should be emphasized.

Price-Earnings Ratios of Different Industry Groups

Because of differences in earnings record and growth expectations, some industry groups usually sell at much higher P/E multiples than other groups. This salient factor should be properly taken into account by investors in the valuation of individual stocks. Table 8-5 shows the average price-earnings ratios (both high and low) of 35 industry groups during the period 1962–66.

The top five P/E groups were office and business equipment, radio and TV manufacturing, electronics, soft drinks, and drugs. They all recorded good earnings growth in the recent past and investors were expecting a continuation of the same pattern in the years ahead.

The lowest five P/E groups, on the other hand, were agricultural machinery, textile, auto parts, rail equipment, and aerospace. The reasons for the low P/E status of these groups are varied. Sensitivity to foreign competition and overcapacity in the industry is likely the reason for the textile group, whereas dependence on government order and the declining importance of the rail industry may account for the low P/E status of aerospace and rail equipment group.

In terms of range of variation between high and low average P/E, the group for bread and cake makers had the least variation of 17 percent, and the radio and TV manufacturing group had the most fluctuation around 67 percent. The mean variation for the 35 groups was 33 percent. This shows clearly that market prices of common stocks are extremely volatile.

A Method of Valuation Based on Anticipated Average Earning Power

Through observations and empirical studies we note that stock prices are strongly influenced by three factors: (1) actual earnings achievements, (2) ex-

TABLE 8-5
Average Price-Earnings Ratios of 35 Industry Groups
During 1962–66

P/E Rank	Industry Group	Average P/E, 1962–66		Range of Variation Between High and Low P/E, Percent
		High	Low	
1	Office and business equipment. . . .	44.3	31.9	39
2	Radio and TV manufacturers	29.9	17.8	67
3	Electronics	27.7	18.4	50
4	Soft drinks . . . . : . .	27.2	21.3	27
5	Drugs	26.9	20.9	28
6	Aluminum	23.5	17.5	34
7	Canned goods	23.0	18.1	27
8	Department stores.	19.9	15.6	28
9	Dairy products.	19.6	15.5	26
10	Paper	19.2	15.1	27
11	Food chains	18.9	14.1	34
12	Amusements	17.4	12.3	41
13	Coal	17.3	13.1	32
14	Rubber fabricating	17.2	13.1	31
15	Bread and cake makers	16.4	14.0	17
16	Roofing and wallpaper	16.2	12.5	29
17	Metal and glass contain..	16.1	13.5	19
18	Lead and zinc	15.9	11.7	36
19	Variety chains	15.6	11.6	35
20	Cement	15.6	11.2	39
21	Distillers	15.5	12.6	23
22	Tobacco	15.5	11.5	35
23	Leather and shoes	15.4	12.6	22
24	International oil	15.4	12.6	22
25	Metal fabricating.	15.3	10.8	42
26	Steel.	15.0	10.8	39
27	Finance companies	15.0	12.0	25
28	Industrial machinery	14.9	11.2	33
29	Domestic oil	14.6	11.9	22
30	Autos	14.5	10.6	37
31	Aerospace	14.0	9.8	43
32	Rail equipment	13.7	10.3	33
33	Auto parts	13.3	11.0	21
34	Textile	13.0	8.5	53
35	Agricultural machinery	12.8	9.5	35

SOURCE: *Industry Survey*, Standard & Poor's Corporation, 1967.

pected earnings in the foreseeable future, especially in the next few years, and (3) historical level of P/E ratios at which the stock was normally selling. To incorporate these findings into a valuation framework, a method[4] of valuation is suggested below. The steps are:

1. Estimate earnings per share of the stock for the current year and the following three years.

[4] Stanley S. C. Huang, *Corporate Earning Power and Valuation of Common Stocks*, Larchmont, N.Y.: Investors Intelligence, Inc., 1968.

2. Compute anticipated average earning power on basis of a seven-year moving average of earnings centered.
3. Divide mean price of yearly high and low by anticipated average earning power to get adjusted P/E ratio. This ratio measures how anticipated average earning power of the stock is appraised in the market.

TABLE 8-6
Valuation of the Common Stock of Abbott Laboratories

Year	(1) Earnings Per Share	(2) Estimated Average Earning Power 7-Year Moving Average Centered	(3) Mean Price of High and Low	(4) Adjusted P/E (3/2)	(5) Basic Multiplier, Average Adjusted P/E, Last 3 years	(6) Final Multiplier After Adjustment of Basic Multiplier	(7) Indicated Value of Stock (2 × 6)
1940	.24		5.0				
1941	.24		4.1				
1942	.23		3.7				
1943	.35	.37	4.9	13.2			
1944	.29	.47	5.1	10.8			
1945	.30	.58	5.9	10.2			
1946	.97	.67	11.1	16.6	11.4		
1947	.91	.76	12.7	16.7	12.5		
1948	.99	.85	11.8	13.9	14.5		
1949	.89	.92	13.7	14.9	15.7		
1950	.97	.89	15.3	17.2	15.2		
1951	.92	.86	17.5	20.4	15.3		
1952	.75	.84	17.6	21.0	17.5		
1953	.78	.84	14.0	16.7	19.5		
1954	.74	.86	15.1	17.6	19.4		
1955	.83	.89	14.3	16.1	18.4		
1956	.93	.94	13.6	14.4	16.8		
1957	1.10	.98	14.6	14.8	16.0		
1958	1.11	1.02	19.3	18.9	15.1		
1959	1.11	1.08	23.0	21.3	16.0		
1960	1.05	1.16	19.7	17.0	18.3		
1961	1.02	1.24	23.0	18.5	19.1		
1962	1.24	1.35	22.7	16.8	18.9		
1963	1.47	1.49	33.5	22.5	17.4		
1964	1.71	1.63	42.0	25.8	19.3		
1965	1.87	1.81	45.5	25.0	21.7		
1966	2.03	1.98	41.8	21.0	24.4		
1967	2.10	2.14	47.5	22.2	23.9		
1968	2.35	2.42	58.7	24.2	22.7		
1969	2.59	2.64	71.0	26.8	22.5		
1970E	2.90	2.88					
1971E	3.10						
1972E	3.40						
1973E	3.80						

(Column between (5) and (7): "To be decided by the analyst")

EEstimated.

4. Take an average of adjusted P/E in the last three years to get a basic multiplier. This basic multiplier indicates the historical level of P/E at which the stock was normally selling.

5. Adjust the basic multiplier upward or downward to get a final multiplier in the light of current conditions and on basis of the judgment of the analyst.

6. Multiply the final multiplier by anticipated average earning power to get valuation of the stock.

As an example, the steps in the valuation of the common stock of Abbott Laboratories are shown in Table 8-6.

A Method of Semimechanical Valuation

For investors and analysts who feel that the adjustment of the suggested basic multiplier is somewhat arbitrary and difficult and that bench marks for valuation are useful, we offer below a model of semimechanical valuation as a supplementary method.

In this method we eliminate the step of adjusting the historically derived basic multiplier and in place of it we impose a restriction: the final multiplier (column 8 in Table 8-7) should be the same as basic multiplier (column 5) if the latter does not deviate more than 15 percent either way from the current adjusted P/E (column 4). Should the basic multiplier exceed by more than 15 percent the current adjusted P/E, we limit our final multiplier at 115 percent of the current adjusted P/E. By the same token, if the basic multiplier falls short more than 15 percent of the current adjusted P/E, we limit the final multiplier at 85 percent of the level of current adjusted P/E. The reason for this step is that the fluctuation of current P/E infrequently goes beyond 15 percent either way in a year. Since in our view commitment in common stocks has to be reviewed at least once a year, it seems unrealistic to apply a final multiplier which deviates more than 15 percent from the current adjusted P/E.

The results from applying the semimechanical valuation method to the common stock of Abbott Laboratories are shown in Table 8-7. The valuation of the stock shown in column 9 is also compared to mean price in column 10.

A Method of Mechanical Valuation

Many investors and analysts, because of either lack of training, experience, or time, are not in a position to formulate their own estimates of earnings of stocks which are under consideration. Therefore they most likely cannot take advantage of the two methods of valuation just described, but nonetheless they are probably anxious to have some indications of value of stocks on basis of their recorded average earning power. For this reason we now offer a method of mechanical valuation on basis of historical average earning power. The method differs from the semimechanical method only in one respect. The average earn-

TABLE 8-7
Semimechanical Valuation of the Common Stock of Abbott Laboratories on Basis of Estimated Average Earning Power

	(1)	(2)	(3)	(4)	(5)	(6)	(7)	(8)	(9)	(10)
						Limit of Basic Multiplier				
Year	Earnings Per Share	Estimated Average Earning Power, 7-Year Moving Average Centered	Mean Price of High and Low	Adjusted P/E (3/2)	Basic Multiplier Average Adjusted P/E, Last 3 Years	115% of Adjusted P/E	85% of Adjusted P/E	Adjusted Basic or Final Multiplier	Indicated Value (2 X 8)	Indicated Value as Percent of Mean Price
1938	.20		3.8							
1939	.22		5.2							
1940	.24		5.0							
1941	.24	.25	4.1	16.4						
1942	.23	.27	3.7	13.7						
1943	.35	.37	4.9	13.2						
1944	.29	.47	5.1	10.8	14.4	12.4		12.4	5.8	113
1945	.30	.58	5.9	10.2	12.6	11.8		11.8	6.8	115
1946	.97	.67	11.1	16.6	11.4		14.1	14.1	9.5	85
1947	.91	.76	12.7	16.7	12.5		14.2	14.2	10.8	85
1948	.99	.85	11.8	13.9	14.5			14.5	12.3	104
1949	.89	.92	13.7	14.9	15.7			15.7	14.4	105
1950	.97	.89	15.3	17.2	15.2			15.2	13.5	88
1951	.92	.86	17.5	20.4	15.3		17.3	17.3	14.8	85
1952	.75	.84	17.6	21.0	17.5		17.8	17.8	14.9	85
1953	.78	.84	14.0	16.7	19.5	19.2		19.2	16.1	115
1954	.74	.86	15.1	17.6	19.4			19.4	16.7	110
1955	.83	.89	14.3	16.1	18.4			18.4	16.3	114
1956	.93	.94	13.6	14.4	16.8	16.6		16.6	15.6	115
1957	1.10	.98	14.6	14.8	16.0			16.0	15.7	108
1958	1.11	1.02	19.3	18.9	15.1		16.0	16.0	16.3	85
1959	1.11	1.08	23.0	21.3	16.0		18.1	18.1	19.6	85
1960	1.05	1.16	19.7	17.0	18.3			18.3	21.2	108
1961	1.02	1.24	23.0	18.5	19.1			19.1	23.8	104
1962	1.24	1.35	22.7	16.8	18.9			18.9	25.5	113
1963	1.47	1.49	33.5	22.5	17.4		19.1	19.1	28.5	85
1964	1.71	1.63	42.0	25.8	19.3		21.9	21.9	35.8	85
1965	1.87	1.81	45.5	25.0	21.7			21.7	39.2	86
1966	2.03	1.98	41.8	21.0	24.4	24.2		24.2	48.0	115
1967	2.10	2.14	47.5	22.2	23.9			23.9	51.0	107
1968	2.35	2.42	58.7	24.2	22.7			22.7	55.0	94
1969	2.59	2.64	71.0	26.8	22.5		22.8	22.8	60.0	85
1970E	2.90	2.88	67.0*	23.2	24.4			24.4	64.5	96
1971E	3.10									
1972E	3.40									
1973E	3.80									

E Estimated.
*Mean price of high and low during January–August 1970.

TABLE 8-8

Mechanical Valuation of the Common Stock of Standard Oil Company of New Jersey

Year	(1) Earnings Per Share	(2) Earnings, 7-Year Moving Average	(3) Mean Price of High and Low	(4) Adjusted P/E (3/2)	(5) Basic Multiplier Mean Adjusted P/E, Last 3-Years	Limit of Basic Multiplier (6) 115% of Adjusted P/E	Limit of Basic Multiplier (7) 85% of Adjusted P/E	(8) Adjusted Basic or Final Multiplier	(9) Indicated Value (2 × 8)	(10) Indicated Value as Percent of Mean Price
1935	.38		7							
1936	.58		9.7							
1937	.87		9.6							
1938	.44		7.7							
1939	.52		7.3							
1940	.70		6.0							
1941	.80		6.2							
1942	.47	.61	5.8	9.5						
1943	.70	.63	8.5	13.5						
1944	.88	.65	8.5	13						
1945	.87	.65	9.6	14.8	12		12.6	12.6	8.2	85
1946	1.01	.71	10.9	15.4	13.8		13.1	13.8	9.8	89
1947	1.53	.76	11.2	14.7	14.4			14.4	10.9	98
1948	2.03	.90	12.6	14	15			15	13.5	107
1949	1.49	1.07	11.4	10.7	14.7	12.3		12.3	13.2	115
1950	2.24	1.22	12.7	10.5	13.1	12.1		12.1	14.8	116
1951	2.91	1.44	20.2	14	11.7		11.9	11.9	17.1	85
1952	2.86	1.72	25.8	15	11.7		12.7	12.7	21.8	84
1953	3.04	2.01	24	12	13.2			13.2	26.5	110
1954	2.98	2.3	30	13	13.7			13.7	31.5	105
1955	3.61	2.51	42	16.8	13.3		14.2	14.2	35.6	85
1956	4.11	2.73	56	20.5	13.9		17.4	17.4	47.5	85
1957	4.08	3.11	59	19	16.8		16.1	16.8	52.5	89
1958	2.72	3.37	54.5	16.2	18.8	18.6		18.6	63	115
1959	2.91	3.34	51.5	15.4	18.6	17.7		17.7	59	115
1960	3.18	3.35	42	12.5	16.9	14.4		14.4	48.5	115
1961	3.50	3.37	46	13.6	14.7	15.6		14.7	49.5	108
1962	3.88	3.44	53	15.4	13.8		13.1	13.8	47.5	90
1963	4.73	3.48	68	19.5	13.8		16.5	16.5	57.5	85
1964	4.87	3.6	87	24	16.2		20.4	20.4	73.5	84
1965	4.74	4.0	82	20.5	19.6			19.6	78.4	96
1966	5.06	4.3	72	16.7	21.3	19.2		19.2	82.6	115
1967	5.54	4.6	65	14.1	20.4	16.2		16.2	74.5	114
1968	5.94	5.0	75.7	15.1	17.1			17.1	85.5	113
1969	5.78	5.3	73	13.8	15.3			15.3	81.0	111
1970E	5.70	5.4	57*	10.7	14.3	12.3		12.3	66.4	116

E Estimated.

*Mean price of high and low during January–August 1970.

ing power of the stock is based on historical earnings. It is computed on basis of a seven-year average—namely, earnings in the last six years and the earnings estimated for the current year. The estimate of earnings for the current year can be looked up in Standard & Poor's Stock Reports or Value Line Investment Survey. The restriction that the final multiplier be not over or under 15 percent of the current adjusted P/E is, however, the same as in the semimechanical method. Table 8-8 shows the results of the valuation of the common stock of Standard Oil Company of New Jersey by the mechanical method just described.

A Method of Comparative Valuation Based on Relative Earnings, Price, and P/E Ratios

In appraising the worth of common stocks, what the investors and analysts are often concerned most is usually the relative rather than the absolute values of individual stocks. What they usually ask themselves is whether the stock or stock group in question is of good value relative to the general market at the moment or relative to itself in the past few years or both.

As illustrated in Table 8-9 and Figure 8-1, we offer a method of comparative valuation which comprises the following steps:

1. *Relative earnings.* Compute a five-year moving average of earnings (four years past and the current year) for the stock in question and the Dow Jones Industrial Average. Divide the five-year average of earnings of DJIA into that of the stock to obtain relative earnings.
2. *Relative price.* Divide the mean price of yearly high and low of the stock by annual mean price of DJIA to obtain relative price.
3. *Relative price-earnings ratio.* Divide annual mean price by 5 year average earning to obtain adjusted P/E. Divide adjusted P/E of the stock in question by the adjusted P/E of DJIA to obtain relative P/E.

After the comparative table is completed and charted, the investor or the analyst can proceed to evaluate the findings in three aspects:

(a) What is the present level of relative P/E of the stock? Is it selling near the upper limits or lower limits of the historical range of its relative P/E? If it is selling at lower limit of its relative P/E, the stock should be considered attractive on basis of past experience. As shown in Figure 8-1, G.M. at 68 in mid-August, 1970 was selling near the upper limit of its relative P/E in the last two decades.

(b) What is the present level of adjusted P/E of DJIA? How is it compared to the average experience in the last ten years or so? A comparison between the present level of adjusted P/E and the average experience in the last decade should give some indications whether the general market is relatively high, low, or neutral. The adjusted P/E of DJIA as shown in Table 8-9 in mid-August 1970 was 13.1 and the average adjusted P/E in the previous ten years was 19.1 Therefore the general market as represented by DJIA at 720 (adjusted P/E 13.1) in

TABLE 8-9
Performance of General Motors Compared to DJIA

Year	Actual Earnings		Earnings, 5-Year Moving Average			Mean Price of Annual High and Low			Adjusted P/E (mean price/5-year Average Earnings)		
	G.M.	DJIA	G.M.	DJIA	G.M. as Percent of DJIA	G.M.	DJIA	G.M. as Percent of DJIA	G.M.	DJIA	G.M. as Percent of DJIA
1938	.36	6.01				6.6	128.7	5.1			
1939	.67	9.11				7.8	138.7	5.6			
1940	.71	10.92				8.2	132.3	6.2			
1941	.74	11.64				6.6	120.0	5.5			
1942	.59	9.22	.61	9.38	6.5	6.2	106.3	5.6	10.1	11.4	89%
1943	.54	9.74	.65	10.12	6.4	8.5	132.5	6.4	13.0	13.1	99
1944	.61	10.07	.64	10.32	6.2	9.8	143.3	6.8	15.3	13.9	110
1945	.67	10.56	.63	10.25	6.1	11.3	173.6	6.5	18.0	16.9	107
1946	.29	13.63	.54	10.64	5.1	10.7	187.8	5.7	19.8	17.1	116
1947	1.04	18.80	.63	12.56	5.0	9.8	175.0	5.6	15.5	14.0	111
1948	1.62	23.07	.85	15.23	5.6	9.9	179.3	5.5	11.6	11.8	98
1949	2.44	23.54	1.21	17.92	6.7	10.2	181.0	5.6	8.4	10.1	83
1950	3.13	30.70	1.70	21.95	7.7	14.4	215.9	6.7	8.5	9.9	86
1951	1.88	26.59	2.02	24.54	8.2	16.7	257.7	6.5	8.3	10.5	79
1952	2.09	24.78	2.23	25.74	8.8	19.0	274.0	6.9	8.5	10.7	79
1953	2.23	27.23	2.35	26.56	8.9	20.0	275.0	7.3	8.5	10.3	82
1954	3.02	28.18	2.47	27.50	9.0	25.5	353.5	7.2	10.3	12.8	80
1955	4.26	35.78	2.70	28.50	9.5	39.0	438.0	8.9	14.5	15.3	95
1956	3.01	33.34	2.92	29.70	9.8	45.0	492.0	9.1	15.4	16.5	93
1957	2.98	36.08	3.10	32.10	9.7	40.5	470.5	8.6	13.1	14.7	89
1958	2.21	27.95	3.10	32.30	9.6	41.0	510.5	8.0	13.2	15.8	83
1959	3.05	34.31	3.10	33.50	9.2	51.0	627.0	8.1	16.4	18.7	88
1960	3.35	32.21	2.92	32.80	8.9	44.0	625.8	7.0	15.1	19.1	79
1961	3.10	31.91	2.94	32.50	9.0	48.0	672.6	7.1	16.3	20.7	79
1962	4.82	36.43	3.31	32.60	10.2	53.5	630.9	8.5	16.1	19.4	83
1963	5.55	41.21	3.97	35.20	11.3	72.0	707.0	10.1	18.1	20.0	91
1964	6.04	46.51	4.57	37.60	12.1	91.0	828.9	11.0	19.8	22.0	90
1965	7.40	53.67	5.38	41.90	12.8	102.5	905.0	11.3	19.1	21.6	88
1966	6.23	57.68	6.01	47.10	12.7	87.0	869.7	10.0	14.5	18.5	78
1967	5.65	53.87	6.17	50.60	12.2	78.5	864.7	9.1	12.7	17.1	74
1968	6.01	57.89	6.27	53.92	11.6	81.2	897.0	9.0	13.0	16.7	78
1969	5.94	57.02	6.25	56.03	11.2	74.5	876.2	8.5	11.9	15.6	76
1970E	5.30	48.00	5.83	54.90	10.6	68.0*	720.0*	9.4	11.7	13.1	89

EEstimated.
*Mean price of high and low during January–August 1970.

mid-August 1970 should be considered quite low on basis of average experience in the last ten years.

(c) What is the present level of adjusted P/E of the stock? How does it compare with its adjusted P/E in the past ten years or so? A comparison between the present level and average past experience will indicate whether the stock is attractive relative to itself in terms of past experience. As shown in Table 8-9, G.M. at 68 in mid-August 1970 was selling at an adjusted P/E of 11.7 compared to 15.7, the average adjusted P/E of the stock in the previous ten years. The stock was therefore selling at reasonable P/E multiples in mid-August 1970 in terms of past experience in the last ten years.

To summarize the findings, the general market was found relatively low, and

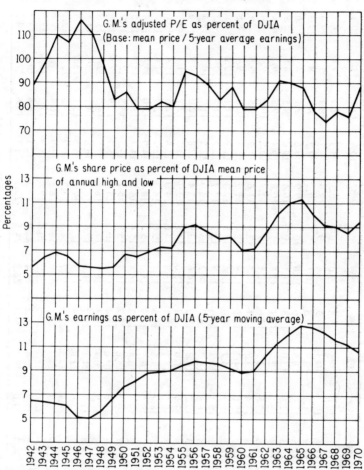

Figure 8-1
Performance of General Motors Compared to DJIA

the G.M. common was selling at a reasonable P/E on basis of past experience. However, G.M. was selling near the upper limit of its relative P/E. This may indicate that GM. is a reasonable "buy" now, but better "buys" can be probably found elsewhere.

If the investor or analyst feels that the DJIA does not represent well the general market, he can substitute the Standard & Poor's "425" industrial index for the DJIA for purpose of comparative evaluation.

Comparative Valuation in Terms of Payout Periods

Another method of comparative valuation is in terms of payout periods. If a stock is currently selling at a P/E ratio of 20, it means that the price is 20 times

TABLE 8-10
Price-Future Earnings Ratios, Payout Periods

Price-Earnings Ratio (Current Earnings)	Estimated Annual Growth Rate of Earnings Per Share													
	1%	2%	3%	4%	5%	6%	7%	8%	9%	10%	12%	15%	20%	25%
12	11.4	10.9	10.4	10.0	9.6	9.3	9.0	8.7	8.5	8.3	7.9	7.4	6.7	6.2
13	12.3	11.7	11.1	10.7	10.3	9.9	9.6	9.3	9.0	8.7	8.3	7.7	7.0	6.5
14	13.2	12.5	11.9	11.3	10.9	10.5	10.1	9.8	9.5	9.2	8.7	8.1	7.3	6.7
15	14.0	13.2	12.6	12.0	11.5	11.0	10.6	10.2	9.9	9.6	9.1	8.4	7.6	7.0
16	14.9	14.0	13.3	12.6	12.0	11.5	11.1	10.7	10.4	10.0	9.5	8.8	7.9	7.2
17	15.8	14.8	13.9	13.2	12.6	12.1	11.6	11.2	10.8	10.4	9.8	9.1	8.1	7.4
18	16.6	15.5	14.6	13.8	13.2	12.6	12.1	11.6	11.2	10.8	10.2	9.4	8.4	7.6
19	17.5	16.3	15.3	14.4	13.7	13.1	12.5	12.0	11.6	11.2	10.5	9.6	8.6	7.8
20	18.3	17.0	15.9	15.0	14.2	13.5	12.9	12.4	11.9	11.5	10.8	9.9	8.8	8.0
21	19.2	17.7	16.5	15.5	14.7	14.0	13.4	12.8	12.3	11.9	11.1	10.2	9.0	8.2
22	20.0	18.4	17.1	16.1	15.2	14.4	13.8	13.2	12.7	12.2	11.4	10.4	9.2	8.4
23	20.8	19.1	17.8	16.6	15.7	14.9	14.2	13.6	13.0	12.5	11.7	10.7	9.4	8.6
24	21.6	19.8	18.3	17.2	16.2	15.3	14.6	13.9	13.4	12.8	12.0	10.9	9.6	8.7
25	22.4	20.5	18.9	17.7	16.6	15.7	15.0	14.3	13.7	13.1	12.2	11.1	9.8	8.9
26	23.2	21.1	19.5	18.2	17.1	16.1	15.3	14.6	14.0	13.4	12.5	11.4	10.0	9.0
27	24.0	21.8	20.1	18.7	17.5	16.5	15.7	15.0	14.3	13.7	12.7	11.6	10.2	9.2
28	24.8	22.5	20.6	19.2	17.9	16.9	16.0	15.3	14.6	14.0	13.0	11.8	10.4	9.3
29	25.6	23.1	21.2	19.6	18.4	17.3	16.4	15.6	14.9	14.3	13.2	12.0	10.5	9.5
30	26.4	23.7	21.7	20.1	18.8	17.7	16.7	15.9	15.2	14.5	13.5	12.2	10.7	9.6
32	27.9	25.0	22.8	21.0	19.6	18.4	17.4	16.5	15.7	15.1	13.9	12.6	11.0	9.8
34	29.4	26.2	23.8	21.9	20.4	19.1	18.0	17.1	16.3	15.5	14.3	12.9	11.3	10.1
36	30.9	27.4	24.8	22.7	21.1	19.7	18.6	17.6	16.8	16.0	14.7	13.3	11.5	10.3
38	32.4	28.5	25.7	23.6	21.8	20.4	19.2	18.1	17.2	16.5	15.1	13.6	11.8	10.5
40	33.8	29.7	26.7	24.4	22.5	21.0	19.7	18.6	17.7	16.9	15.5	13.9	12.1	10.7
45	37.3	32.4	28.9	26.3	24.2	22.5	21.0	19.8	18.8	17.9	16.4	14.7	12.6	11.2
50	40.7	35.0	31.0	28.0	25.7	23.8	22.2	20.9	19.8	18.8	17.2	15.3	13.2	11.7
60	47.2	39.8	34.8	31.2	28.4	26.2	24.4	22.8	21.5	20.4	18.6	16.5	14.1	12.4
70	53.3	44.2	38.3	34.0	30.8	28.3	26.2	24.5	23.1	21.8	19.8	17.5	14.9	13.1

SOURCE: Bell, "The Price-Future Earnings Ratio," *Financial Analysts Journal*, August 1958, p. 28, formula:

$$x = \frac{(1+i)^n - 1}{i}$$

where x = price earnings ratio, current earnings
n = price-future earnings ratio
i = growth rate in per share earnings

the current earnings. Alternatively, it can also mean that it will take 20 years to recover the price of the stock from flow of earnings if the earnings remain constant during the period. The payout period for the stock is therefore 20 years. However, earnings of the majority of companies will normally grow through retention and reinvestment of a part of their earnings; therefore the payout period will be less than the current price-earnings ratio. Table 8-10 shows payout periods for different combinations of price-earnings ratios and earnings growth rates. By referring to the table, the analyst can look up the payout periods of different stocks with varying growth prospects. He can then determine which stock is most attractive on basis of comparison of duration of payout periods. For illustration, the adjacent table shows the payout periods of IBM, Colgate-Palmolive, Burroughs Corporation, and DJIA as of mid-August 1970 on basis of assumed earnings growth rates.

	Current P/E	Estimated Earnings Growth Rates, Percent	Pay out Periods
IBM	27	15	11.6
Colgate-Palmolive	13	8	9.3
Burroughs Corporation	30	20	10.7
DJIA	14	4	11.3

Valuation on Basis of Correlation Analysis

Another approach to valuation of indidivual stocks can be based on correlation analysis. In a multiple correlation analysis, the first step is to select several factors or variables which are believed to be the main factors influencing or determining the price of a stock. For purpose of illustration, a multiple correlation analysis was applied below to a selected sample of 27 large companies in the electronic industry in 1968.

The Independent Factors or Variables Selected. On basis of deductive reasoning and observations of past experience in the stock market, we are of the view that the price of an individual stock in the long run is greatly influenced by a combination of five factors:

1. Average rate of return on equity earned by the corporation in past five years or so.
2. Extent of variation in rates of return earned on equity in last five years.
3. Earnings growth rate in past five years.
4. Estimate of earnings per share for the current year.
5. Projected level of earnings per share in three to five years.

Brief Explanations of the Selected Independent Variables in Table 8-11. In Table 8-11, X_1 represents average rate of return on equity during 1963–67. Rate

TABLE 8-11
Factors Affecting Stock Price

Company	Mean Price of High and Low January–September 1968	Average Rate of Return on Equity Past 5 Years	Variation of Rate of Return on Equity Past 5 years, percent	Growth of Earnings Past 5 Years, Percent	Estimated of Earning for Current Year (1968)	Projected Earning Level in 3–5 Years by Value Line
	Y	X_1	X_2	X_3	X_4	X_5
Beekman Instruments	52.5	8.6	16	16	1.50	4.90
Gen. Instruments	53.5	9.4	1	465	2.65	3.30
Litton Industries	83	18.5	5	250	2.30	5.25
Raytheon	43.5	9.5	1	70	2.05	2.70
Texas Instruments	100.5	14.5	19.3	150	2.65	7.00
AMP, Inc.	33.5	22.3	5.7	86	1.30	2.00
G. E.	91	15.7	4.1	35	4.25	7.00
R. C. A.	50	16.9	1	176	2.30	3.00
Sperry-Rand	52.5	6.5	3	335	2.15	3.70
Westinghouse	69	9.4	3	104	3.45	4.25
Addressograph-Multigraph . . .	71.5	13.6	10	22	2.90	4.70
Burroughs	188	9.8	1	200	5.00	8.50
Nat'l Cash Register	127	10.0	3	48	4.25	7.00
Pitney-Bowes	63.5	15.4	6.5	35	2.20	4.65
S. C. M.	49	8.7	1	174	2.50	4.50
Xerox	278	35.6	21.5	515	5.50	10.75
Zenith Radio	58	21.3	3	102	2.40	3.70
Sanders Associations	54	15.8	40	90	1.35	2.70
Magnavox	45.5	26.2	3	130	2.45	3.85
Int. Tel. & Tel.	52	11.2	1	86	2.50	3.75
Honeywell	115	13.7	8.3	53	3.30	6.35
Gen. Precision	40	9.1	1	75	2.40	4.05
Fairchild Camera	72	12.0	36	15	1.90	8.50
Collins Radio	77	8.6	3	270	4.25	6.50
Ampex	26.5	13.0	4.3	87	1.40	2.20
Consolidated Electric	39.5	11.0	1	78	2.75	5.40
I. B. M.	350	17.9	6.7	102	6.75	11.00

of return on equity is obtained by dividing net income after tax per share by book value per share.

X_2 represents extent of variation in rates of return earned on equity during 1963–67. For companies whose rate of return on equity was increased every year in past five years, the trend was favorable, and therefore a minimum 1 percent variation was assigned. For companies whose rate of return on equity was increased four out of five years, a 3 percent variation was arbitrarily assigned. For companies whose rate of return was decreased every year in the past five years, the trend was unfavorable and a 40 percent variation was arbitrarily assigned. For the remaining companies, the rates of variation were computed on basis of the average deviation method.

X_3 represents growth of earnings per share from 1962 to 1967 in percent.

X_4 represents estimate of earnings per share for the year 1968.

X_5 represents projected level of earnings per share during 1971–73 by Value Line Investment Survey.

Y represents the dependent variable, the mean price of high and low during January–September 1968.

The Regression Equation. A multiple correlation analysis was applied to the data in Table 8-11. The resultant regression equation was

$$Y = -96.254 + 1.778X_1 + 1.192X_2 + 0.014X_3 + 40.201X_4 + 5.658X_5$$

The coefficient of correlation R was 93.7 percent.

Calculated Values for Stocks. Once the correlation equation is arrived at, the final step of arriving at calculated values for stocks is very simple. If the numerical values for $X_1 - X_5$ for stocks are already available as in Table 8-11, calculated values for stocks will be obtained by simply substituting these numerical values for $X_1 - X_5$ in the equation above. However, if the same equation is to be used for following years, then the first step is to ascertain the numerical values for $X_1 - X_5$, and then substitute them in the equation.

Evaluation of Statistical Findings

In terms of order of importance on Y, the five independent variables ranked as X_4, X_2, X_1, X_5, and X_3. X_4, the estimate of earnings per share for the current year, was the most important factor influencing mean price of a stock and X_3, growth rate of earnings in the last five years, was found the least important among the five factors.

The coefficient of correlation R was 93.7 percent which means that 88 percent (R^2) of the variations in mean price of stocks were accounted for by factors $X_1 - X_5$, leaving only about 12 percent of the variations unexplained due to other causes. In addition, the correlation coefficient of 93.7 percent on basis of 27 observations is statistically significant.

To conclude, the mean prices of stocks were found highly correlated to the selected five factors mentioned above. Consequently, the valuation procedure on basis of correlation analysis of data on these factors seems quite meaningful and worthy of further exploration by analysts.

SUMMARY

Methods of Valuation

A number of approaches to the valuation of common stocks are discussed above. The four main methods are

1. Present worth approach—using preconstructed tables by various investment writers.
2. Valuation methods on basis of capitalizing anticipated average earning power.
3. Comparative valuation methods based on relative earnings, price, and P/E ratio; and in terms of payout periods.
4. Valuation on basis of correlation analysis.

Valuation of IBM as an Illustration

Table 8-12 shows valuation of IBM by the present-worth approach under various assumptions about the stock. It shows also the valuation of IBM using the valuation method on basis of correlation analysis.

TABLE 8-12
Valuation of the Common Stock of International Business Machine (IBM)

Stock	Key Assumptions about the Stock				P/E or Price-Dividend Ratio Derived	Current Earnings or Dividend	Valuation
	Earnings or Dividend Growth Rate	Duration of Growth, Years	Rate of Return Desired or Discount Rate	P/E Ratio at Time of Sale			
Present-worth approach							
IBM	15%, 10% (D)	10, 10	6½%		87 × D	4.80 (D)	$417
	(using Soldovsky & Murphy's table)						
IBM	10% (E)	20	7%	20	45.6 × E	8.85 (E)	$404
	(using S. E. Guild's table)						
IBM	12% (E)	10	7%		43.8 × E	8.85 (E)	$388
	(using Molodovsky, May & Chottiner's table)						

Valuation based on correlation analysis

$$Y = -96.254 + 1.778x_1 + 1.192x_2 + 0.014x_3 + 40.201x_4 + 5.658x_5$$

where
X_1: Rate of return in past 5 years   = 17.9
X_2: Variation of rate of return on equity   = 6.7
X_3: Growth of earnings in past 5 years in % = 102
X_4: Estimated current earnings per share (1970) = 8.85
X_5: Projected earnings level in 3–5 years   = 13

Valuation of IBM $Y = \$373$

NOTE: Estimates of X_1, X_2, X_4 and X_5 are obtained from Table 8-11.

Key Variables in Valuation

As shown in Table 8-12, the present worth or the "normal value" of a stock depends primarily on three factors:

(a) Expected rate of growth of earnings or dividends.
(b) The duration of growth of earnings.
(c) Rate of return desired by investors from the stock or, in other words, the rate used by investors to discount future earnings of the stock.

Any change in any one or any combination of these three factors will affect the valuation of a stock as can be seen in the valuation of IBM in Table 8-12.

The rate of return desired by investors (discount rate of future earnings) is primarily a function of riskiness of the stock. Investors generally do not like risk, the higher the risk in receiving future returns (dividend and capital gain) from the stock, the greater will be the rate of return demanded by investors. Therefore, investors usually require lower rate of return on stocks of seasoned companies or of companies of established growth record. They demand, on other hand, higher return on lower-grade stocks whose future performance are relatively unclear and uncertain.

Guidelines on Choice of Discount Rate

Since the choice of higher or lower discount rate affects substantially the valuation of a stock, proper care should be given to the final selection of a discount rate applicable to a given stock. The best approach to this matter is probably to follow these logical steps:

1. To find out what rates of return the investors received in the past decade or so on stocks listed on the New York Stock Exchange, on indexes such as Standard & Poor's 425 Industrials, and Dow Jones Industrial Average
2. To find out what has been the rate of return from this particular stock in question in the last decade
3. To find out what adjustments, if any, should be made in the historical rate of return of the stock in the light of prospects about the stock and the equity market in general.

For purpose of reference for the first step, some empirical evidences are offered below:

(a) Professors Fisher and Lorie found from their extensive studies that the rate of return before tax on all common stocks listed on the New York Stock Exchange during the entire period from 1926 to 1960 was about 9 percent.[5]

(b) The rate of return on Dow Jones Industrial Average (30 large industrials) in the past ten years from 1960 to 1970 was estimated by the author at about 7¼ percent, of which dividend yield accounted for 3½ percent and the remaining 3¾ percent was price appreciation.

(c) The rate of return on Standard & Poor's 425 Industrials during the same period from 1960 to 1970 was about 8½ percent, of which 3¼ percent was dividend yield and 5¼ percent was price appreciation.

(d) Professors Weston and Brigham made some estimates of their own on the rates of returns on common stocks that investors probably have

[5] L. Fisher and J. H. Lorie, "Rates of Return on Investments in Common Stocks," *The Journal of Business*, University of Chicago, January 1964.

experienced in the past. Their estimates for three types of companies are[6]

Company Characteristics	Estimated Rates of Return on Common Stocks Under Normal Stock Market Conditions, Percent
Low risk, high marketability	7
Average risk and marketability	8–10
High risk, low marketability	12

The empirical evidence cited above should be useful as a frame of reference. If the analyst follows judiciously the other two steps suggested above, he should be in all likelihood making good judgment in the selection of an appropriate discount rate for the stock in question.

SUGGESTED READINGS

Bauman, W. Scott, *Estimating the Present Value of Common Stocks by the Variable Method*. Ann Arbor: University of Michigan, Bureau of Business Research, Graduate School of Business Administration, 1963; "Investment Returns and Present Values," *Financial Analysts Journal*, November–December 1969.

Bernhard, Arnold, *The Evaluation of Common Stocks*. New York: Simon and Schuster, 1959.

Factors Affecting the Stock Market—A Staff Report to the *Committee on Banking and Currency*, U.S. Senate, Washington, D.C.: Government Printing Office, 1965.

Fredrikson, E. Bruce (ed.), *Frontiers of Investment Analysis*. Rev. ed. Scranton, Pa.: Intext Educational Publishers, 1971.

Gordon, Myron J., *The Investment, Financing and Valuation of the Corporation*. Homewood, Ill.: Richard D. Irwin, Inc., 1962.

Graham, Benjamin, et al., *Security Analysis*. 4th ed. New York: McGraw-Hill Book Company, 1962.

Guild, Samuel E., *Stock Growth and Discount Tables*. New York: Financial Publishing Co., 1931.

Hayes, Douglas A., *Investments: Analysis and Management*. New York: The Macmillan Company, 1966.

Huang, Stanley S. C., *Corporate Earning Power and Valuation of Common Stock*. Larchmont, N.Y.: Investors Intelligence, Inc., 1968.

Institute of Chartered Financial Analysts, *C.F.A. Readings in Financial Analysis*. Homewood, Ill.: Richard D. Irwin, Inc., 1966.

Latané, H. A., D. L. Tuttle, and C. P. Jones, "E/P Ratios vs. Changes in Earnings," *Financial Analysts Journal*, January–February 1969.

[6] J. Fred Weston and Eugene F. Brigham, *Managerial Finance*, 3d ed. (New York: Holt, Rinehart & Winston, 1969), p. 325.

Lerner, Eugene M. (ed.), *Readings in Financial Analysis and Investment Management.* New York: Institute of Chartered Financial Analysts, Inc., 1963.

Molodovsky, Nicholas, Catherine May, and Sherman Chottiner, "Common Stock Valuation," *Financial Analysts Journal,* March–April, 1965.

Murphy, J. E., Jr., and J. Russell Nelson, "Stability of P/E Ratios," *Financial Analysts Journal,* March–April 1969.

Soldofsky, R. M., and J. T. Murphy, *Growth Yields on Common Stock – Theory and Tables.* Ames, Iowa: State University of Iowa, Bureau of Business and Economic Research, 1961.

Wendt, Paul F., "Current Growth Stock Valuation Methods," *Financial Analysts Journal,* March–April 1965.

Wu, H. K., and A. J. Zakon (eds.), *Elements of Investments, Selected Readings.* New York: Holt, Rinehart and Winston, Inc., 1965.

QUESTIONS AND PROBLEMS

1. Indicate the pros and cons of using the present-worth approach and discount tables in the valuation of common stocks.
2. Give two illustrations of your own of valuation of common stocks by using any one of the discount tables reproduced and included in this chapter.
3. Prepare a table listing the current price-earnings ratios for 30 industry groups. Explain why some industry groups are selling at high P/E, whereas a few others are selling at very low P/E.
4. If the value of common stock is dependent on earnings, why is it that common stock of companies without earnings still has a market value?
5. What is the significance of the P/E ratio, and how can it help us determine whether the price of a stock is reasonable or not?
6. Prepare a valuation for a selected company on basis of any one of the methods suggested by the author in this chapter.
7. Prepare a valuation of the common stock of Sears, Roebuck based on comparative valuation method as discussed in the text.
8. What are the dangers involved in purchasing a high P/E growth stock?

9. Market Analysis

MARKET ANALYSIS VS. SECURITY ANALYSIS

One often hears that there are two approaches to the stock market, the fundamental approach and the technical approach. The fundamental approach concerns itself with the study of earnings and dividends record, the quality of management, and prospects of individual companies and industries. It is in the domain of security analysis. The technical approach on the other hand concerns itself with the study of the action of the market itself, with the aim to predict short-term price movements. It is therefore in the domain of market analysis.

Since it is important for the stock buyers of all types and inclinations to understand thoroughly the differences between the two approaches, we compare them as follows:

	Technical Approach (market analysis)	Fundamental Approach (security analysis)
Objective	To predict short-term movements of stock prices.	To gauge long-term security values.
Object of study	Action of the stock market, particularly price and volume changes of individual issues and the general market.	Earnings and dividends record, sales, product mix, profit margins, the quality of management, outlook of profit of the individual companies, industries and the whole economy.
Type of buyer	Mostly in-and-out short-term traders.	Mainly the long-term security holders.
Strategy and tactics	Follow trading rules such as placing stop loss orders, cut losses short and let profits run; identify and take advantage of trends in movements of security prices.	Buy issues at reasonable prices in terms of both historical record and outlook; ignore short-term price movements.

176

	Technical Approach	Fundamental Approach
	(market analysis)	(security analysis)
Philosophy or conviction	Short-term price movements can be predicted on basis of price-volume study, chart pattern of individual stocks and other technical market indicators.	Long-term security values can be gauged on basis of fundamental factors. Short-term price changes, to say the least, are difficult to forecast.

THE DOW THEORY

The Dow theory is the foundation from which much of modern-day technical market analysis originates. The theory was formulated by Charles H. Dow and expressed in articles and editorials written by him for the *Wall Street Journal* around the turn of the century. The theory was later interpreted, expanded, and refined by William P. Hamilton and Robert Rhea. Present-day Dow theory is therefore a synthesis of the thoughts of Dow, Hamilton, and Rhea. The basic tenets of their theory are:[1]

Dow's three movements
Determining the primary trend
Principle of confirmation
The "line" formation
Relationship between volume and price movement

Dow's Three Movements

The "market," meaning the price of stocks in general, is always to be considered as having three movements, all going on at the same time. The first and the most important one is the primary trend, which is a broad upward or downward movement lasting usually a few years. The upward movement is also known as a *bull market*, and the downward movement as a *bear market*. The second movement represents intermediate reactions of the major trend—namely, important declines in a bull market or advances in a bear market. These interruptions of the major trend last usually several weeks to several months, retracing one-third to two-thirds of the price change in the preceding primary swing. The third movement represents day-to-day changes in security prices. Except as building blocks of the secondary movement, these daily fluctuations are not considered important by the Dow theorists.

[1] Readers interested in the development and more detailed exposition of the Dow theory are advised to consult William P. Hamilton, *The Stock Market Barometer* (New York: Richard Russel Associates, 1960); Robert Rhea *The Dow Theory* (Boulder, Colo.: Rhea, Greiner & Co., 1959); and Richard Russel, *The Dow Theory Today* (New York: Richard Russel Associates, 1961).

Determining the Primary Trend

A major upward trend is said to be in existence when successive rallies penetrate preceding high points with ensuing declines terminating above preceding low points. Conversely, a major downward movement is signified by successive rallies failing to reach preceding high points with ensuing declines carrying below preceding low points.

Principle of Confirmation

However, a major upward movement found in the Dow Jones Industrial Average does not automatically signal that a bull market is in existence. For a bull market to be in existence, a similar upward movement has to be found also in the Dow Jones Transportation Average. Conversely, a bear market is signaled when both averages are found in a major downward movement. Should the Dow Jones Transportation Average fail to confirm the major movement of the Dow Jones Industrial Average, the current movement of the DJIA is held in suspect and the previous trend is considered still intact.

The "Line" Formation

A "line" formation in Dow theory parlance represents a sidewise movement of several weeks duration during which the price variation of both Dow Jones Industrial and Transportation Average move within a range of approximately 5 percent. The formation indicates that supply and demand is more or less in equilibrium. Simultaneous advances beyond the narrow range signifies stronger forces of demand and predict higher prices whereas simultaneous decline below the "line" formation indicates lower prices to follow.

Relationship Between Volume and Price Movement

The Dow Theory as originally formulated by Charles H. Dow was based primarily on price movements of two averages. However, Dow had the belief that volume pointed out the trend of prices. Whereas William P. Hamilton rarely discussed the relation of volume to price movement, Robert Rhea stated clearly the relationship between the two.

> A market which has been overbought becomes dull on rallies and develops activity on declines; conversely, when a market is oversold, the tendency is to become dull on declines and active on rallies. Bull markets terminate in a period of excessive activity and begin with comparatively light transactions.[2]

Nevertheless, volume in Dow theory serves primarily as supporting evidence which may aid interpretation in practice. Trend signals are still dictated by changes solely in price movements.

[2] Robert Rhea, *The Dow Theory* (Boulder, Colo.: Rhea, Greiner & Co., 1959), p. 15.

Defects of the Dow Theory

After explaining the basic tenets of the Dow theory as above, we now come to indicate several deficiencies or criticisms of the theory as seen by its critics.

First, the theory is always late in identifying the major trend because of the requirement of confirmation of the two averages.

Second, the Dow theory is designed to identify the major trend, and therefore renders little help to the intermediate trend investor.

Third, the Dow theory is designed to tell the direction of major trend, but tells nothing about what stocks to buy or sell.

Fourth, the Dow theory is based primarily on study of price movement. Volume data are not receiving sufficient attention.

TECHNICAL INDICATORS OF STOCK PRICE LEVEL

As mentioned earlier, the followers of the technical approach or market analysis believe that the short-term price movements of the general market and individual stocks are by and large predictable. Their tools are price-volume studies, chart patterns of individual stocks, and a collection of technical market indicators. The technical indicators are derived from the study of the actions consummated in the stock market itself. The more important technical indicators are reviewed below.

Trends and Moving Average

Students and followers of the technical market approach are firmly convinced that stock prices tend to move in trends. To identify the major trend of price movement of an individual stock or stock average, market analysts often use a 200-day moving average, or alternatively a 30-week moving average of weekly prices. Granville has suggested eight basic rules for successful trading through the use of 200-day moving-average price charts as follows.

The eight basic ways of trading successfully by using these 200-day moving average price charts are as follows:

(1) If the 200-day average line flattens out following a previous decline, or is advancing, and the price of the stock penetrates that average line on the upside, this comprises a major buying signal.

(2) If the price of the stock falls below the 200-day moving average price line while the average line is still rising, this also is considered to be a buying opportunity.

(3) If the stock price is above the 200-day line and is declining toward that line, fails to go through and starts to turn up again, this is a buying signal.

(4) If the stock price falls too fast under the declining 200-day average line, it is entitled to an advance back toward the average line and the stock can be bought for this short-term technical rise.

(5) If the 200-day average line flattens out following a previous

rise, or is declining, and the price of the stock penetrates that line on the downside, this comprises a major selling signal.

(6) If the price of the stock rises above the 200-day moving average price line while the average line is still falling, this also is considered to be a selling opportunity.

(7) If the stock price is below the 200-day line and is advancing toward that line, fails to go through and starts to turn down again, this is a selling signal.

(8) If the stock price advances too fast above the advancing 200-day average line, it is entitled to a reaction back toward the average line and the stock can be sold for this short-term technical reaction.[3]

These rules are, of course, simply guidelines suggested by a well-known market analyst and should not be blindly adopted by the stock trader as a system for playing the market.

To identify the intermediate trend of price movement, a short span of moving average, usually 20 days to 60 days, is often used.

Confirmation Between Stock Averages

The Dow Jones Industrial Average represents the price index of 30 "blue chip" stocks. The Standard & Poor's "425" Industrials Index represents price index of 425 larger industrial issues on the New York Stock Exchange, and the New York Stock Exchange Composite Index includes all issues on the exchange. Advance in the DJIA confirmed by proportionate gain of S&P's 425 or the NYSE composite index indicates a more universal advance and signals that the advance is more likely to continue. Conversely, a decline of similar magnitude registered in several stock averages would indicate the decline will more likely continue. The technical indicator of confirmation between stock averages differs from the principle of confirmation in the Dow theory in two respects: (1) the latter requires a confirmation between Dow Jones industrial and rail averages, and (2) the latter is designed to identify the major trend whereas the former is concerned more or less with day to day changes in stock prices.

The Advance-and-Decline Line

The advance-and-decline line measures the cumulative net differences between the number of issues advanced and declined. The starting point can be any time. Table 9-1 shows the computation of advance-decline line together with changes in DJIA for the period of July 20 to August 21, 1970. The basic idea underlying the advance-and-decline line is to find out whether the daily price changes registered in a stock average such as DJIA are shared by the market as a whole in terms of number of issues advanced or declined. It is believed that continued price advances in 30 blue-chip stocks in the DJIA cannot be main-

---

[3] Joseph E. Granville, *A Strategy of Daily Stock Market Timing for Maximum Profit* (Englewood Cliffs, N.J.: Prentice-Hall, Inc., 1960), pp. 237-238.

TABLE 9-1
Cumulative Advance-Decline Differential and Changes in DJIA

Date	Number of Issues Advanced	Number of Issues Declined	Cumulative Advances	Cumulative Declines	Cumulative Net Advance (+) or Decline (−)	Trend	DJIA	Net Changes
7-20-70	810	510	810	510	300	−	733.9	−
21	398	900	1,208	1,410	−202	Down	722.1	−11.8
22	765	496	1,973	1,906	67	Up	724.7	+ 2.6
23	855	420	2,828	2,326	502	Up	732.7	+ 8.0
24	638	607	3,466	2,933	533	Up	730.2	− 2.5
27	625	636	4,091	2,569	522	Down	730.1	− .1
28	671	564	4,762	4,133	629	Up	731.5	+ 1.4
29	809	457	5,571	4,590	981	Up	735.6	+ 4.1
30	597	614	6,168	5,204	964	Down	734.7	− .9
31	644	617	6,812	5,821	991	Up	734.1	− .6
8-3-70	385	855	7,197	6,676	521	Down	723.0	−11.1
4	569	628	7,766	7,304	462	Down	725.9	+ 2.9
5	599	617	8,365	7,921	444	Down	724.8	− 1.1
6	474	705	8,839	8,626	213	Down	722.8	− 2.0
7	666	505	9,505	9,131	374	Up	725.7	+ 2.9
10	328	973	9,833	10,104	−271	Down	713.9	−11.8
11	364	826	10,197	10,930	−733	Down	712.6	− 1.3
12	486	673	10,683	11,603	−920	Down	710.6	− 2.0
13	411	780	11,094	12,383	−1,289	Down	707.4	− 3.2
14	628	558	11,722	12,941	−1,219	Up	710.8	+ 3.4
17	556	637	12,278	13,578	−1,300	Down	709.1	− 1.7
18	843	411	13,121	13,989	−868	Up	716.7	+ 7.6
19	803	471	13,924	14,460	−536	Up	724.0	+ 7.3
20	701	530	14,625	14,990	−365	Up	729.6	+ 5.6
21	1,116	275	15,741	15,265	476	Up	745.4	+15.8

tained long if these advances are not shared by majority issues on the New York Stock Exchange. Conversely, if more issues are going up than down and if the DJIA is also going up, it is considered that price advance is more likely to continue. Many market analysts believed that the advance-decline line when compared with DJIA is of much predictive value of price movement.

New Highs and New Lows

A rising market should normally witness an expanding number of new highs and a decreasing number of new lows. Conversely, a declining market is often accompanied by increasing number of new lows and decreasing number of new highs.

In order to smooth out daily erratic fluctuations for the purpose of finding trend of movement, some kind of moving average is usually applied to the data of new highs and new lows. In Table 9-2 we suggest two ways of computing an index for new highs and new lows. Under the first method, we get a new high as percentage of a combined total of new high and new low, and than take a

TABLE 9-2
New High—New Low Indexes

(A)

Date	New High on NYSE	New Low on NYSE	Total	New High as Percent of Total	3-Day Moving Average	DJIA
7-20-70	14	20	34	41.0	—	733.9
21	7	36	43	16.3	—	722.1
22	2	21	23	8.7	22.0	724.7
23	9	19	28	32.0	19.0	732.7
24	7	17	24	29.2	23.3	730.2
27	3	19	22	13.7	25.0	730.1
28	8	18	26	30.8	24.6	731.5
29	16	21	37	43.4	29.3	735.6
30	9	23	32	28.0	34.1	734.7
31	11	18	29	38.0	36.5	734.1
8-3-70	5	32	37	13.5	26.5	723.0
4	5	31	36	13.9	21.8	725.9
5	7	29	36	19.5	15.6	724.8
6	7	35	42	16.7	16.7	722.8
7	10	29	39	25.6	20.6	725.7

(B)

Date	New High on NYSE	New Low on NYSE	Difference	5-Day Moving Average	DJIA
7-20-70	14	20	− 6	—	733.9
21	7	36	−29	—	722.1
22	2	21	−19	—	724.7
23	9	19	−10	—	732.7
24	7	17	−10	−14.8	730.2
27	3	19	−16	−16.8	730.1
28	8	18	−10	−13.0	731.5
29	16	21	− 5	−10.2	735.6
30	9	23	−14	−11.0	734.7
31	11	18	− 7	−10.4	734.1
8-3-70	5	32	−27	−12.6	723.0
4	5	31	−26	−15.8	725.9
5	7	29	−22	−19.2	724.8
6	7	35	−28	−22.0	722.8
7	10	29	−19	−24.4	725.7

three-day moving average. Under the second method, we take a difference between the new highs and new lows and then apply a five-day moving average to the differences between new highs and new lows.

The new-high-new-low indicator should normally correspond to the movement in stock averages. However, when there is divergency between the two, the new-high-new-low indicator provides often the clue to future price movement.

Confidence Indicator: Speculative vs. Blue Chips

When the market is advancing and full of optimistic forecasts, investors are willing to take higher risks and buy speculative stocks. Conversely, when the market is declining and investors are wary about market outlook, they usually return to high-grade common stocks. Many market analysts believe that a comparison between the prices of speculative stocks and high grade commons as in Table 9-3 provides clues to future price movements.

TABLE 9-3
Confidence Index Speculative vs. High Grade
Common Stock Prices

Date	S&P's 20 Low-Price Common	S&P's 25 High-Grade Common	Confidence Index: Low-Price Common to High-Grade Common	S&P's 425 Industrials
3-4-70	155.52	82.74	1.89	98.44
11	154.63	81.52	1.90	96.97
18	151.98	81.03	1.88	95.74
25	153.86	82.18	1.87	98.22
4-1-70	152.06	82.66	1.84	98.55
8	145.00	82.11	1.77	96.74
15	140.49	80.58	1.75	94.83
22	133.30	77.70	1.72	92.21
29	124.41	75.51	1.65	89.58
5-6-70	120.84	73.75	1.64	86.95
13	113.30	70.61	1.60	83.67
20	107.61	68.44	1.57	80.27
27	102.75	67.56^L	1.52	79.49^L
6-3-70	117.27	71.69	1.63	86.08
10	110.70	70.21	1.58	82.79
17	111.60	70.83	1.58	83.49
24	104.62	69.30	1.51	81.23
7-1-70	100.08	69.05	1.45	80.26
8	97.02	69.18	1.40	79.92
15	95.25^L	70.93	1.35^L	82.37
22	101.28	71.73	1.42	84.42
29	103.37	72.58	1.43	85.63
8-5-70	102.83	71.22	1.44	84.63
12	99.26	70.10	1.42	82.56
19	99.40	71.16	1.40	84.30

NOTE: Data from "The Outlook," Standard & Poor's Corporation.
^{L}Lowest point during the period.

The probable pattern of such a confidence index according to Leo Barnes, at intermediate and major turning points is likely as follows:

1. At the bottom of a decline, investors' confidence is typically negligible and the confidence index is low and declining. But as investors' hopes start to revive, the drop in the confidence index comes to a

halt and reverses itself. This is usually one of the first clues to the end of a bear market.

2. During the first stages of a bull market or an extended intermediate rise, the confidence index usually lags as investors rush to find bargains among the "blue chips." Then—

3. As the advance speeds up, speculation is rampant and the confidence index rises to the high point of its cycle. But—

4. Before the top of a major rise, investors lose confidence and sell speculative issues, so that the index falls prior to a peak.[4]

The Odd-Lot Index

An odd-lot transaction is a purchase or sale of a lot less than 100 shares. Odd-lot transactions are usually made by small investors. There is a popular theory in the financial community that the small investors are usually wrong. The reason is probably that the small investors are less sophisticated in the art of investment and easily influenced by the prevalent wave of optimism or gloom. Market analysts who subscribe to the theory follow the pattern of odd-lot transactions for clues to future price movement.

Odd-Lot Sales/Purchases. The odd-lot index is usually derived by dividing odd-lot purchases into sales. Normally, the odd-lot purchases exceed sales. The ratio is about 11 to 10. According to the odd-lot theory, the small investors are usually timid in the initial stage of a bull market, and therefore buy less than normal. However, at a later stage of the bull market the small investors cannot resist the lure of the advancing market and become bold in their purchases. Conversely, at the initial stage of a declining market the small investor resists selling, but, as the market declines more precipitously, they get panicky and pour in sale orders. Mr. William L. Jiler, a famous market analyst, enunciated his rules for interpreting the odd-lot index as follows:

1. Odd-lot buying is invariably much less than normal during a bull move. This can help to confirm a rise in the market as a valid major move.
2. Toward the end of an advance, odd-lotters begin to buy more than normally. They continue to do so while the market is making its top. Often their buying becomes frenzied close to the very top.
3. They also buy more than normally during the beginning stage of a decline in the market. This tapers off as the decline continues.
4. Around a valid bottom, odd-lot buying is usually well below normal.[5]

Odd-Lot Short Sales/Sales. This is an odd-lot short sales ratio measuring the extent of short sales in total odd-lot sales. The odd-lot short seller is a specu-

---

[4] Leo Barnes, *Your Investments* (New York: American Research Council, 1968), p. 182.

[5] William L. Jiler, "How Charts Can Help You in the Stock Market," *Trendline*, Standard & Poor's Corporation, 1962, p. 173.

lator. According to the odd-lot theory, he is usually more wrong than the average odd lotter. The odd-lot short sellers tend to increase their short sales sharply near the bottom of a declining market. As soon as the market turns around, they tend to lose courage and conviction, reducing sharply their short sales. Table 9-4 shows the calculation of odd-lot index and short-sales ratio for a brief recent period, July 1 to August 19, 1970. Even though the period is brief, it should be interesting to compare these statistics with the tenets of odd-lot theory as mentioned above.

TABLE 9-4
Odd-Lot Index and Odd-Lot Short-Sales Index

Date	Purchases, Thousands of Shares*	Sales, Thousands of Shares*	Short Sales, Thousands of Shares*	Odd-Lot Index Sales/Purchases	Odd-Lot Short-Sales Index Short Sales/Sales	DJIA
7-1-70	293.8	259.6	9.584	.89	3.68%	687.6
2	326.9	274.4	17.670	.84	6.45%	689.1
6	386.1	350.8	23.405	.91	6.65%	675.7
7	345.6	327.4	26.563	.95	8.15%	669.4
8	306.4	274.0	16.607	.90	6.05%	682.1
9	329.5	281.8	12.421	.86	4.40%	692.8
10	322.7	257.2	9.662	.80	3.75%	700.1
13	306.5	249.0	9.949	.81	4.00%	702.2
14	250.6	279.9	13.569	1.12	4.85%	703.0
15	240.1	254.7	8.382	1.06	3.28%	711.7
16	292.3	308.9	8.912	1.06	2.88%	723.4
17	383.2	326.1	13.752	.85	4.25%	735.1
20	396.8	324.0	10.280	.82	3.18%	733.9
21	307.1	316.4	16.101	1.03	5.10%	722.1
22	283.0	293.4	14.804	1.04	5.05%	724.7
23	263.5	267.6	8.260	1.02	3.08%	732.7
24	259.4	255.3	7.564	.98	2.95%	730.2
27	265.9	261.3	4.870	.98	1.87%	730.1
28	249.6	265.1	5.939	1.06	2.24%	731.5
29	262.1	292.6	4.237	1.12	1.45%	735.6
30	237.0	255.6	6.098	1.08	2.38%	734.7
31	264.2	269.8	11.598	1.02	4.30%	734.1
8-3-70	256.2	269.7	12.159	1.05	4.52%	723.0
4	233.5	260.8	12.709	1.12	4.85%	725.9
5	219.6	232.0	7.417	1.05	3.20%	724.8
6	217.4	247.6	8.762	1.14	3.52%	722.8
7	242.5	267.1	8.986	1.10	3.36%	725.7
10	252.5	292.5	12.156	1.16	4.15%	713.9
11	236.5	282.2	12.433	1.19	4.40%	712.6
12	204.1	260.8	9.999	1.28	3.91%	710.6
13	228.6	270.9	13.017	1.18	4.80%	707.3
14	216.8	255.8	10.993	1.18	4.30%	710.8
17	216.7	258.5	8.406	1.19	3.25%	709.1
18	240.9	292.2	11.111	1.21	3.80%	716.7
19	244.7	296.2	6.131	1.21	2.05%	724.0

*On New York Stock Exchange.

Diffusion Index of Stock Prices of Industry Groups

In Chapter 2 on analysis and forecast of trend of general business, we introduced and discussed diffusion index as one of the tools for short-term forecast of general business. It is worthwhile to restate what we said about the nature of a diffusion index.

The diffusion index is a statistical series indicating the percentage of items in a group which is rising at any given time. By nature, it resembles rates of change of the aggregate to which it applies. *The diffusion index tends to change direction ahead of the aggregate. When the diffusion index starts to descend from a high level, the aggregate will continue to ascend. Conversely, when the diffusion index begins its rise from a low level, the aggregate will continue its decline.* Only after the diffusion index rises to the 50 percent line, will the aggregate cease to decrease.

The diffusion index in a similar manner can be also used as a tool for short-term forecast of the trend of stock prices. Table 9-5 shows the computation of a diffusion index on basis of weekly reports of advances and declines of Barron's 32 industry groups. A three-week moving average of the proportion of advances is taken in order to smooth out its irregular fluctuations. The table

TABLE 9-5
Diffusion Index of Stock Price Among Industry Groups

Week Ending	Barron's 32 Industry Groups				
	Number of Advances	Number of Declines	Percent of Advances	3-Week Moving Average, Percent	DJIA
4-2-70	17	15	53.0	–	792.4
9	6	26	18.8	–	792.5
16	2	30	6.2	26.0	775.9
23	2	30	6.2	10.4	750.6
30	5	27	15.6	9.3	736.1
5-7-70	5	27	15.6	12.5	723.1
14	0	32	0	10.4	684.8
21	1	31	3.1	6.2	665.3
28	21	11	65.5	22.9	684.2
6-4-70	27	5	84.5	51.0	706.5
11	4	28	12.5	54.2	684.4
18	26	6	81.5	59.5	712.7
25	3	29	9.4	34.5	693.6
7-2-70	4	28	12.5	34.5	689.1
9	25	7	78.0	33.3	692.8
16	30	2	94.0	61.5	723.4
23	24	8	75.0	82.3	732.7
30	24	8	75.0	81.3	734.7
8-7-70	7	25	22.0	57.3	725.7
14	2	30	6.2	34.4	710.8
20	25	7	67.0	35.4	729.6
27	30	2	94.0	59.4	759.8

covers a short period, April 2, 1970 to August 27, 1970, for purpose of illustration of computation of the diffusion index. However, even during this brief period it is interesting to note that while the DJIA reached its low at 665.3 on May 21, 1970, the proportion of advances reached its low a week earlier. In subsequent weeks the proportion of advances rose sharply, signaling the possibility of higher level for DJIA.

While the usefulness of the diffusion index as a tool of short-term forecast of trend in stock prices is acknowledged by some sophisticated market analysts, one should not lose sight of the limitations of this statistical tool. Besides flushing occasionally invalid signals, the diffusion index cannot anticipate the happening of major events which will have strong impact on the level and trend of stock prices.

Comparison Between Price and Volume Changes

Market analysts generally pay close attention to volume data in relation to changes in stock prices. The relationship between volume and price changes is generally interpreted as follows:[6]

1. When volume is increasing during price declines, it is considered a bearish indication.
2. When volume is increasing during price advances, it is considered a bullish indication.
3. When volume is decreasing during price declines, it is considered a bullish indication.
4. When volume is decreasing during price advances, it is considered a bearish indication.

While these interpretations of the relationships between price and volume changes are widely accepted by most students of technical market analysis, we are skeptical of the validity and usefulness of some of the interpretations. The views of the author will be presented later in a separate section on price-volume relationships.

Comparison of Direction of Movement Between DJIA and DJRA

In Dow theory the confirmation between Dow Jones Industrial Average and Dow Jones Rail (Transportation) Average is one of the two basic requirements for identifying a major upward or downward trend in security prices. Some market analysts used the idea and compare the direction of movements between DJIA and DJRA to provide clues for near-term price changes. Granville suggested interpretations of the movements of the two indexes as follows:

When the Dow Jones Rail Average moves more negatively than the Dow

---

[6] H. D. Schultz and S. Coslow (eds.), *A Treasury of Wall Street Wisdom* (Palisades Park N.J.: Investors' Press, Inc., 1966), p. 250.

Jones Industrial Average, then this is considered to be a signal for a near-term decline in the Dow Jones Industrial Average.

When the Dow Jones Rail Average moves more positively than the Dow Jones Industrial Average, then this is considered to be a signal for a near-term advance in the Dow Jones Industrial Average.[7]

Other Indicators

There are many other indicators followed by various students of technical market analysis. Among them, two receive wide attention by many market analysts. One is the size of round-lot short interest in relation to normal market volume, and the other is the amount of brokers' loans and customers' debit and credit balances. These indicators, however, suffer two common drawbacks. First, only monthly figures are available. Indications tend to be late compared to other indicators mentioned above. Second, the interpretation of both indicators is by no means simple and straightforward. For instance, a large short interest can be interpreted as both bearish and bullish. It is bearish because it indicates widespread expectation of price decline among many traders. However, a large short interest can be also considered a bullish factor because it represents potential demand from the short-sellers who must eventually cover. A large credit balance in the accounts of customers of brokerage firms can be likewise considered both bearish and bullish. Because of difficulty in interpretation as well as poor timing, the two indicators, short interest and customers' balance of brokerage firms, are considered of less value as market indicators and therefore are not fully discussed here.

TECHNICAL MARKET ANALYSIS—INDIVIDUAL STOCKS

In deciding which specific stock to buy and when, technical market analysts usually have to examine two factors. First, what is the outlook of the general market? Second, what is the chart pattern of the stock? The first factor has been examined in detail above and now we turn to the examination of the second factor, chart pattern of individual stocks.

Theory of Chart Reading and Analysis

Chartists claim that stock prices move in trend and that price fluctuations usually form characteristic patterns that are of predictive value through signaling the likely course of further movement. Edwards and Magee enunciated their theory of chart reading as follows.

No one of experience doubts that prices move in trends and trends tend to continue until something happens to change the supply-demand balance. Such changes are usually detectable in the action of the market

[7] Joseph E. Granville, *op. cit.*, p. 23.

itself. Certain patterns or formations, levels or areas, appear on the charts which have a meaning, can be interpreted in terms of probable future trend development. They are not infallible, it must be noted, but the odds are definitely in their favor.[8]

Another market analyst, William L. Jiler, also explained the theory of chart reading in his recent book in these words:

> The purpose of "chart reading" or "chart analysis" is to determine the probable strength of demand versus pressure of supply at various price levels, and thus to predict the probable direction in which a stock will move, and where it will probably stop.

> The clues are provided by the history of a stock's price movements, as recorded on a chart. In the market, history does repeat itself—often. On the charts, price fluctuations tend, with remarkable consistency, to fall into a number of patterns, each of which signifies a relationship between buying and selling pressures. Some patterns, or "formation," indicate that demand is greater than supply, others suggest that supply is greater than demand, and still others imply that they are likely to remain in balance for some time.[9]

Some Basic Premises in Chart Reading

Trends. The most basic premise or belief of the chartist is that stock prices tend to move in trend. The movement of stock prices is often likened to the physical law of inertia or momentum—that is, an object in motion will continue in motion in the same direction until it meets an opposing force. The chartists agree that stock prices in like manner are more likely to continue to move in the same direction (up, down, or sideways) than not, until they meet a change in the supply-demand relationship.

"Volume Goes with Trend." This is one of the tenets of the Dow theory as discussed earlier. The idea is that in a major upward trend, volume normally increases with price advances and decreases with price declines. In a major downward trend, the reverse will happen. Volume will usually increase as price decline and dwindle on price rallies. Most chartists subscribed to this thesis and applied it to the price movement of individual stocks. This become another basic premise in chart reading.

Support and Resistance Levels. Another basic premise is in relation to assumed behavior of investors. The typical pattern of the behavior of investors according to the chartists is as follows. When investors make mistakes and find prices declining after purchase, they usually grit their teeth and hang on, hoping that they will later be able to get out without a loss. When prices actually start to recover, they usually grasp the first chance to get out at prices they originally paid for. This kind of behavior creates the phenomenon that at certain price

[8] Robert D. Edwards and John Magee, *Technical Analysis of Stock Trends* (Springfield, Mass.: John Magee, 1951), p. 6.
[9] William L. Jiler, *op. cit.*, p. 21.

levels there will be a considerable increase in supply and the price of a stock will find it difficult to go beyond this level, which in the language of the chartists is called the resistance level." Since more investors buy high then low and there is usually high volume at former highs, the resistance level for a stock tends to establish at its former highs.

A support level on the other hand is the level at which a falling stock may expect a considerable increase in demand. The support level is usually established at the level where a stock had previously been rising from and where there was much volume of transactions done. At this support level, a variety of investors may come in to buy the stock. They include (1) those who regretted that they did not buy before when the stock was advancing, (2) short sellers who sold short before and now buy back to take profits, and (3) "value" conscious investors.

In Figure 9-1, support and resistance levels are shown in pattern F.

Figure 9-1
Typical Graphic Patterns Used in Technical Market Analysis

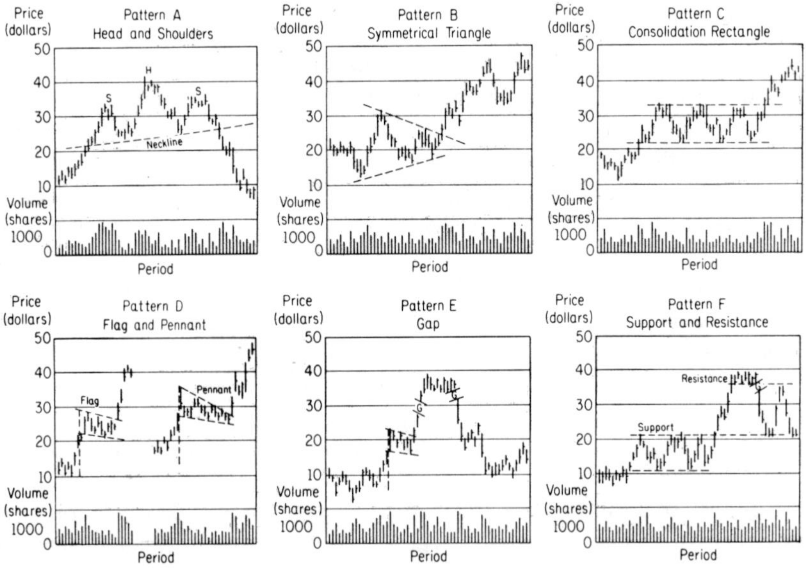

SOURCE: Sidney M. Robbins, *Managing Securities* Boston Houghton Mifflin Company 1954, p. 502.

Important Chart Patterns

As mentioned earlier, chartists believe that several characteristic formations or patterns on charts of stock prices do have predictive value. Their interpretations of these chart formations, however, rely heavily on the three basic premises just discussed above.

1. Stock prices move in trends.
2. Volume goes with trend.
3. The typical pattern of behavior of investors shows up in establishing support and resistance levels.

A few important chart patterns are selected and described below. They are: head and shoulders; triangles or coils; rectangles; flags and pennants; gaps; line and saucer formation; and V formation.

Head and Shoulders. Chartists consider the head-and-shoulders formation one of the most important and reliable of the major *reversal* patterns. It is a bearish pattern. A typical head and shoulder formation as shown in Pattern A in Figure 9-1 consists of four basic elements.

> A. A strong rally, climaxing a more or less extensive advance, on which trading volume becomes very heavy, followed by a minor recession on which volume runs considerably less than it did during the days of rise and at the top. This is the "left shoulder."
> B. Another high volume advance which reaches a higher level than the top of the left shoulder and then another reaction on less volume which takes prices down to somewhere near the bottom level of the preceding recession, somewhat lower perhaps or somewhat higher but, in any case, below the top of the left shoulder. This is the "head."
> C. A third rally, but this time on decidedly less volume than accompanied the formation of either the left shoulder or the head, which fails to reach the height of the head before another decline sets in. This is the "right shoulder."
> D. Finally, decline of prices in this third recession down through a line (the "neckline") drawn across the bottoms of the reactions between the left shoulder and head and the head and right shoulder, respectively, and a close below that line by an amount approximately equivalent to 3% of the stock's market price. This is the "confirmation" or "breakout."[10]

The inverted head and shoulders looks exactly the same in the figure as a normal head and shoulders except that it is upside down. It signals the end of a downward trend rather than the end of an advance.

Triangle or Coil. Triangle or coil represents a pattern of uncertainty. It is difficult to predict which way price will break out. The triangle can be of four different shapes. They are shown in the sketch and are called respectively symmetrical triangle, ascending triangle, descending triangle, and inverted triangle. William L. Jiler suggested several guidelines on market tactics toward the triangles as follows:

> The analysis of triangles should, of course, be tied in with other chart information such as trendlines, support and resistance, and other

[10] Edwards and Magee, *op. cit.*, p. 50.

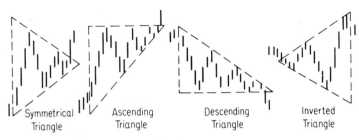

Symmetrical Triangle   Ascending Triangle   Descending Triangle   Inverted Triangle

Triangles

formations. The following guidelines are offered as a checklist in following triangle developments:

1. Odds are favorable that any triangle will eventually result in a continuation of the trend that preceded it.
2. The odds favoring a continuation decrease according to which of the four basic triangles develops, in the following order; ascending, symmetrical, descending, inverted.
3. Purchases should be made at the lowest possible levels within a triangle, or after the subsequent trend has been well defined, because triangles are especially treacherous. They are subject to many false moves, and are among the least reliable of all chart formations. [11]

Rectangles. Rectangles represent another chart pattern of uncertainty. Like triangles, a rectangular area pattern may either represent a consolidation or the beginning of a reversal movement. However, more often than not it represents a consolidation rather than a reversal formation. Pattern C in Figure 9-1 shows a consolidation rectangle.

Flags and Pennants. Pattern D in Figure 9-1 shows formations described commonly as flags and pennants which often appear after a swift, upward movement of price. These area patterns represent usually consolidation or continuation pattern. In other words, they represent usually a pause after which the previous price trend will likely resume.

Gaps. A gap represents a price range at which no shares changed hands. A gap occurs when the lowest price at which a stock is traded on a given day is higher than the highest price of the preceding day. Technicians recognized several types of gaps such as breakaway gap, runaway gap, and exhaustion gap. Depending on their location, they may have little significance or may signify the vigor or the start of an important move.

Line and Saucer Formation. These formations are easy to recognize and they are reliable. They constitute the dream pattern of the chartist. However, they are rare among popular, actively traded stocks. The line formation represents a narrow range within which price has been moving sideways for a long period of time. It represents usually a long base from which a meaningful up-

[11] William L. Jiler, *op. cit.*, p. 120.

ward move will eventually start. Only infrequently does it represent major top from which a subsequent decline develops. The saucer formation is characterized by a curving upward or downward movement of prices. The curve indicates usually the probable direction of price movement.

V Formation. Many chartists brush off the existence of V formation, yet their existence cannot be denied. Not infrequently stocks are found to turn around and move in the other direction without making reversal patterns and without any warning. William L. Jiler, contrary to the views of others, not only recognized the V formation but considered it as one of the important reversal patterns. However, because it strikes with little warning, he acknowledged that the V formation is the most difficult to analyze.[12]

RANDOM-WALK THEORY AND TECHNICAL MARKET ANALYSIS

As mentioned before, the most basic premise of the technical approach is the belief that stock prices move in trends. Should this belief be proven untrue or cast in serious doubt, the theoretical foundation of the approach will likewise become vulnerable.

The random-walk theory which enjoys a growing number of advocates among economists and statisticians from the academic circle says just the contrary. They maintain that where trends seem to be observable, they are merely interpretations, read in after the fact, of a process that really follows a random walk. The future changes in speculative prices are independent of previous changes. To prove their theory, they have conducted various statistical analysis of past experience of speculative prices and have found no positive serial correlation of successive changes of speculative prices. In other words, knowledge of past price changes does not enable a person to predict successfully future price changes.[13]

However, the random-walk thesis of speculative prices is by no means universally accepted by statisticians. Some statisticians argued that the statistical tests employed to support the random-walk thesis were either too simple or too inflexible that they cannot really capture the principles the technical analysts were supposed to follow. Others countered with their own statistical findings

---

[12] William L. Jiler, *op. cit..* pp. 97-103.

[13] For purpose of reference, a few important articles on the controversy of random-walk theory of speculative prices are P. H. Cootner, "Stock Prices: Random vs. Systematic Changes," *Industrial Management Review*, Spring 1962; M. G. Kendall, "The Analysis of Economic Time Series—Part I: Prices," *Journal of the Royal Statistical Society*, Vol. 96, 1953; H. Houthakker, "Systematic and Random Elements in Short-Term Price-Movements," *American Economic Review*, May 1961; Robert A. Levy, "Random Walks: Reality or Myth," *Financial Analysts Journal*, November-December 1967; M. C. Jensen, "Random Walks: Reality or Myth—Comment," *Financial Analysts Journal*, November-December 1967; H. C. Wallish, "Random Walk and Security Analysts," *Financial Analysts Journal*, March-April 1968; P. A. Rinfret, "Investment Managers are Needed," *Financial Analysts Journal*, March-April 1968.

indicating nonrandomness in the changes of stock prices. For illustration, we cite briefly the methods and findings of two statistical studies.

Findings by Sidney Alexander

Professor Alexander attacked the problem this way: If it is true that stock prices are a random walk, there should be no strategy that will consistently yield profits. On the other hand, if such strategy is found in existence, then price changes cannot be considered random. He outlined his strategy as follows:[14]

> Suppose we tentatively assume the existence of trends in stock market prices but believe them to be masked by the jiggling of the market. We might filter out all movements smaller than a specified size and examine the remaining movements. The most vivid way to illustrate the operation of the filter is to translate it into a rule of speculative market action. Thus, corresponding to a 5% filter we might have the rule: if the market moves up 5% go along and stay long until it moves down 5% at which time sell and go short until it again moves up 5%. Ignore moves of less than 5%. The more stringent the filter, the fewer losses are made, but also the smaller the gain from any move that exceeds the filter size.

He applied this filter technique to daily closing prices of two indexes, the Dow Jones Industrials from 1897 to 1929 and the Standard & Poor's Industrials from 1929 to 1959. He concluded his findings as follows:[15]

> Taken altogether the evidence runs strongly against the hypothesis that from 1928 to 1961 the movement of the Standard & Poor's Industrials is consistent with a random walk with drift. The inconsistency of the data with that hypothesis may be largely linked with the "special events" of 1928-1940, but that is just a plausible conjecture. The formulas tested show substantial profits over the entire period, formulas which would be expected to do only a little better than break even if applied to a random walk with drift equal to the observed drift, since they go short as often as they go long.

Findings by Robert Levy

An important tenet of technical analysis is that relative strength of individual securities tends to persist for a significant period of time. If this tenet is valid, replacing weak issues with currently strong issues should prove to be a successful portfolio strategy. With a view to test the validity of this tenet of technical analysis, Levy constructed a number of variable ratio models whereby the portfolios would be composed of both stocks and bonds and the stock portion will increase if the market has been relatively strong; and decrease if the market has been relatively weak. The performances of these portfolios operated

[14] Sidney S. Alexander, "Price Movement in Speculative Markets: Trends or Random Walks," *Industrial Management Review*, May 1961.
[15] Sidney S. Alexander, "Price Movements in Speculative Markets–Trends or Random Walks, Number 2," *Industrial Management Review*, Vol. 5, No. 2, Spring 1964, p. 44.

on basis of this upgrading strategy were found much better than a random buy-and-hold policy could produce during the period 1960-65. Based on these findings, Levy argued that "Stock prices followed discernible trends and patterns which have predictive significance; and the theory of random walks has been refuted."[16]

In spite of the fact that there have been statisticians like Alexander and Levy expressing dissenting view to the random-walk thesis, the dominant view today still favors the idea of random-walk thesis. Therefore, the random-walk thesis represents a serious challenge to the theoretical foundation of the technical approach. Unless and until the technical analysts produce more rigorous evidence to validate their claims that they can predict stock prices from past trends and patterns, their approach will remain suspicious at least in the academic circle.

PRICE VS. VOLUME CHANGES

As mentioned above, students of technical market analysis consider the relationships between stock price and volume changes of vital importance in predicting further future movement of stock prices, both of stock averages and individual issues. Generally they believe that volume goes with trend of price. Specifically, they mean:[17]

1. When volume tends to increase during price declines, it is a bearish indication.
2. When volume tends to increase during advances, it is a bullish indication.
3. When volume tends to decrease during price declines, it is bullish.
4. When volume tends to decrease during price advances, it is bearish.

Since the pattern of price-volume relationships constitutes one of the cornerstones of technical market analysis, more careful analysis of price-volume relationships seems very worthwhile. Two types of analysis are accordingly introduced below. First, the stock market pricing mechanism is examined in terms of basic principles of economics, observations, and deductive reasoning to see whether there is a pattern between changes in volume and stock price. Second, the pattern of changes in price and volume is examined on basis of empirical evidence.

Supply and Demand in the Stock Market. The stock market is usually cited in basic economic texts as a classic example of pure competition where the price of a stock at any given moment is determined by "bids" and "asks" of many buyers and sellers.

---

[16]Robert A. Levy, "Random Walks: Reality or Myth," *Financial Analysts Journal,* November-December 1967, p. 76.

[17]H. D. Schultz and S. Coslow (eds.), *A Treasury of Wall Street Wisdom* (Palisades Park, N.J.: Investors' Press, Inc., 1966), p. 250.

Changeability and Volatility of Demand for Stocks. The factors underlying demand for stocks are many. The more important factors are (1) previous stock price rise and expectation of the same in the near future, (2) fear of erosion of purchasing power of fixed income from more inflation, (3) expectation of increase of dividend and earnings from cyclical upturn or growth of the company or from the secular growth of the economy, (4) expectation of better overall return (dividend and appreciation) over bonds and other financial media, and so forth. From the above factors it can be seen that the demand for stocks is strongly influenced by the *expectations of investors*. Expectations, however, are highly psychological. They can be quickly changed not only by future developments of all sorts (social, economic, political, domestic, or international), but also by interpretations of those developments. Therefore the demand for a specific stock or stocks in general is subject to frequent and swift changes, both upward or downward.

Supply of Stocks is Less Changeable and Less Volatile. Relying on observations and common sense, we know that owners of stocks have a special attachment to the original purchase price. Theoretically, decision of sale should be made in terms of what one thinks one can gain from it in the future rather than what it cost in the past. However, the behavior of human beings is seldom dominated wholly by logical reasoning. Besides, even if we adhere to logic, who knows for sure what the future would bring us from it? On the other hand, it is hard to admit to oneself and others that the purchase was a failure and has to be written off at whatever salvage value. Because of the special attachment to original purchase price and the influence of inertia, the sellers as a group, in our view, are more passively motivated than buyers. Consequently the change of supply tends to be less frequent and of smaller magnitude compared to change in demand.

Changes in Demand vs. Changes in Supply. The demand for and supply of stocks at a given moment of time are influenced by more or less the same set of circumstances. If a favorable set of circumstances or factors is reflected in increase of demand, the latter must be accompanied by less willingness to sell on the part of owners. In other words, we should normally expect increase in demand to be associated with reduction in supply, and vice versa. However, in view of the special characteristics of sellers as a group as mentioned above, an increase in demand is likely to be accompanied by smaller change (reduction) in supply. By the same token, a reduction in demand should be associated with a smaller increase in supply. In other words, demand is a more dynamic force than supply in determining changes in stock prices.

Price and Volume Changes Under Changing Demand and Supply. Case A in Figure 9-2 shows changes in prices and volume under conditions of increasing demand with less than proportionate reduction in supply, and case B under conditions of decreasing demand with less than proportionate increase in supply. What we find in both cases is that price advances with volume increasing, and

Figure 9-2

Case A. Increase in demand with less than proportionate reduction in supply.

Case B. Decrease in demand with less than proportionate increase in supply.

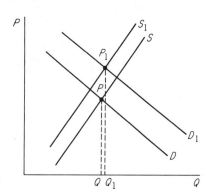
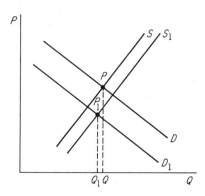

Conventional chart of price and volume as reported in daily newspapers.

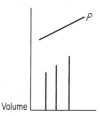
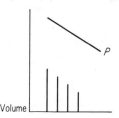

price declines with volume decreasing. In other words, changes in price and volume usually go together in the same direction. This contradicts partly the assumptions of the technical market students on price-volume relationships. The suggestion that volume decrease during price declines is bullish does not seem to correspond to what we find deductively on basis of basic economic principles and observations of the behavior pattern of stock buyers and sellers.

Empirical Study on Market Prices and Volume of Sales. Careful empirical studies on relationships between changes in market prices and changes in volume of sales were conducted by C. Ying.[18] His findings are:

1. A small volume is usually accompanied by a fall in price.
2. A large volume is usually accompanied by a rise in price.
3. A large increase in volume is usually accompanied by either a large rise in price or a large fall in price.
4. A large volume is usually followed by a rise in price.
5. If the volume has been decreasing consecutively for a period of five

[18]C. Ying, "Market Prices and Volumes of Sales," *Econometrica*, July 1966, pp. 676-685.

trading days, there will be a tendency for the price to fall over the next four trading days.

6. If the volume has been increasing consecutively for a period of five trading days, there will be a tendency for the price to rise over the next four trading days.

The above empirical findings seem to correspond closely to what we find on basis of deductive reasonings. A declining market should normally be accompanied by small volume of transactions. The view of the technical market students that volume decrease during price declines is bullish may be seriously in error.

EVALUATION OF TECHNICAL MARKET ANALYSIS

After a lengthy discussion of the various aspects of the technical market analysis approach, a few summary comments are now in order.

The Dow Theory

Despite its limitations as noted earlier, the Dow theory provided most of the basic tenets on the basis of which the modern day technical market analysis is developed. Whatever merit the technical approach may claim must be partly attributable to the Dow theory.

The Dow theory was designed to identify major trends. The identification of major trends, though somewhat late, is followed not only by technical market analysts but also by many students of the fundamental approach.

Though the Dow theory was based primarily on price movements, the importance of volume data in relation to price changes was also pointed out. Present-day technical analysts still relied heavily on Dow's suggestion that volume follows trend of price and did not seem to go much beyond that.

Technical Indicators of Stock Price Level

The technical students are of the conviction that they can predict short-term changes in the level of stock prices. Their method is to rely on a group of technical indicators. Some of the important indicators mentioned above are identification of trend by moving average, confirmation of stock averages, the advance-decline line, new highs and new lows, speculative vs. "blue chips," the odd-lot index, the diffusion index of prices of industry groups, price vs. volume changes, and comparison between DJIA and DJRA.

Although we do not share fully their views on ability of near-term forecast, the present author is inclined to acknowledge that most of the indicators mentioned above are usually helpful to gauge the probable near-term changes in stock prices. A judicious use of these indicators should be helpful not only to short-term traders but also to long-term investors in implementing flexible portfolio policies. However, a warning should be given in respect to these indicators.

They are useful only in normal circumstances. They cannot anticipate sudden, unexpected developments in politics or elsewhere. When these important developments do take place, they tend to overwhelm the indicators.

Technical Market Analysis—Individual Stocks

Much of the underlying rationale of the technical analysis of individual stocks as noted above is originated from the technical analysis of the general market and the Dow theory. However, the basic contention that characteristic chart patterns are of predictive value is basically unproved. Most technical analysts agree that the best chart patterns of individual stocks will either collapse or yield false signal when the general market turns downward. The moral is quite obvious. Even if one believes in the validity of the claim of the chartist on chart patterns, one should always forecast the general market first and then proceed to take advantage of the assumed characteristic patterns of stock charts. In our view, chart patterns by themselves are of doubtful predictive value. However, they could provide near-term guidance to short-term traders if they are accompanied by (1) a near-term forecast of the general market on basis of various indicators mentioned above, and (2) a near-term earnings forecast of the stock in question.

Random-Walk Theory and Technical Market Analysis

The findings by S. Alexander confirmed our observation that stock prices do tend to move in trend. However, the duration of trend, upward or downward, is of various length and it is difficult to tell at the time how much longer the existing trend will continue to run.

The use of the various indicators of general level of stock prices mentioned above can be helpful in gauging the near-term prospects of stock prices. However, they cannot help predict how long the existing trend will last.

Certain randomness in the changes of stock prices from day to day or week to week is discernible from observations of past experience. The influence of random factors and the changeable nature of investors' psychology had much to do with the randomness of price fluctuations. However, such randomness is not sufficient proof that stock prices fluctuate at random and that stock prices do not tend to move in trend. Students of the fundamental approach, although they differ with the technical students on many grounds, do share the view of the latter that stock prices do tend to move in trend.

Price and Volume Changes

Price changes and volume of sales in the stock market are joint products of a single market mechanism. A technical analysis aiming at the near-term forecast of stock prices should logically examine the trend of price changes as well as fluctuations in volume of transactions. However, the common interpretation of price-volume changes by the technical students is found partly in error on basis of empirical evidence and our deductive analysis discussed above. Consequently, a reevaluation of their beliefs about price-volume changes on basis of carefully designed deductive and empirical analysis seems a very necessary endeavor on the part of technical market students in order to enhance the usefulness of their cherished approach.

SUGGESTED READINGS

Barnes, Leo, *Your Investments*, New York: American Research Council, Inc., 1970.

Baumol, William, Jr., *The Stock Market and Economic Efficiency*, New York: Fordham University Press, 1965.

Crouch, Robert L., "Market Volume and Price Changes," *Financial Analysts Journal*, July-August 1970.

Drew, Garfield A., *New Methods for Profit in the Stock Market*, Wells, Vt.: Fraser Publishing Co., 1966.

Edwards, R D., and J. Magee, *Technical Analysis of Stock Trends*, Springfield, Mass.: John Magee, 1958.

Eiteman, W. J., et al., *The Stock Market*, New York: McGraw-Hill Book Company, 1966.

Gordon, William, *The Stock Market Indicators*, Palisades Park, N.J.: Investors' Press, Inc., 1968.

Granville, Joseph E., *A Strategy of Daily Stock Market Timing for Maximum Profit*, Englewood Cliffs, N.J.: Prentice-Hall, Inc., 1960, *Granville's New Key to Stock Market Profits*, Englewood Cliffs, N.J.: Prentice-Hall, Inc., 1963.

Hamilton, William P., *The Stock Market Barometer*, New York: Richard Russel Associates, 1960.

Jiler, William L., *How Charts Can Help You in the Stock Market*, Trendline, Standard & Poor's Corporation, 1962.

Levy, Robert A., "Conceptual Foundations of Technical Analysis," *Financial Analysts Journal*, July-August 1966.

Mindell, Joseph, "Chart Patterns," *Financial Analysts Journal*, May-June 1964.

Nelson, S. A., *The ABC of Stock Speculation*, Wells, Vt.: Fraser Publishing Co., 1964.

Pinches, George E., "The Random Walk and Technical Analysis," *Financial Analysts Journal*, March-April 1970.

Rhea, Robert, *The Dow Theory*, Boulder, Colo.: Rhea, Greiner & Co., 1959.

Robbins, Sidney M., *Managing Securities*, Boston: Houghton Mifflin Company, 1954.

Russel, Richard, *The Dow Theory Today*, New York: Richard Russel Associates, 1961.

Schultz, H. D., and S. Coslow (eds.), *A Treasury of Wall Street Wisdom*, Palisades Park, N.J.: Investors' Press, Inc., 1966.

Schulz, John W., *The Intelligent Chartist*, New York: WRSM Financial Service Corp., 1962.

Seligman, Daniel, "Playing the Market with Charts," *Fortune*, February 1962; "The Mystique of Point-and-Figure," *Fortune*, March 1962.

Vaughn, Donald E., *Survey of Investments*, New York: Holt, Rinehart and Winston, Inc., 1967.

QUESTIONS AND PROBLEMS

1. What is the rationale of technical or market analysis?
2. Indicate the differences between security analysis and market analysis.
3. What is the essence of the Dow theory? Is there any connection between Dow theory and modern-day technical analysis?
4. How may the advance-decline line be used by the students of technical analysis?
5. What is a "new high and new low index," and what is it supposed to measure?
6. How do you construct a confidence indicator and odd-lot index? What are they supposed to measure?
7. Prepare a diffusion index of weekly stock prcies of Barron's 32 industry groups in the last six months, compare it with weekly price of Dow Jones Industrial Average, and indicate your findings, if any.
8. Is there any relationship between changes in stock prices and changes in volume of transactions? How should we correctly interpret the relationships, if any, between stock price and volume changes?
9. What is the theory of chart reading? Explain a few important chart patterns from the point of view of a technician.
10. What is the random-walk theory? Does it weaken or strengthen the technical market analysis?
11. What do you think of the technical approach?
12. Is there any possibility for a combined use of both technical and fundamental approach by an investor? How?
13. What are some of the important technical indicators of the stock market?
14. Predict the short-term outlook of the stock market on basis of some of the technical devices discussed in this chapter.

10. Portfolio Management

FINANCIAL STATUS AND REQUIREMENTS OF THE INVESTOR, INDIVIDUAL OR INSTITUTIONAL

The first step in the setting up of a meaningful investment program in securities is to ascertain and enumerate the circumstances of the investor in respect to current financial status and prospective financial needs. For the individual investor, it is necessary to reveal and consider the following:

(a) Number of people in the family, their age and health.
(b) Source and size of current income.
(c) Nature of occupation.
(d) Amount and adequacy of life insurance.
(e) Size of budgeted current expense.
(f) Size of funds for investment in securities.
(g) Size of other assets, if any, including equity in home.
(h) Is there any need to require income from securities portfolio to supplement current income? How much?
(i) Temperament, training, experience, and time available in managing his own securities portfolio.

In the case of institutional investor, it is necessary to identify and examine these factors:

(a) Nature of the institution.
(b) Tax status of the institution.
(c) Legal restrictions on investment policy.
(d) Size of funds for investment. Is there periodic net addition of funds for investment? What size? Is there any need or threat of periodic withdrawal of funds from the securities portfolio? How much?
(e) Size of current expense and size of current income required from securities portfolio to cover whole or part of current expense.
(f) Nature of future claims or requirements—are they expressed in fixed amount of dollars? Or roughly rising with inflation?

PORTFOLIO OBJECTIVES AND RISK ASSUMPTION

The second step in the formulation of a meaningful investment program in securities is to arrive at a set of portfolio objectives. These realistic objectives can be obtained after carefully considering three somewhat conflicting factors: (1) the financial status and prospective requirements of the investor, (2) the extent of desire for capital appreciation, and (3) the ability of the investor to shoulder various types of investment risks.

Not infrequently one finds that the people who can least afford investment risks in securities are the ones to set up the most ambitious portfolio objectives. The lack of a set of reasonable and realistic portfolio objectives is probably the most important reason for the disastrous investment results experienced not infrequently by millions of individual investors in the United States. According to U.S. Government income tax statistics, almost 1.6 million investors and speculators ended the year 1963 with a net capital loss of almost $4 billion. In the five years 1959 through 1963, American investors had net capital losses of $14.4 billion.

Classification of Investment Risks

Investment management is, in a real sense, "risks management." Each investor should be thoroughly familiar with the nature of several different types of investment risks and the securities which are mostly exposed to each of these risks.[1] Table 10-1 indicates the five distinct types of investment risks, their nature, and the types of securities which are most sensitive to each risk.

Formulation of Specific Portfolio Objectives

The final selection of specific portfolio objectives should be consistent with two basic factors: (1) the financial circumstances of the investor, and (2) the ability of the investor to evaluate and manage risks. However, not infrequently the desire for fast growth of one's capital interferes with a logical selection of appropriate objectives. This inconsistency between one's ability and desire no doubt constitutes the most common reason for unsatisfactory performance of numerous portfolios.

Once the objectives are logically selected, they should be expressed as specifically as possible in terms of the rate of return desired from current income and the rate or appreciation the investor is aiming for. These specific objectives should help guide the investor himself or the manager of the portfolio to make appropriate investment policy decisions for the purpose of fulfilling the desired objectives.

[1] See Chapter 1.

TABLE 10-1
Classification of Investment Risks

Types	Nature of Risk	Securities Mostly Exposed to This Type of Risk
Business or financial risk	Due to bankrupcy, insolvency, and more frequently, declining profitability to the issuing corporation.	Common stocks, particularly unseasoned companies, also lower grade of bonds and preferred stocks.
Price level risk	Loss of purchasing power of fixed money claim.	Fixed income securities: bonds and preferred stocks.
Interest rate risk	Due to fluctuation in the level of interest rate.	High-grade bonds and preferred stocks.
Market risk	Due to cyclical change in general business and profits, and alternate swings between enthusiasm and pessimism among investors.	Common stocks in general, particularly small companies and "glamour" growth stocks; also medium and low grade of bonds and preferred stocks.
Psychological risk	Due to emotional instability of the investor; overly enthused when market is rising and overly pessimistic when the market suffers sharp decline.	

PORTFOLIO POLICY AND MANAGEMENT

Portfolio objectives can be conveniently classified into three groups: (1) conservative, (2) moderately aggressive, and (3) very aggressive.

The conservative investor aims for safety of principal and dependable present and future income. The very aggressive investor has a primary objective in capital appreciation and treats current income as relatively insignificant. The moderately aggressive investor falls somewhere in between. He desires moderate appreciation varying, say from 5 to 15 percent per year plus a satisfactory current return.

The discussions that follow on various aspects of portfolio policy and management are organized along these three broad groups of portfolio objectives.

Composition of Portfolio

The first step in the implementation of chosen investment objectives of a portfolio is to decide what types of assets and what percent of each should be in the portfolio.

For the conservative portfolio, since the emphasis is on safety of principal and dependable income, the majority of the portfolio should be in high-grade fixed-income securities. A ratio between fixed-income securities and common stocks around 60–40 or 70–30 percent seems quite reasonable.

For the more aggressive portfolio, the fixed-income-equity ratio should be probably just the opposite of the conservative investor. A ratio of 40-60 or 30-70 percent in favor of equity seems advisable. Since only moderate appreciation is desired, high grade for both fixed-income and equity issues should be maintained.

For the very aggressive portfolio, the fixed-income securities should constitute a negligible portion of the portfolio. Since the aim is for high rate of appreciation, it is perhaps necessary to seek out attractive issues in medium to small companies. The "blue chips" can at most serve as a balancing portion in the portfolio.

Extent of Diversification

Security prices can drop substantially over a short or longer time span for a variety of reasons:

(a) Cyclical downturn in general business and profits.

(b) Adverse industry developments.

(c) Changes in the level of interest rates.

(d) A general swing to pessimism.

(e) Error in the forecast of earnings.

(f) Unexpected important developments in politics, social or foreign affairs, and the like.

In order to protect against some of these risks, a sound investment policy should adhere to the *principle of diversification*. Generally speaking, diversification of portfolio can be achieved through (1) maintaining an appropriate number of issues in the portfolio, and (2) selecting issues among a variety of companies in terms of stability and growth potential among industries relatively independent from one to another.

For the conservative portfolio of individual investor, the number of issues should preferably be set somewhere between 10 and 15 issues. As a general rule, a portfolio should not include more issues than can be diligently reviewed periodically. On the other hand, for the conservative portfolio, a good rule may be that no more than 10 percent of funds should be invested in a single issue, with the exception of government securities. The industries to be favored should be those relatively stable and moderately growing. So far as individual companies are concerned, the more established ones are to be preferred.

For the moderately aggressive portfolio of an individual investor, the number of issues in a portfolio should be similiar to that of a conservative portfolio composed of issues anywhere from 10 to 15. However, in terms of the type of companies to be favored, both medium-size companies and industry leaders should be equally considered. In terms of industry diversification, the faster-growing industries should have at least some representation in the portfolio.

For the very aggressive portfolio of an individual investor, the number of issues in the portfolio should probably be within ten but not less than five at any time. In terms of industry diversification, the fast-growing and moderately growing industries deserve more attention than the average industries. As far as types and size of companies are concerned, more attention should be probably directed toward medium- to small-size companies with high growth potential or turnaround possibilities. However, this does not mean that there should not be some representation of more established companies to anchor the portfolio.

Large institutional investors such as open-end and closed-end investment companies usually have 100 to 200 issues in their portfolio. Generally speaking, the higher the goal of capital appreciation the smaller should be the number of issues in the portfolio. However, even for the most ambitious goal of capital appreciation it is not advisable for such an institution to have less than 50 issues in the portfolio.

Selection of Individual Security

Selection of individual security belongs more to the area of security analysis than portfolio management. In the case of institutional investor, the customary procedure is that the security analysts will first initiate a list of attractive securities for the consideration of the investment committee or portfolio managers who will in turn make the final decisions to buy or sell given issues and in what quantities. *The individual investor when managing his own portfolio, however, has to serve, in a sense, in a dual capacity: analyst as well as portfolio manager.* What concerns the portfolio manager most is, of course, the valuation of securities in comparison with their market prices.

For the conservative portfolio, the selection of individual security should be logically oriented toward higher grade of fixed-income securities and, in the case of equity, more seasoned companies. Moreover, the emphasis is on purchase of each issue at prices that will yield a good current return as well as reasonable "value" based on both realized and prospective earnings of the corporation.

For the moderately aggressive portfolio, the selection will favor, as mentioned earlier, both medium-size companies and industry leaders. Since the aim is for moderate growth of capital and the companies concerned are fairly large, the problem of valuation should not be too difficult.

For the very aggressive portfolio, since the selection is oriented toward high-risk and high-reward situations, the problem of valuation can be quite vexing. Because of this serious difficulty the average investor is wise to stay away from very high portfolio goals. Even the professional managers of some "performance" mutual funds cannot claim that they have overcome this problem. The record of these "performance" funds as a whole in recent years was far from the desired goals. Worse, they could not even compare favorably with other institutional investors with more modest portfolio objectives.

Timing of Purchase and Sale

Equity prices are known for their volatility. The stock market has its cycles. Though these are related to the business cycle in most cases, they differ from the latter in terms of timing, magnitude, and frequency. It is also noticeable from past experience that there is rotation of favoritism among investors for different industries. The timing of purchase and sale ranks as the most vexing aspect in portfolio policy decision and management.

The timing of purchase and sale of securities has two aspects. One way to consider it is in relation to the whole portfolio. The policy decision pertains to the problem of whether the portfolio policy should be aggressive, neutral, or defensive at the time. The second aspect is in relation to the timing of purchase or sale of individual security. The two aspects of course overlap to some extent. However, one is concerned with overall policy, and the other is concerned with over- or underpricing of individual issues in the market place. They should be treated as distinct entities.

For the conservative portfolio, the question of timing ranks perhaps next to selection. Between the two aspects of timing discussed above, the second aspect should be more important. In other words, what should be stressed is purchasing of individual issues at reasonable price and selling when they are overpriced. The portfolio policy should not be designed to take advantage of short swings in security prices.

For the moderately aggressive portfolio, both aspects of timing should be considered equally important. In other words, while selection and over- or underpricing of individual issues should be stressed, some attention should also be directed toward the appraisal of whether the general market is high, low, or somewhat neutral.

For the very aggressive portfolio, since the goal is high annual rates of return, the portfolio should if at all possible be made flexible to take advantage, fully or partly, of short swings in security prices. While selection is always important for any type of portfolio, it probably ranks next to timing in the case of high objective portfolio.

Periodic Evaluation of Portfolio Performance

To improve the performance of a portfolio, a periodic evaluation is necessary—say at the interval of every six months. The performance of the portfolio should be first compared to its objectives, which may be expressed by certain level of current dividend yield and certain percent of capital appreciation at broadly defined levels of risk exposure. In addition, the performance of the portfolio should also be compared to a broad market average such as Standard & Poor's 425 Industrials or New York Stock Exchange Composite Index. The relative record of performance of the portfolio should be then analyzed in relation to the several aspects of portfolio policy and management discussed above. The purpose is to find out whether any improvement or changes should be made in relation to

(a) The composition of the portfolio.
(b) The degree of diversification.
(c) The selection criteria of individual security.
(d) The technique of forecast of the general market, and the timing of purchase and sale of individual stocks.
(e) The investment decision-making process itself.

SUGGESTED READINGS

Baumann, W. Scott, "Investment Experience with Less Popular Common Stocks," *Financial Analysts Journal*, March-April 1964 and January-February 1965.

Belfer, Nathan, "Determining the Construction and Composition of an Individual Securities Portfolio," *Financial Analysts Journal*, May-June 1965.

Bellemore, Douglas H., *The Strategic Investor*, New York: Simmons-Boardman Publishing Corporation, 1963.

Block, Frank E., "Elements of Portfolio Construction," *Financial Analysts Journal*, May-June 1969.

Dietz, Peter O., "Investment Goals: A Key to Measuring Performance of Pension Funds," *Financial Analysts Journal*, March-April 1968.

Dowrie, G. W., et al., *Investments*, New York: John Wiley & Sons, Inc., 1961.

Fredrikson, E. Bruce, *Frontiers of Investment Analysis*, Rev. ed. Scranton, Pa: International Textbook Company, 1971.

Goodrich, Frederick N., "How to Manage Individual Portfolios," *Commercial and Financial Chronicle*, June 2, 1966.

Graham, Benjamin, et al., *Security Analysis*, New York: McGraw-Hill Book Company, 1962.

Hall, J. Parker III, "Toward Effective Portfolio Management," *Financial Analysts Journal*, January-February 1966.

Hartwell, John M., "Performance: Its Promise and Problems," *Financial Analysts Journal*, March-April 1969.

Hayes, Douglas H., "Institutional Investors and Selection Criteria," *Financial Analysts Journal*, July-August 1965.

Hooper, Lucien O., "The Specialist Should be a Generalist Too," *Financial Analysts Journal*, November-December 1965.

Institute of Charted Financial Analysts, *C.F.A. Readings in Financial Analysis*, Homewood, Ill.: Richard D. Irwin, Inc., 1966.

Latané, Henry A. and William E. Young, "Test of Portfolio Building Rules," *The Journal of Finance*, September 1969.

Lori, James H., "New Rules for Analysts and Portfolio Managers," *Commercial and Financial Chronicle*, Nov. 21, 1968.

Mennis, Edmund A., "Investment Policy for a Growing Pension Fund," *Financial Analysts Journal*, March-April 1968.

O'Brien, John W., "How Market Theory Can Help Investors Set Goals, Select

Investment Managers and Appraise Investment Performance," *Financial Analysts Journal*, July-August 1970.

Reilly, F. K., G. L. Johnson, and R. E. Smith, "Inflation Hedges and Common Stocks," *Financial Analysts Journal*, January-February 1970.

Richardson, Lemont K., "Do High Risks Lead to High Returns?," *Financial Analysts Journal*, March-April 1970.

Sauvain, Harry C., "Problems of Portfolio Policy," *Financial Analysts Journal*, May-June 1965; also *Investment Management*, Englewood Cliffs, N.J.: Prentice-Hall, Inc., 1967.

Smith, Keith V., "Needed: A Dynamic Approach to Investment Management," *Financial Analysts Journal*, May-June 1967.

Stern, Walter P., "Performance—Transitory or Real," *Financial Analysts Journal*, January-February 1968.

Wu, H. K., and A. J. Zakon, *Elements of Investments*, *Selected Readings*, New York: Holt, Rinehart and Winston, Inc., 1965.

QUESTIONS AND PROBLEMS

1. What is responsible for the fact that many people did a poor job of managing their own funds?
2. What is the purpose of diversification? How much diversification should one have for his portfolio?
3. Plan a portfolio of seven securities having a total value of $10,000 with the objective of high capital appreciation.
4. Plan a conservative portfolio of five securities with a total value of $5,000.
5. For a young family interested in growth, recommend a portfolio of five growth stocks with a total $10,000. Defend your selection and composition of the portfolio.
6. "Choose the best securities, then put them away and forget them." Is this good advice?
7. How does analysis of individual securities relate itself to the formulation and execution of an investment program?
8. Other things being equal, portfolio managers generally prefer securities listed on exchanges rather than stocks traded over the counter. Why?

Index

Advance-decline line, 180–181

Business and consumer surveys, 22–23

Chart reading
  basic premises in, 189–190
  chart patterns, 190–193
  theory of, 188–189
Company analysis
  adequacy of working capital, 110–112
  capital expenditures, 120
  cashflow analysis, 115
  causes of growth in earnings, 109–110
  degree of leverage, 110–112
  growth of earnings, 106–107, 120
  growth of sales, 103, 115–117
  least-squares method, 107–109
  management and current programs, 120–125
  outlook of sales and profits, 125–127
  rate of return on common equity, 106
  stability of profit margin, 103–105, 120
  turnover of capital, 105–106
Confidence indicator, 183–184
Control of costs and profitability, 120
Corporate data, comparability of
  accounting for merger, 114
  consolidation practice, 113
  convertible senior security, 113–114
  inventory valuation, 112–113
  methods of depreciation, 113
  research and development expenditures, 114–115, 117
Corporate profits
  aggregate measures, 34–36
  factors affecting profit margins, 39–40
  level in last two decades, 37–38
  long-term perspective of, 43–44
  net profit margins, 37–39
  rates of return on equity, 37–39
  short-term forecast, 44–47
  turnover of capital, 37–39

Depreciation, method of, 113
Difussion index, 14, 20–21, 186–187
Dow theory, 177–179, 198

Economic indicators, 13–14

Federal Reserve policy, 68–71
Forecasts
  long-term, 6–12
  short-term, 12–29
Forecasts of trend of interest rates
  estimates of demand for and sources of funds, 63–67
  financial forecast for 1971, 62–63
  implications for interest rates, 67–68
  by supply and demand analysis, 62

Industries
  advantages of faster growing, 74–76
  changing importance of, 74
  classification of the economy into, 76–81
  stages of development of, 81–84
Industry analysis
  composite industry data, 90
  cost considerations and profitability, 85–86
  industry performance in the stock market 1965–68, 92–97
  market valuation, 90–91
  nature and prospect of demand, 85
  outlook of sales and profits, 86–87
  performance of the industry, 90–91
  structure of industry and state of competition, 85
  technology and research, 86
Input-output analysis, 29–32
Interest rates
  cyclical variation, 60–61
  Federal Reserve policy in 1969–1970 and, 68–71
  influence of Federal Reserve policy on, 61
  seasonal variation, 56
  secular trends, 57–58
  structure of, 49–54
  yield curve, 55–56
Inventory valuation, 112

Management performance yardstick, 87–90
Merger, accounting for, 114

National income and product accounts, 23–25
Net profit margins, 37–39
New highs and new lows, 181–182

Odd-lot index, 184–185

Portfolio management
    composition of portfolio, 204–205
    extent of diversification, 205–206
    objectives, 202–203
    periodic evaluation, 207–208
    risk assumption, 203
    selection of individual security, 206
    timing of purchase and sale, 207
Price vs. volume changes
    empirical study on market prices and volume of sales, 197–198
    supply and demand in the stock market, 195–197
Profit margins, 39–40

Random-walk theory, 193–195, 199
Rates of return on equity, 37–39
Research expenditures, 117
Risks of investment
    business or financial, 3
    interest rate, 3–4
    market, 4
    price level, 3
    psychological, 4

Trends of moving average, 179–180
Turnover of capital, 37–39

Valuation of common stocks
    based on anticipated average earning power, 159–162
    on basis of correlation analysis, 169–171
    capitalization approach, 158–159
    comparative valuation, 165–169
    guidelines on choice of discount rate, 173–174
    key variables in valuation, 172–173
    mechanical valuation, 162–164
    present-worth approach and discount tables, 150–158
    semimechanical valuation, 162–163
    theories of valuation, 133–135
Valuation of the "general market"
    on basis of anticipated average earning power, 145–148
    on basis of present-worth approach, 144–145
    on basis of price-actual earnings ratio, 140–144
    capitalization approach, 134–135
    concept of price-earnings ratio, 139–140
    theory of present worth, 133

Working capital, 110–111